# Ethnicity and Nationalism

# Anthropology, Culture and Society

Series Editors:
Professor Vered Amit, Concordia University
and
Dr Jon P. Mitchell, University of Sussex

Published titles include:

# ETHNICITY AND NATIONALISM

## Anthropological Perspectives

Third Edition

Thomas Hylland Eriksen

PlutoPress
www.plutobooks.com

First published 1994
This edition published 2010 by Pluto Press
345 Archway Road, London N6 5AA

www.plutobooks.com

Distributed in the United States of America exclusively by
Palgrave Macmillan, a division of St. Martin's Press LLC,
175 Fifth Avenue, New York, NY 10010

British Library Cataloguing in Publication Data
A catalogue record for this book is available from the British Library

ISBN    978 0 7453 3043 3    Hardback
ISBN    978 0 7453 3042 6    Paperback

Library of Congress Cataloging in Publication Data applied for

This book is printed on paper suitable for recycling and made from fully managed
and sustained forest sources. Logging, pulping and manufacturing processes are
expected to conform to the environmental standards of the country of origin.


10   9   8   7   6   5   4


Typeset from disk by Stanford DTP Services, Northampton, England
Simultaneously printed digitally by CPI Antony Rowe, Chippenham, UK and
Edwards Bros in the United States of America

# Contents

# Series Preface

Anthropology is a discipline based upon in-depth ethnographic works that deal with wider theoretical issues in the context of particular, local conditions – to paraphrase an important volume from the series: *large issues* explored in *small places*. This series has a particular mission: to publish work that moves away from an old-style descriptive ethnography that is strongly area-studies oriented, and offer genuine theoretical arguments that are of interest to a much wider readership, but which are nevertheless located and grounded in solid ethnographic research. If anthropology is to argue itself a place in the contemporary intellectual world, then it must surely be through such research.

We start from the question: 'What can this ethnographic material tell us about the bigger theoretical issues that concern the social sciences?' rather than 'What can these theoretical ideas tell us about the ethnographic context?' Put this way round, such work becomes *about* large issues, *set in* a (relatively) small place, rather than detailed description of a small place for its own sake. As Clifford Geertz once said, 'Anthropologists don't study villages; they study *in* villages.'

By place, we mean not only geographical locale, but also other types of 'place' – within political, economic, religious or other social systems. We therefore publish work based on ethnography within political and religious movements, occupational or class groups, among youth, development agencies, and nationalist movements; but also work that is more thematically based – on kinship, landscape, the state, violence, corruption, the self. The series publishes four kinds of volume: ethnographic monographs; comparative texts; edited collections; and shorter, polemical essays.

We publish work from all traditions of anthropology, and all parts of the world, which combines theoretical debate with empirical evidence to demonstrate anthropology's unique position in contemporary scholarship and the contemporary world.

Professor Vered Amit
Dr Jon P. Mitchell

# Preface to the Third Edition

It would be an exaggeration to claim that our entire way of thinking about ethnicity and nationalism has changed since the second edition of this book was completed in 2002, but it cannot be denied that research agendas have moved on and shifted somewhat in response to changing historical circumstances; new themes have been introduced, and some old themes have been rephrased, sometimes for the better. A few new topics in this edition, dealt with cursorily or not at all in the first two editions of this book, are cultural property rights, the role of genetics in the public understanding of identification, commercialisation of identity, and the significance of the internet. Arguments about globalisation, hybridisation and the need for a more inclusive concept of identity politics have been developed further, as have the sections about the relative degree of group cohesion, the role of culture in ethnic identification, the concept of race, and migration. Apart from these fairly major revisions, I have updated the text and made minor changes where necessary.

As always, I am grateful to my students, colleagues and translators to languages other than English for their encouragement, but also for pointing out inconsistencies, debatable points, lacunae and incomplete arguments, and I have done my best to deal with relevant objections.

Oslo, November 2009

# Preface to the Second Edition

The manuscript for the first edition of this book was completed in the summer of 1992, that is a decade ago; during the Serbian-Croatian war, a year and a half after the Gulf War, in the midst of the transition of the European Community into the European Union, in the early days of the Rushdie affair, and shortly after the regime changes in Eastern Europe. It seems a very long time ago. The worlds of academia and of identity politics change rapidly in this era of accelerated change, and this revision is long overdue. Although ethnicity studies in anthropology may have peaked, quantitatively speaking, some time in the 1980s, the concerns that initially animated *Ethnicity and Nationalism* remain at the core of the discipline: reflexive identity and social change, identity politics, social complexity and group dynamics. Although new research agendas focusing on transnationalism, hybridity and globalisation (in the 1990s, this word was all over the place!) were developed, the more general issues remain relevant.

This edition has been extensively revised and updated. New research and new theoretical agendas have been taken into account, and I have often seen the need (sometimes prompted by critical remarks from colleagues) to clarify and rephrase vague or misleading formulations; in one or two cases, I have also taken the liberty of changing my mind. Moreover, a new chapter has been added on multiculturalism, culture and rights, a major recent research topic and a public preoccupation in many countries.

I would like to take this opportunity to thank Pluto Press for their continued support of my work, and my postgraduate students for bringing so much intriguing ethnographic material to my desk.

Oslo, February 2002

# Preface to the First Edition

This book was written thanks to an invitation from Richard Wilson and Pluto Press. Upon receiving the invitation, I believed I would not have the time to undertake the task. Having reflected on the matter, I quickly realised I would be unable not to. I have not regretted this decision: it has been a pleasure to work on this book, which deals with a topic about which I feel great enthusiasm.

The study of ethnicity and nationalism forms the empirical focus of much contemporary anthropological research, and it has also been instrumental in raising theoretical and methodological issues of great importance, as well as providing models for understanding the contemporary world. Ethnic relations can be identified in virtually every society in the world and, contrary to much popular opinion, they may just as well be balanced and peaceful as they may be violent and volatile. Social anthropology is unique among the social sciences in offering a variety of research methods to investigate these phenomena, while simultaneously providing theoretical concepts and models that enable us to understand, account for and compare diverse ethnic phenomena.

Several people have been involved – wittingly or unwittingly – in the process of writing this book. Richard Wilson and Leif John Fosse have both read the entire manuscript critically, and their comments have been enlightening and very useful. Several of my colleagues and students have commented on ideas and concepts, especially concerning the relationship of ethnicity to gender and class. My former teachers at the Department and Museum of Anthropology, University of Oslo – Eduardo Archetti, Harald Eidheim and Axel Sommerfelt – should also be acknowledged for having taught me, among other things, that ethnicity is not self-explanatory. Finally, a nod of recognition must be directed towards the people who invented word processing, which enables authors to remain in total command of their own work until it is completed.

Oslo, June 1993

# 1
# What is Ethnicity?

It takes at least two somethings to create a difference ... Clearly each alone is – for the mind and perception – a non-entity, a non-being. Not different from being, and not different from non-being. An unknowable, a *Ding an sich*, a sound from one hand clapping.

Gregory Bateson (1979: 78)

Words like 'ethnic groups', 'ethnicity' and 'ethnic conflict' have become common terms in the English language, and they keep cropping up in the press, in TV news, in political discourse and in casual conversations. The same can be said for 'nation' and 'nationalism', and it has to be conceded that the meaning of these terms frequently seems ambiguous and vague.

There has been a parallel development in the social sciences. In the last few decades, there has been an explosion in the growth of scholarly publications on ethnicity and nationalism, particularly in the fields of political science, history, cultural studies, sociology and social anthropology. This growth is probably only paralleled by the explosion in studies featuring the terms 'globalisation', 'identity' and 'modernity', which incidentally refer to phenomena closely related to ethnicity and nationalism. The relationship of ethnicity to other forms of collective identification, including gender, local and religious identity, will be discussed in the final chapters of this book.

In social and cultural anthropology, ethnicity has been a main preoccupation since the late 1960s, and it remains a central focus for research today. Although I hope the relevance of this book extends beyond the confines of academic anthropology, it is built around the contributions of anthropology to the study of ethnicity and kindred phenomena. Through its dependence on long-term fieldwork and its bottom-up perspective on social life, anthropology has the advantage of generating first-hand knowledge of social life at the level of everyday interaction. To a great extent, this is the locus where ethnicity is created and re-created. Ethnic relations emerge and are made relevant through social situations and encounters, and through people's ways of coping with the demands and challenges of life. From its vantage point right at the centre of local life, social anthropology is in a unique position to investigate these processes at the micro level, although it needs to be supplemented by other approaches such as history and macrosociology in order to develop a full picture of ethnicity and nationalism.

Anthropological approaches, moreover, enable us to explore the ways in which ethnic relations are being defined and perceived by people; how they talk and think about their own group and its salient characteristics as well as those of other groups, and how particular worldviews are being maintained, contested and transformed. The personal significance that ethnic membership has to people can best be investigated through that detailed on-the-ground research which is the hallmark of anthropology. Finally, social anthropology, being a comparative discipline, studies both differences and similarities between discrete inter-ethnic situations and settings. It is thereby capable of providing a nuanced and complex vision of ethnicity in the contemporary world.

An important reason for the current academic interest in ethnicity and nationalism is the fact that such phenomena have become so visible in many societies that it has become impossible to ignore them. In the early twentieth century, a leading social theorist such as Max Weber discarded 'ethnic community action' (*Gemeinschaftshandeln*) as an analytical concept, since it referred to a variety of very different kinds of phenomena (Weber 1980 [1921]). Weber also held that 'primordial phenomena' like ethnicity and nationalism would decrease in importance and eventually vanish as a result of modernisation, industrialisation and individualism. Many early to mid-twentieth-century social scientists shared this view. However, it was eventually proven wrong. In fact, ethnicity, nationalism and other forms of identity politics grew in political importance in the world after the Second World War, continuing into the twenty-first century.

Wars and other armed conflicts in the 1990s and 2000s have typically been internal conflicts, and many of them – from Sri Lanka and Fiji to Rwanda, Congo and Bosnia – could plausibly be described as ethnic conflicts. An influential theory of geopolitical conflict from the post-Cold War era even claims that future conflicts would largely take place in 'the faultlines' between 'civilizations' (Huntington, 1996), although this particular view has been argued against on empirical grounds (Fox, 1999). Ethnic or nationalist struggles for recognition, power and autonomy, however, often takes a non-violent form, like in the Québecois independence movement in Canada. Moreover, in many parts of the world, nation-building – the creation and consolidation of political cohesion and national identity in former colonies or imperial provinces – is high on the political agenda.

In a very different kind of context, ethnic and national identities have become fields of contestation following the continuous influx of labour migrants and refugees to Europe and North America, which has led to the establishment of new, permanent ethnic minorities in these areas. Since the Second World War, and especially since the 1970s, indigenous populations such as Inuit, Sami, Native Americans and Australian Aborigines have organised themselves politically, and are demanding that their ethnic identities and territorial entitlements should be recognised by the state. Finally, the political dynamics in Europe has moved issues of ethnic and national identities to the forefront of political life since the 1990s. At one extreme of the continent, the erstwhile Soviet Union split into over a dozen states, most of them based on ethnic and linguistic identities. With the disappearance of the strong socialist state in the countries of Central and Eastern Europe, issues of nationhood and minority problems emerged with unprecedented force. At the other extreme of the continent, the reverse appears be happening, as the nation-states of Western Europe have been moving towards a closer economic, political and possibly cultural integration within the framework of the European Union, since the early 2000s. But here, too, national and ethnic identities have become important issues in recent years, as witnessed, for example, in the growth of right-wing nationalist parties at the European elections in 2009. Many Europeans fear that cultural standardisation following tight European integration will result in the loss of their national or ethnic identity. Others, who take a more positive view of such processes, welcome the possibilities for a pan-European identity to replace ethnic and national ones in a number of contexts. During the electoral campaign preceding the first Danish referendum on the Maastricht Treaty in June 1992, one of the main anti-EU slogans was: 'I want a country to be European in.' This slogan suggested that personal identities were intimately linked with political processes and that social identities, for example as Danes or Europeans, were not given once and for all, but were subject to negotiation. Both of these insights are crucial to the study of ethnicity. At the same time, debates about multiculturalism and the integration of immigrants have also, from a different perspective, raised important questions about national identity.

This book will show how social anthropology can shed light on concrete issues of ethnicity; what questions social anthropologists ask in relation to ethnic phenomena, and how they proceed to answer them. In this way, the book will offer a set of conceptual tools which go far beyond the immediate interpretation of day-to-day politics in their applicability. Some of the questions that will be discussed are:

- How do ethnic groups remain distinctive under varying social conditions?
- Under what circumstances does ethnicity become important?
- What is the relationship between ethnic identification and ethnic political organisation?
- Is nationalism always based on ethnicity?
- What is the relationship between ethnicity and other forms of identification, social classification and political organisation, such as class, religion and gender?
- What happens to ethnic relationships in situations of rapid social and cultural change?
- In what ways can history be important in the creation of ethnicity?
- What is the relationship between ethnicity and culture?

This introductory chapter will present the main concepts to be used throughout the book. It also explores their ambiguities and thereby introduces some principal theoretical issues.

## THE TERM ITSELF

Writing in the 1970s, Glazer and Moynihan argued that '[e]thnicity seems to be a new term' (1975: 1), pointing to the fact that the word's earliest dictionary appearance is in the *Oxford English Dictionary* in 1972. Its first usage is attributed to the US sociologist David Riesman in 1953. The word 'ethnic', however, is much older. It is derived from the Greek *ethnos* (which in turn derived from the word *ethnikos*), which originally meant heathen or pagan (R. Williams, 1976: 119). It was used in this sense in English from the mid fourteenth century until the mid nineteenth century, when it gradually began to refer to 'racial' characteristics. In the United States, 'ethnics' came to be used around the Second World War as a polite term referring to Jews, Italians, Irish and other people considered inferior to the dominant 'WASP' group (White Anglo-Saxon Protestants). None of the founding fathers of sociology and social anthropology – with the partial exception of Weber – granted ethnicity much attention. In early modern Anglophone sociocultural anthropology, fieldwork ideally took place in a single society and concentrated on particular aspects of its social organisation or culture (Eriksen and Nielsen, 2001). British anthropology in the tradition of Radcliffe-Brown or Malinowski, moreover, tended to favour synchronic 'snapshots' of the society under study. With its emphasis on intergroup dynamics, often in the context of a modern state, as well as its frequent insistence on historical depth, ethnicity studies represents a specialisation which was not considered particularly relevant by the early twentieth-century founders of modern anthropology.

Since the 1960s, 'ethnic groups' and 'ethnicity' have become household words in Anglophone social anthropology, although, as Ronald Cohen (1978) remarked more than thirty years ago, few of those who use the terms bother to define them. In the course of this book, I shall examine a number of approaches to ethnicity. Many of them are closely related, although they may serve different analytical purposes. Sometimes heated argument arises as to the nature of the object of inquiry and the appropriate theoretical framework. All of the approaches of anthropology nevertheless agree that ethnicity has something to do with the *classification of people* and *group relationships*.

In everyday language the word 'ethnicity' still has a ring of 'minority issues' and 'race relations', but in social anthropology it simply refers to aspects of relationships between groups which consider themselves, and are regarded by others, as being culturally distinctive. Although it is true that 'the discourse concerning ethnicity tends to concern itself with subnational units, or minorities of some kind or another' (Chapman *et al.*, 1989: 17), majorities and dominant peoples are no less 'ethnic' than minorities. This will be particularly evident in chapters 6–8, which discuss nationalism and minority–majority relationships.

## ETHNICITY AND RACE

A few words must be said initially about the relationship between ethnicity and 'race'. The term 'race' has deliberately been placed within inverted commas in order to stress that it is not a scientific term. Whereas it was for some time fashionable to divide humanity into four main races, and racial labels are still used to classify people in some countries (such as the USA), modern genetics tends not to speak of races. There are two principal reasons for this. First, there has always been so much interbreeding between human populations that it would be meaningless to talk of fixed boundaries between races. Second, the distribution of hereditary physical traits does not follow clear boundaries (Cavalli-Sforza *et al.*, 1994). In other words, there is in many respects greater genetic variation within a 'racial' group than there is systematic variation between two groups. Third, no serious scholar today believes that hereditary characteristics explain cultural variations. The contemporary neo-Darwinist views in social science often lumped together under the heading 'evolutionary psychology' (see e.g. Buss, 2005), are with few exceptions strongly universalist; they generally argue that people everywhere have the same inborn abilities, and that interesting variations exist at the level of the individual, not that of the group.

Concepts of race can nevertheless be relevant to the extent that they inform people's actions; at this level, race exists as a cultural construct, whether it has a biological reality or not (see also Banks, 1996: 54; Jenkins, 2008: 23–4). Racism, obviously, builds on the assumption that personality is somehow linked with hereditary characteristics which differ systematically between 'races', and in this way race may assume sociological importance even if it has no 'objective' existence. Social scientists who study race relations in Great Britain and the United States need not themselves believe in the objective existence of racial difference, since their object of study is the social and cultural relevance of the *notion* that race exists, in other words the social construction of race. If influential people in a society had developed a similar theory about the hereditary personality traits of red-haired people, and if that theory gained social and cultural significance, 'redhead studies' would for similar reasons have become a field of academic research, even if the researchers themselves did not agree that redheads were different from others in a relevant way. In societies where ideas of race are important, they must therefore be studied as part of local discourses on ethnicity.

Should the study of race relations, in this meaning of the word, be distinguished from the study of ethnicity or ethnic relations? Pierre van den Berghe (1983) does not think so, but would rather regard 'race' relations as a special case of ethnicity. Others, among them Michael Banton (1967), have argued the need to distinguish between race and ethnicity. In Banton's view, race refers to the (negative) categorisation of people, while ethnicity has to do with (positive) group identification. He argues that ethnicity is generally more concerned with the identification of 'us', while racism is more oriented to the categorisation of 'them' (Banton, 1983: 106; cf. Jenkins, 1986: 177). This would imply that race is a negative term of exclusion, while ethnic identity is a term of positive inclusion. However, ethnicity can assume many forms, and since ethnic ideologies tend to stress common descent among their members, the distinction between race and ethnicity is a problematic one, even if Banton's distinction between groups and categories can be useful (see chapter 3). Nobody would suggest that the horrors of Yugoslavia and Rwanda in the 1990s were racial, but they were certainly ethnic – in other words, there is no inherent reason why ethnicity should be more benign than race. Besides, the boundaries between race and ethnicity tend to be blurred, since ethnic groups have a common myth of origin, which relates ethnicity to descent, which again makes it a kindred concept to race. It could moreover be argued that some 'racial' groups are ethnified, such as American blacks who have gradually come to be known as African-Americans; but also that some ethnic groups are racialised, as when immutable traits are accorded to ethnic minorities; and finally, there are strong tendencies towards the ethnification of certain religious groups, such as European Muslims. Formerly known by their ethnic origin, they are increasingly lumped together as primarily 'Muslims'. Finally, Martin Barker's notion of *new racism* (Barker, 1981; cf. also Fenton, 1999: chapter 2) seems to elide the distinction. The new racism talks of cultural difference instead of inherited characteristics, but uses it for the same purposes; to justify a hierarchical ordering of groups in society.

The relationship between race and ethnicity is complex. Ideas of 'race' may or may not form part of ethnic ideologies. It could nevertheless be argued that the main divisive mechanism of US society is race as opposed to ethnicity. Discrimination on ethnic grounds is spoken of as 'racism' in Trinidad and as 'communalism' in Mauritius (Eriksen, 1992a), but the forms of imputed discrimination referred to can be nearly identical. On the other hand, it is doubtless true that groups who look different from majorities or dominating groups may be less liable to become assimilated into the majority than others, and that it can be difficult for them to escape from their ethnic identity if they wish to. However, this may also hold good for minority groups with, say, an inadequate command of the dominant language. In both cases, their ethnic identity becomes an imperative status, an ascribed aspect of their personhood from which they cannot escape entirely.

In the first two editions of this book, I concluded that race could simply be seen as a form of ethnicity; a subset of ethnic variation where the physical appearance of different groups or categories is brought to bear on intergroup relations. In the US, the term 'visible difference' is often used to this effect. However, I have revised my position somewhat since then, and have come to believe in the utility of keeping the two concepts apart.

Ethnicity is a wider concept than race, as pointed out by Richard Jenkins (2008: 23). Quite clearly, there exist important ethnic differences which are not thought of as 'racial' in the sense of being based on group-specific, immutable characteristics. On the other hand, as argued by Peter Wade (2002), Michel Wieviorka (1997) and others, the boundary between what is perceived as natural, biological differences between groups, and acquired, cultural differences is often fuzzy in practice. Ethnic differentiation frequently entails, to a greater or lesser extent, the existence of folk notions of inborn group differences that are assumed to explain some cultural differences.

On the other hand ethnicity can arguably exist without accompanying notions of race, as witnessed among people of European descent in the USA, which often maintain ethnic (or national) identities as Germans, Italians, Irish, etc. without implying any form of genetic determinism. The case of Bosnia is also an obvious one in this respect, as Bosnian Muslims, Catholics and Orthodox (Bosniacs, Croats and Serbs) maintain ethnic differences with no reference to separate 'racial' origins. But could it equally well be said that race can exist without ethnicity?

It may be no coincidence that Wade (1997, 2002), one of the strongest defenders of the view that race and ethnicity should be kept conceptually apart, is a Latin Americanist. In the countries of South and Central America, the relationship between race and ethnicity is complex, and the two kinds of distinctions are only partly overlapping. The conventional view is that 'the study of blacks is one of racism and race relations, while the study of Indians is that of ethnicity and ethnic groups' (Wade, 1997: 37). Although this contrast does refer to different forms of social classification, with distinctive analytical implications, the boundary is fuzzy. In Brazil, the black–brown–white continuum in terms of pigmentation is a dimension of classification which has an obvious class element which may indeed overrule phenotype (wealth 'makes people paler'), but which does not imply the existence of separate ethnic categories based on cultural distinctiveness, as is the case with Brazilian Indians.

The North American situation, while different from the Brazilian one, reflects a similar complexity and ambiguity in the relationship between race and ethnicity. Whereas Brazilians have a great number of terms used to designate people of varying pigmentation, the 'one-drop principle' prevalent in the USA entails that people are either black or white, and that 'a single drop of black blood' (*sic*) contaminates an otherwise pale person and makes him or her black. Conversely, ethnic identity in the USA is, as mentioned above, not necessarily correlated with 'race'. At the same time, African-American identities are associated with social solidarity and specific sets of shared practices and values, thus resembling ethnic identities.

A final point is the fact that discrimination based on presumed inborn and immutable characteristics (race) tends to be stronger and more inflexible than ethnic discrimination which is not based on 'racial' differences. Members of a presumed race cannot change their assumed inherited traits, while ethnic groups can change their culture and, ultimately, become assimilated into a dominant group.

To conclude, race and ethnicity should be seen as kindred terms which partly overlap. Notions about cultural uniqueness and social solidarity tend to be stronger with respect to ethnic categorisations, while the idea of biological, nowadays dubbed 'genetic', difference is stronger in racist thought and practice. Strictly speaking, members of a 'race' do not need to have specific shared cultural character-istics in order to be subjected to the same treatment by others. Although members of an ethnic category generally assume that they have the same origins, current commonalities at the level of culture and social integration tend to be more important as sources of solidarity and collective identification. As later chapters will show, ideas about 'racial purity' may or may not be invoked as part of the ideological toolkit justifying ethnic cohesion, but notions of biological or genetic uniqueness are not a necessary component of ethnic identity, just as ideas of common cultural heritage do not necessarily enter into discourses of racial difference.

## ETHNICITY, NATION AND CLASS

The relationship between the terms 'ethnicity' and 'nationality' is nearly as complex as that between 'ethnicity' and 'race'. Like the words 'ethnic' and 'race', the word 'nation' has a long history (R. Williams, 1976: 213–14) and has been used with a variety of different meanings in European languages. I shall refrain from discussing these meanings here, and will concentrate on the sense in which nation and nationalism are used analytically in academic discourse. Like ethnic ideologies, nationalism stresses the cultural similarity of its adherents and, by implication, it draws boundaries vis-à-vis others, who thereby become outsiders. The distinguishing mark of nationalism is, by definition, its relationship to the state. A nationalist holds that political boundaries should be coterminous with cultural boundaries (Gellner, 1983: 1), whereas most ethnic groups, even if they ask for recognition and cultural rights, do not demand command over a state. When the political leaders of an ethnic movement make demands to this effect, the ethnic movement therefore by definition becomes a nationalist movement. Although nationalisms tend to be ethnic in character, it is debatable whether there is a necessary ethnic foundation for national identity (A.D. Smith, 1986; Eriksen, 2004b), and we shall look more carefully into the relationship between ethnicity and nationalism in chapters 6–8.

The term 'ethnicity' refers to relationships between groups whose members consider themselves distinctive, and these groups are often ranked hierarchically within a society. It is therefore necessary to distinguish clearly between ethnicity and social class.

In the literature of social science, there are two main definitions of classes. One derives from Karl Marx, the other from Max Weber. Sometimes elements from the two definitions are combined.

The Marxist view of social classes emphasises economic aspects. A social class is defined according to its relationship to the productive process in society. In capitalist societies, according to Marx, there are three main classes. First, there is the capitalist class or bourgeoisie, whose members own the means of production (factories, tools and machinery and so on) and buy other people's labour-power (employ them). Second, there is the petit-bourgeoisie, whose members own means of production but do not employ others. Owners of small shops are typical examples. The third and most numerous class is the proletariat or working class, whose members depend upon selling their labour-power to a capitalist for their livelihood. There are also other classes, notably the aristocracy, whose members live by land interest, and the lumpenproletariat, which consists of unemployed and underemployed people – vagrants, petty thieves and so on.

Since Marx's time in the mid-nineteenth century, the theory of classes has been refined in several directions, not least through studies of peasants in the Third World (Wolf, 1964) and through Bourdieu's and others' analyses of cultural classes defined through symbolic power rather than property (Bourdieu, 1984). Its adherents nevertheless still stress the relationship to property in their delineation of classes. A further central feature of this theory is the notion of class struggle. Marx and his followers held that oppressed classes would eventually rise against their oppressors, overthrow them through a revolution, and alter the political order and the social organisation of labour. This, in Marx's view, was the chief way in which societies evolved.

The Weberian view of social classes, which has partly developed into theories of social stratification, combines several criteria in delineating classes, including income, education and political influence. Unlike Marx, Weber did not regard classes as potential corporate groups; he did not believe that members of social classes necessarily would have shared political interests. Weber preferred to speak of 'status groups' rather than classes.

Theories of social class always refer to systems of social ranking and distribution of power. Ethnicity, on the contrary, does not necessarily refer to rank; ethnic relations may well be egalitarian in this regard. Still, many polyethnic societies are ranked according to ethnic membership. The criteria for such ranking are nevertheless different from class ranking: they refer to imputed cultural differences or even inborn racial differences, not to property or achieved statuses.

There may be a high *correlation* between ethnicity and class, which means that there is a high likelihood that persons belonging to specific ethnic groups also belong to specific social classes. There can be a significant interrelationship between class and ethnicity, both class and ethnicity can be criteria for rank, and ethnic membership can be an important factor in class membership. Both class differences and ethnic differences can be pervasive features of societies, but they are not one and the same thing and must be distinguished from one another analytically.

## THE CURRENT CONCERN WITH ETHNICITY

If one were to run a word-search programme through a representative sample of English-language anthropological publications since 1950, one would note significant changes in the frequency of a number of key words. Words like 'structure' and 'function', for example, have gradually grown unfashionable, whereas Marxist terms like 'base and superstructure', 'means of production' and 'class struggle' were widespread from around 1965 until the early 1980s. Terms like 'ethnicity', 'ethnic' and 'ethnic group', for their part, have steadily grown in currency from the late 1960s until the 1990s, and have remained widely used since then. There may be two main causes for this. One of them is changes in the world, while the other concerns changes in the dominant way of thinking in anthropology.

Whereas early to mid-twentieth-century anthropology, as exemplified in the works of Malinowski, Boas, Radcliffe-Brown, Lévi-Strauss, Evans-Pritchard and others, would characteristically focus on single traditional societies, changes in the world after the Second World War have brought many of these societies into increased contact with each other, with the state, capitalism and global society. Many of the peoples studied by social anthropologists have become involved in national liberation movements or ethnic conflicts in post-colonial states. Many of them, formerly regarded as 'tribes' or 'aboriginals', have become redefined as 'ethnic minorities'. Furthermore, many former members of tribal or traditional groups have migrated to cities or to Europe or North America, where their relationships with the host societies have been studied extensively by sociologists, social psychologists and social anthropologists.

Many traditional peoples have moved to towns or regional centres where they are brought into contact with people with other customs, languages and identities, and where they frequently enter into competitive relationships in politics and the labour market. A major change taking place worldwide in the twentieth century was urbanisation, and reportedly (Davis, 2006), in 2007, for the first time in human history, more than half the world's population was urban. Frequently, people who migrate try to maintain their old kinship patterns, cultural practices and neighbourhood social networks in the new urban context, and both ethnic quarters and ethnic political groupings often emerge in such urban settings. Although the speed of social and cultural change can be high, many retain their ethnic identity generations after having moved to a new environment. This kind of social change was investigated in a series of pioneering studies in North American cities from the 1920s to the 1950s and in Southern Africa from the early 1940s to the 1960s, and we will return to these studies in the next chapter.

In an influential study of ethnic identity in the United States, Glazer and Moynihan (1963) claimed that the most important point to be made about the 'American melting-pot' is that it never occurred. They argued that, rather than eradicating ethnic differences, modern American society has actually created a new form of self-awareness in people, which is expressed in a concern about roots and origins.

Moreover, many Americans continue to use their ethnic networks actively when looking for jobs or a spouse. Many prefer to live in neighbourhoods dominated by people with the same origins as themselves, and they continue to regard themselves as 'Italians', 'Poles' and so on in a hyphenated way (Italian-American etc.) several generations after their ancestors left the country of origin.

An insight from anthropological research has been that ethnic organisation and identity, rather than being 'primordial' phenomena radically opposed to modernity and the modern state, are frequently reactions to processes of modernisation. As Jonathan Friedman has put it, '[e]thnic and cultural fragmentation and modernist homogenization are not two arguments, two opposing views of what is happening in the world today, but two constitutive trends of global reality' (1990: 311).

Does this mean that ethnicity is chiefly a *modern* phenomenon? This is a tricky but highly relevant question. The contemporary ethnic processes referred to above can be described as modern in character. In an influential statement on political ethnicity, Abner Cohen (1974a) argued that the concept is perhaps most useful in the study of the development of new political cultures in situations of social change in the Third World. It must be added, however, that some of the most important studies of ethnicity have been carried out in non-modern societies, though if quantity were anything to go by, ethnic studies are most vigorously pursued in Western societies.

The contemporary concern with ethnicity and ethnic processes is partly related to historical changes such as the ones alluded to above. It could nevertheless also be argued that the growing interest in ethnicity reflects changes in the dominant anthropological mode of thought. Instead of viewing 'societies' or even 'cultures' as more or less isolated, static and homogeneous units as the early structural-functionalists and Boasians would have tended to do, anthropologists now typically try to depict flux and process, ambiguity and complexity in their analyses of social worlds. In this context, ethnicity has proven a highly useful concept, since it suggests a dynamic situation of variable contact, conflict and competition, but also mutual accommodation between groups.

## FROM TRIBE TO ETHNIC GROUP

As already mentioned, there has been a shift in Anglophone anthropological terminology concerning the nature of the social units we study. While one formerly spoke of 'tribes', the term 'ethnic group' is nowadays much more common. In the late 1970s, Ronald Cohen could well remark: 'Quite suddenly, with little comment or ceremony, ethnicity is an ubiquitous presence' (1978: 379). Although the peak of ethnicity studies was possibly reached a few years later, quantitatively speaking (Banks, 1996: 1), the study of intergroup dynamics and cultural variation has reached a point of no return in the sense that it is difficult to envision future social scientists talking about 'alien tribes'. This change in terminology implies more than a mere replacement of one word with another. Notably, the use of the term 'ethnic group' suggests contact and interrelationship and, ultimately, that we all live in one, 'continuous' world. To speak of an ethnic group in total isolation is as absurd as to speak of the sound from one hand clapping (see Bateson, 1979: 78). By definition, ethnic groups remain more or less discrete, but they are aware of – and in contact with – members of other ethnic groups. Moreover, these groups or categories are in a sense *created* through that very contact. Group identities must always be defined in relation to what they are not – in other words, in relation to non-members of the group.

The terminological switch from 'tribe' to 'ethnic group' may also mitigate or even transcend an ethnocentric or Eurocentric bias which anthropologists have often been accused of promoting covertly (most famously, perhaps, by Said, 1978). When we talk of tribes, we implicitly introduce a sharp, qualitative distinction between ourselves and the people we study; the distinction generally corresponds to the distinction between modern and traditional or so-called primitive societies. If we instead talk of ethnic groups or categories, such a sharp distinction becomes difficult to maintain. Virtually every human being belongs to an ethnic group, whether he or she lives in Europe, Melanesia or Central America, although the significance of their ethnic membership is bound to vary. There are ethnic groups in English cities, in the Bolivian countryside and in the New Guinea highlands. Anthropologists themselves belong to ethnic groups or nations. Moreover, the concepts and models used in the study of ethnicity can be applied to modern as well as non-modern contexts, to North Atlantic as well as Asian or African societies. In this sense, the concept of ethnicity can be said to bridge two important gaps in social anthropology: it entails a focus on dynamics rather than statics, and it relativises the boundaries between 'Us' and 'Them', between moderns and tribals (see also Jenkins, 2008: chapter 2).

## SO WHAT IS ETHNICITY?

When we talk of ethnicity, we indicate that groups and identities have developed in mutual contact rather than in isolation. But what is the nature of such groups?

When A.L. Kroeber and Clyde Kluckhohn investigated the various meanings of 'culture' in the early 1950s (Kroeber and Kluckhohn, 1952), they identified 162 different definitions. Most of those who write on ethnicity do not bother to define the term, and the actual usages of the term vary. Instead of going through the various definitions of ethnicity here, I will point out significant differences between analytical perspectives as we go along. As a starting point, let us examine the recent development of the term as it is used by social anthropologists.

The term 'ethnic group' has come to mean something like 'a people'. But what is 'a people'? Does the non-immigrant population of Britain constitute a people, does it comprise several peoples (as Nairn, 1977, argued), or does it rather form part of a Germanic, or an English-speaking, or an Atlantic, or a European people? All of these positions may have their defenders, and this very ambiguity in the designation of peoples has been taken on as a challenge by anthropologists. In a pioneering study of ethnic relations in Thailand, Michael Moerman (1965) asked, rhetorically: 'Who are the Lue?' The Lue were the ethnic group his research focused on, but when he tried to describe who they were – in what ways they were distinctive from other ethnic groups – he quickly encountered problems. His problem, a very common one in contemporary anthropology, concerned the boundaries of the group. After listing a number of criteria commonly used by anthropologists to demarcate cultural groups, such as language, political organisation and territorial contiguity, he states: 'Since language, culture, political organization, etc., do not correlate completely, the units delimited by one criterion do not coincide with the units delimited by another' (Moerman, 1965: 1215). When he asked individual Lue what were their typical characteristics, they would mention cultural traits which they in fact shared with other, neighbouring groups. They lived in close interaction with other groups in the area; they had no exclusive livelihood, no exclusive language, no exclusive customs, no exclusive religion. Why was it appropriate to describe them as an ethnic group? After posing these problems, Moerman was forced to conclude that '[s]omeone is Lue by virtue of believing and calling himself Lue and of acting in ways that validate his Lueness' (1965:

1219). Being unable to argue that this 'Lueness' can be defined with reference to objective cultural features or clear-cut boundaries, Moerman defines it as an *emic category of ascription*.[1] This way of delineating ethnic groups has become very influential (see chapter 3).

Does this imply that ethnic groups do not necessarily have a distinctive culture? Can two groups be culturally identical and yet constitute two different ethnic groups? This is a complicated question, which will be dealt with at length in later chapters. At this point it should be noted that, contrary to a widespread commonsense view, the existence of cultural differences between two groups is not the decisive feature of ethnicity. Two distinctive, endogamous groups, say, somewhere in New Guinea, may well have widely different languages, religious beliefs and even technologies, but that does not necessarily mean that there is an ethnic relationship between them. For ethnicity to come about, the groups must have a minimum of contact with each other, and they must entertain ideas of each other as being culturally different from themselves. If these conditions are not fulfilled, there is no ethnicity, for ethnicity is essentially an aspect of a relationship, not a property of a group.[2] This is a key point. Conversely, some groups may seem culturally similar, yet there can be a socially highly relevant (and even volatile) interethnic relationship between them. This would have been the case with the relationship between Serbs and Croats following the break-up of Yugoslavia, or the tension between coastal Sami and ethnic Norwegians. There may also be considerable cultural variation within a group without ethnic differences (Blom, 1969). Only in so far as cultural differences are perceived as being important, and are made socially relevant, do social relationships have an ethnic element. Indeed, the similarities between bounded, competing ethnic groups may in fact be highlighted, as shown by Simon Harrison (2002) in an article describing intense ethnic boundary-making between groups which see each other as similar in important respects.

Ethnicity is an aspect of social relationship between persons who consider themselves as essentially distinctive from members of other

1. In anthropology, it is common to use the term *emic* to refer to 'the native point of view'. It is contrasted with *etic*, which refers to the analyst's concepts, descriptions and analyses. The terms are derived from phonemics and phonetics.
2. Glazer and Moynihan (1975: 1) nevertheless define ethnicity as 'the character or quality of an ethnic group'. Hopefully, the advantages of seeing it as a relationship instead, as something which is *between* and not *inside*, will become apparent in later chapters.

groups of whom they are aware and with whom they enter into relationships. It can thus also be defined as a social identity (based on a contrast vis-à-vis others) characterised by metaphoric or fictive kinship (Yelvington, 1991: 168). When cultural differences regularly make a difference in interaction between members of groups, the social relationship has an ethnic element. Ethnicity refers both to aspects of gain and loss in interaction, and to aspects of meaning in the creation of identity. In this way it has a political, organisational aspect as well as a symbolic, meaningful one.

Ethnic groups have myths of common origin, and they nearly always have ideologies encouraging endogamy, which may nevertheless be of highly varying practical importance.

## KINDS OF ETHNIC RELATIONS

This very general and tentative definition of ethnicity lumps together a great number of very different social phenomena.[3] My relationship with my greengrocer (who was born in Pakistan) has an ethnic element, however minor; so, it could be argued, did the wars in ex-Yugoslavia and 'race riots' in American cities. Do these phenomena have anything interesting in common, justifying their comparison within a single conceptual framework? The answer is both yes and no.

One of the contentions from anthropological studies of ethnicity is that there may be mechanisms of ethnic processes which are relatively uniform in every interethnic situation: to this effect, we can identify certain shared formal properties in all ethnic phenomena.

On the other hand, there can be no doubt that the substantial social contexts of ethnicity differ enormously, and indeed that ethnic identities and ethnic organisations themselves may have highly variable importance in different societies, for different individuals and in different situations. We should nevertheless keep in mind that the point of anthropological comparison is not necessarily to establish similarities between societies; it can also reveal important differences. In order to discover such differences, we must initially possess some kind of measuring rod, a constant or a conceptual bridgehead, which can be used as a basis of

3. It would have been perfectly possible, but ultimately fruitless, to delve into the nuances and differences between extant definitions of ethnicity. Banks (1996: 4–5), for example, lists about a dozen slightly different definitions of ethnicity, as well as a short quotation from A.P. Cohen (1985), who sees the exercise of trying to give an accurate, robust definition of ethnicity as counterproductive.

comparison. If we first know what we mean by ethnicity, we can then use the concept as a common denominator for societies and social contexts which are otherwise very different. In this way the concept of ethnicity can not only teach us something about similarity, but also about differences.

Although the concept of ethnicity should always have the same meaning lest it cease to be useful in comparison, it is inevitable that we distinguish between the social contexts under scrutiny. Some interethnic contexts in different societies are very similar and may seem easily comparable, whereas others differ profoundly. In order to give an idea of the variation, I shall briefly describe some typical empirical foci of ethnic studies, some standard kinds of ethnic relations.

(a) Modern migrants. This category would include, among others, non-European immigrants in European cities and 'Hispanics' in the United States, as well as migrants to urban areas in Africa, Koreans in Japan and Chinese in Indonesia. Research on immigrants has focused on problems of adaptation, on ethnic discrimination from the host society, racism, and issues relating to identity management and cultural change (see chapters 4, 7 and 8). Anthropologists who have investigated urbanisation in Africa have focused on change and continuity in political organisation and social identity following migration to totally new settings (see chapter 2). Although they have political interests, these ethnic groups rarely demand political independence or statehood, and they are as a rule integrated into a capitalist system of production and consumption.

(b) Indigenous peoples. This word is a blanket term usually referring to aboriginal inhabitants of a territory, who are politically relatively powerless and who are only partly integrated into the dominant nation-state. Indigenous peoples are associated with a non-industrial mode of production and a stateless political system (Minority Rights Group, 1990; cf. Paine, 1992, 2000). The Basques of the Bay of Biscay and the Welsh of Great Britain are not considered indigenous populations, although they are certainly as indigenous, technically speaking, as the Sami of northern Scandinavia or the Jívaro of the Amazon basin. The concept 'indigenous people' is thus not an accurate analytical one, but rather one drawing on broad family resemblances and contemporary political issues (see chapters 4 and 7).

(c)  Proto-nations (ethnonationalist movements). These groups, the most famous of ethnic groups in the news media, include Kurds, Sikhs, Palestinians and Sri Lankan Tamils. By definition, these groups have political leaders who claim that they are entitled to their own nation-state and should not be 'ruled by others'. These groups, short of having a nation-state, may be said to have more substantial characteristics in common with nations (see chapter 6) than with either urban minorities or indigenous peoples. They are always territorially based; they are differentiated according to class and educational achievement, and they are large groups. In accordance with common terminology, these groups may be described as 'nations without a state'. Anthropologists have studied such movements in a number of societies, including Euzkadi or the Basque country (Heiberg, 1989), Brittany (McDonald, 1989) and Québec (Handler, 1988).

(d)  Ethnic groups in 'plural societies'. The term 'plural society' usually designates colonially created states with culturally heterogeneous populations (Furnivall, 1948; M.G. Smith, 1965). Typical plural societies would be Kenya, Indonesia and Jamaica. The groups that make up the plural society, although they are compelled to participate in uniform political and economic systems, are regarded as (and regard themselves as) highly distinctive in other matters. In plural societies, secessionism is usually not an option and ethnicity tends to be articulated as group competition. As Jenkins (1986) has remarked, most contemporary states could plausibly be considered plural ones.

(e)  Post-slavery minorities:[4] the descendants of slaves, largely in the New World. Neither immigrants nor indigenous peoples, their ancestors were transformed from being members of distinctive, African ethnic groups to simply 'labour, negroes, "niggers"' (Fenton, 1999: 42). These groups have later redefined themselves along different lines depending on the society and context in question. Some of the more striking expressions of a rediscovered Africanness are the *négritude* movement of the French-speaking areas, Jamaican rastafarianism and, more recently, US Afrocentric ideology (Asante, 1988) on the one hand, and a celebration of hybridity on the

---

4.  Thanks to Steve Fenton (1999: 31–2) for alerting me to the significance of this category.

other (Gilroy, 1987; Hall, 1991; Werbner and Modood, 1997). Their identity politics tend to be based on their shared history of enforced uprooting and suffering.

The definition of ethnicity proposed above would include all of these kinds of interethnic relationship, no matter how different they are in other respects. Surely, there are aspects of politics (competition for power and recognition) as well as meaning (social identification and belonging) in the ethnic relations reproduced by urban minorities, indigenous peoples, proto-nations and the component groups of plural societies alike. Despite the great variations between the problems and substantial characteristics represented by the respective kinds of groups, the term 'ethnicity' may, in other words, meaningfully be used as a common denominator for them. In later chapters, it will be shown how anthropological approaches to ethnicity may shed light on both similarities and differences between the various social contexts and historical circumstances that will be explored.

## ANALYTICAL CONCEPTS AND 'NATIVE' CONCEPTS

The final problem to be discussed in this chapter concerns the relationship between anthropological concepts and their subject-matter. This is a problem with complex ramifications, and it concerns the relationships between (i) anthropological theory and 'native theory', (ii) anthropological theory and social organisation, and (iii) 'native theory' and social organisation.

It can be argued that the terminological shift from 'tribe' to 'ethnic group' mitigated the formerly strong distinction between 'moderns' and 'primitives'. The growing anthropological interest in nationalism entails a further step towards 'studying ourselves'. For if ethnicity can be non-modern as well as modern, nationalism must be identified with the modern age, with the French Enlightenment and German Romanticism as parallel starting points. Nationalist slogans, movements and symbols later penetrated into the heartlands of anthropological research. Nationalism, as it is a modern state ideology, is present in the social worlds in which the anthropologists themselves live. Although there are interesting differences between particular nationalisms, nationalism as such is a modern ideology. When studying nationalism in a foreign country, it is therefore difficult to use one's own society as an implicit contrast as anthropologists frequently have done when studying what they regard as exotic societies. In fact, as Handler (1988) has observed, nationalism and social science, including anthropology, grew out of the same historical circumstances of modernisation, industrialisation and the growth of individualism in the nineteenth century. For this reason, Handler argues, it has been difficult for anthropologists to attain sufficient analytical distance vis-à-vis nationalisms; the respective concepts and ways of thinking are too closely related (see also Boyer and Lomnitz, 2005; Herzfeld, 1987; Just, 1989).

Handler's point is also valid in relation to modern ethnopolitical movements. Those who speak for these movements tend to invoke a concept of culture which is in fact often directly inspired by anthropological concepts of culture, and in some cases they self-consciously present themselves as 'tribes' reminiscent of the 'tribes' depicted in classical anthropological monographs (Roosens, 1989). In these cases, there is an intrinsic relationship between anthropological theorising and 'native theory'. Additionally, when anthropologists study contested issues in their own societies, there is a real risk that the scholarly conceptual apparatus will be contaminated by the inaccurate and perhaps ideologically loaded everyday meanings of the words. For this reason, we should be particularly cautious in our choice of analytical terms and interpretations when we study phenomena such as ethnicity and nationalism.

The points made by Handler and others in relation to the study of nationalism and modern ethnopolitics can nevertheless be seen as general problems of social anthropology. The main problem concerns how to articulate the relationship between anthropological theory, 'native theory' and social organisation (Mitchell, 1974; cf. also Baumann, 1996). In a sense, ethnicity is created by the analyst when he or she goes out into the world and raises questions about ethnicity. Had one instead been concerned with gender, one would doubtless have found aspects of gender instead of ethnicity. On the other hand, individuals or informants who live in the societies in question may themselves be concerned with issues relating to ethnicity, and as such the phenomenon clearly does exist outside of the mind of the observer. But since our concepts, for example ethnicity and nationalism, are our own inventions, we must not assume that the actors themselves have the same ideas about the ways in which the world is constituted – even if they are using the very same words as ourselves! History and social identity are constructed socially, sometimes with a very tenuous relationship with established, or at least official, facts (see chapter 4).

There are often discrepancies between what people say and what they do, and there will nearly always be discrepancies between informants' descriptions of their society and the anthropologist's description of the same society. Indeed, many anthropologists (for instance Holy and Stuchlik, 1983) hold that it is a chief goal of the discipline to investigate and clarify the relationship between notions and actions, or between what people say and what they do. One may disagree with their 'rationalist' perspective, which seems to assume that a simple, 'economic' means–end rationality underlies all social action, but the general problem remains important: why is it that people say one thing and then proceed to do something entirely different, and how can this be investigated?

This discrepancy is relevant for ethnic studies, and it requires that we are clear about the distinctions between our own concepts and models, 'native' concepts and models, and social process. In some societies, people will perhaps deny that there is systematic differential treatment between members of different groups, although the anthropologist will discover that such discrimination exists. Conversely, I have met many Christians during fieldwork who have sworn, in conversations, that they would (for ostensibly sound reasons) have nothing to do with Muslims; later on, it has turned out that they in fact entertain enduring and sometimes confidential social relationships with Muslims. It is, indeed, frequently contradictions of this kind that lead to anthropological insights.

## FURTHER READING

Guibernau, Montserrat and John Rex, eds (1997) *The Ethnicity Reader: Nationalism, Multiculturalism and Migration*. Cambridge: Polity. An authoritative, well edited collection of short texts covering the main approaches and theoretical positions.

Jenkins, Richard (2008) *Rethinking Ethnicity*, 2nd edn. London: SAGE. Lucid and comprehensive introduction to the field, with comprehensive ethnographic examples and engaging theoretical discussions.

# 2
# Ethnic Classification: Us and Them

He came of good class, had a light olive complexion and hair with large waves ('good' hair, Miss Henery thought of it as; as a member of the West Indian coloured middle class, she conceived of human hair in terms of 'good' and 'bad' – sometimes 'good' and 'hard'; 'good' hair is hair that is European in appearance; 'bad' or 'hard' hair is of the kinky, negroid type).

Edgar Mittelholzer (1979 [1950]: 58)

The first fact of ethnicity is the application of systematic distinctions between insiders and outsiders; between Us and Them. If no such principle exists there can be no ethnicity, since ethnicity presupposes an institutionalised relationship between delineated categories whose members consider each other to be culturally distinctive. From this principle, it follows that two or several groups who regard themselves as being distinctive may tend to become more similar *and* simultaneously increasingly concerned with their distinctiveness if their mutual contact increases. Ethnicity is thus constituted through social contact. This chapter will present general aspects of these processes of contact. In later chapters, wider contexts for ethnic relations at the interpersonal level will be elucidated – from the formation of ethnic groups (chapter 3) and the creation of ethnic identities and ideologies (chapter 4), to the historical conditions for ethnicity (chapter 5), the relationship between ethnicity and the state, including debates about nationalism, indigenous peoples and multiculturalism (chapters 6, 7 and 8), and the implications of globalisation for identity politics (chapters 8 and 9). Although ethnicity is not wholly created by individual agents, it can simultaneously provide agents with meaning *and* with organisational channels for pursuing their culturally defined interests. It is very important to be aware of this duality.

## THE ECOLOGY OF THE CITY

Some of the earliest empirical research on complex polyethnic societies was undertaken by the group which has come to be known as the Chicago School, comprising urban sociologists as

23

well as anthropologists (Park, 1950; cf. Hannerz, 1980). Among
the main problems investigated by Robert Park and his associates
in the 1920s and 1930s was how it could be that ethnic groups
remained distinctive in American cities – and to what extent they
did so through time. In other words, they were concerned with
continuity and change in ethnic relations. We owe the widespread
use of concepts of 'acculturation' and 'the American melting-pot'
to the efforts of Park and his colleagues. By acculturation, they
meant the adaptation of immigrants to their new cultural context.
It could, but did not have to, eventually lead to total assimilation
or loss of ethnic distinctiveness.

Park regarded the city as a kind of ecological system with its own
internal dynamic, creating diverse opportunities and constraints
for different individuals and groups. At the same time it contained
several distinct 'social worlds' based on class, 'race' or national
origin. These social worlds corresponded to distinctive physical
neighbourhoods, divided by unequal access to economic resources as
well as ethnic differences. The combination of economic adaptation
and ethnic identity thus created 'natural areas', such as Little Sicily
and the 'Black Belt' in Chicago, more or less sharply distinguished
from each other through their respective places in the division of
labour and the cultural identities of their inhabitants. Economic,
political and cultural resources were to a great extent pooled within
each ethnic subsystem so that the individual could achieve many of
his or her goals through ethnic networks. Mobility within the system
as a whole could be achieved through acculturation – the adoption
of the white, English-speaking majority's values and ways of life –
which in turn depended on the economic success of individuals or
groups. 'The typical "race relations" cycle', remarks Ulf Hannerz
(1980: 44) in an assessment of the Chicago School, 'would lead
from isolation through competition, conflict, and accommodation
to assimilation.' Park generally assumed that 'acculturation' would
eventually replace ethnic entrenchment, except in the case of the
blacks. Another influential analysis of 'acculturation' from the same
period is Bateson's article about culture contact and schismogenesis,
published in 1935 (Bateson 1972a), where Bateson argues that,
contrary to what many expect, group differences may just as well
be accentuated as reduced in situations of contact.

A main point in Park's work is that every society is a more or
less successful melting-pot, where diverse populations are merged,
acculturated and eventually assimilated, at different rates and

in different ways, depending on their place in the economic and political systems.

## THE MELTING-POT METAPHOR

The American notion of the melting-pot has a long pedigree. It seems to have been used first in Crèvecoeur's *Letters from an American Farmer* (1904 [1788]), where the author asked 'What is the American, this new man?' and answered: 'here individuals of all nations are melted into a new race of men, whose labours and posterity will one day cause great changes in the world'.[1] The philosopher Emerson spoke about 'the smelting pot' in the mid nineteenth century, and with Israel Zangwill's immensely popular play *The Melting Pot* from 1908, the term became a label of self-description for many new Americans.

The interethnic contexts investigated by the Chicago School were transient, recently constituted and perhaps atypical. In 1900, almost 80 per cent of Chicago's population consisted of immigrants and their children; as late as 1930, about 35 per cent of the population were foreign-born. Following the 'ethnic revival' of the 1960s and 1970s, it has become commonplace to criticise the notion of the melting-pot for having been empirically wrong since it predicted the demise of ethnicity. As a matter of fact, the critics would maintain, the diverse ethnic groups never merged, and indeed the differences between them seem to have been accentuated after two generations or more of mutual adaptation.

This kind of development (see chapter 7) might have been surprising, but not incomprehensible to Park. He stressed that ethnicity, and ethnic conflict (or race prejudice), was an aspect of the relationship between groups and that it was caused by threats, real or imaginary, to an existing 'ecological pattern' of mutual adjustment. In other words, the social mobility – downwards or upwards – of any ethnic group would lead to tension in relation to the other groups.

Park was also aware of the *fluid* character of ethnic categorisations. As an individual moves between social contexts in the flux and transience of urban life, the relative importance of his or her ethnic membership changes. Thus an 'individual may have many "selves" according to the groups to which he belongs and the extent

1. I owe this example to John Davidson.

to which each of these groups is isolated from the others' (Park, 1955 [1921], quoted in Lal, 1986: 290).

Later scholars have criticised some of the premises from the Chicago School. Expanding his critique to include later representatives of the school, notably Robert Redfield, A.P. Cohen mentions three 'myths' of the Chicago school (A.P. Cohen, 1985: 28ff.): The myth of *simplicity* (the idea that rural societies were by default simpler than urban ones); the myth of *egalitarianism* (also assumed to be typical of rural societies), and the myth of *inevitable conformity* (in rural society). While they doubtless exaggerated the contrast between urban complexity and (assumed) rural simplicity, several insights of the Chicago School have proved to be of lasting value in the study of ethnicity: they showed that ethnic relations are fluid and negotiable; that their importance varies situationally; and that, for all their claims to primordiality and cultural roots, ethnic identities can be consciously manipulated and invested in economic competition in modern societies. The trend in American ethnicity studies (as well as in sociology more generally) known as symbolic interactionism (Gans, 1979) was initiated by the Chicago School. As will now be made clear, conclusions which were by and large compatible with those of the Chicago School also emerged, slightly later, from anthropological studies of 'tribalism' and interethnic relations in urbanising Southern Africa.

## COMMUNICATING CULTURAL DIFFERENCE

The intergroup contacts that constitute ethnicity may be caused by a variety of factors, among them population growth, the establishment of new communication technologies facilitating trade, inclusion of new groups in a capitalist system of production and exchange, political change incorporating new groups in a single political system, and/or migration.

In the 1930s, there was a growing demand for labour in the copper mines in the part of Northern Rhodesia (now Zambia) known as the Copperbelt. This spurred a stream of migration from rural areas to the mining towns, and the workers were settled in large barracks. There were several important changes to the social situation of these workers. They had until recently been subsistence farmers in rural villages; now they had become wage labourers in towns with a predominantly monetary economy. In most cases, their social organisation had formerly been based on kinship; now they were tied to the mining enterprise through individual labour contracts. Most of the workers lived alone in the barracks. If they were married, their families were left behind in the village, at least at the early stages. Finally, they were taking part in a social system of a much larger scale and greater complexity than formerly. Whereas the villagers were more or less self-sufficient and had only sporadic contacts with members of other ethnic groups, as town-dwellers they were in continuous interaction with a large number of individuals from ethnic groups other than their own. They shared housing, workplaces and leisure facilities with others. In some of the towns, dozens of 'tribes' were represented.

This process of urbanisation was investigated by anthropologists based at the Rhodes-Livingstone Institute in Lusaka, North Rhodesia, now the capital of Zambia. Among the most prominent of these were Godfrey Wilson, Max Gluckman, J. Clyde Mitchell and A.L. Epstein. This group is today known as the Manchester School because of its members' later affiliation with the University of Manchester. Some of their studies, including Wilson's *Essay on the Economics of Detribalization* (G. Wilson, 1941–2), focused almost exclusively on change, whereas others, such as Mitchell's small monograph *The Kalela Dance* (Mitchell, 1956), looked into the relationship between social and cultural change and continuity. More recently, James Ferguson (1999) has produced an updated ethnography of the Copperbelt, tracing historical changes over the decades. Whereas Wilson described what he saw as a process of *detribalisation*, Mitchell emphasised that a form of *retribalisation* (what we would today call modern ethnicity) was taking place in the mining towns.

Although kin groups and 'tribes' were economically relatively unimportant in the towns, group membership was emphasised to the extent of being *overcommunicated* (Goffman, 1959) in public rituals as well as in casual interaction. This means that ethnicity was deliberately 'shown off'. In other polyethnic situations ethnicity may rather be *undercommunicated*, which means that the actors tried to play it down and not to make it an important aspect of the definition of a situation.

Although people in the towns were not socially organised along tribal or ethnic lines, they grew strongly self-conscious of their ethnic identity under these circumstances of extensive contact with others. They developed standardised ways of behaving vis-à-vis each other, and oriented themselves socially according to ethnic 'maps' which would have been quite superfluous in a village setting, where most of one's contacts were intraethnic. Many of the new social subsystems that developed in the urban environment, such as clubs and peer groups assembling in beer-halls, were based on ethnic membership.

Mitchell (1956) focuses on one such new institution, the kalela dance. It was performed every Sunday afternoon in Luanshya by male members of the Bisa category. They were dressed in a modern way, and the dance did not form part of the group's traditional cultural repertoire. However, the kalela dance and accompanying songs were conspicuous and overt markers of group identity: most of the songs ridiculed the other groups and praised the homeland of the Bisa. Similar performances were carried out by other groups as well. In this way people's social identities were established and emphasised in a striking way. In a village setting such rituals would have been unnecessary, both because the inhabitants knew each other and because villages were as a rule mono-ethnic.

## STEREOTYPING

In the Copperbelt, cultural differences were communicated in private situations as well. When two individuals met for the first time, the first information they would gather about one another would be their ethnic membership. When this fact was established they would know roughly how to behave towards each other, since there were standardised relationships between groups. Some groups had a 'friendly' relationship, some had a 'hostile' one, and yet others had 'joking' relationships. If one knew someone's ethnic identity, one would know what kind of behaviour towards them would be appropriate. The members of each group had particular notions about the vices and virtues of the others, and these notions were articulated and dramatised in public rituals such as the kalela dance.

When such notions become part and parcel of the 'cultural knowledge' of a group and thus regularly and more or less predictably guide their relationships with others, we may describe them as ethnic stereotypes. Mitchell explains:

> Town-dwellers display their ethnic origin by the language they speak and their way of life generally. This enables members of other tribal groups immediately to fit their neighbours and acquaintances into categories which determine the mode of behaviour towards them. For Africans in the Copperbelt 'tribe' is the primary category of social interaction, i.e. the first significant characteristic to which any African reacts in another. (Mitchell, 1956: 32)

Stereotypes are often mentioned in connection with racism and discrimination, so that, for example, white Americans may justify discrimination against blacks by referring to the latter's 'lazy and erratic ways'. Stereotypes tend to be more or less pejorative, although this is not necessarily the case. Many Europeans have positive stereotypes of 'primitive peoples', arguing that their quality of life is higher than their own. Used analytically in social anthropology, the concept of stereotyping refers to the creation and consistent application of standardised notions of the cultural distinctiveness of a group. Stereotypes are held by dominated groups as well as by dominating ones, and they are widespread in societies with siginficant power differences as well as in societies where there is a rough power equilibrium between ethnic groups. In most polyethnic societies, ethnic stereotypes exist, although there always exist individuals who do not hold such stereotypes – as well as individuals who are acknowledged to be 'exceptions'.

In the polyethnic Indian Ocean island society of Mauritius, the entire population of slightly over 1 million consists of the descendants of immigrants who have arrived in successive waves since the French colonisation in 1715. The most important ethnic categories are Hindus and Muslims (of Indian descent), Creoles (of largely African and Malagasy descent), Coloureds (of 'mixed' descent), Sino-Mauritians (of Chinese descent) and Franco-Mauritians (of French and British descent). The groups tend to have mutual stereotypes of each other and of themselves (Eriksen, 1988, 1998; see also Boswell, 2006). The most important of these stereotypes are summarised in Figure 2.1.

Here, we should keep in mind that actual interethnic relations may very well diverge from stereotypes as they are presented in casual conversations; that there may be a discrepancy between what people say and what they do. In a famous study of the relationship between attitudes and actions in the US, La Piere (1934) toured the American West Coast with a Chinese couple and visited a large number of restaurants and hotels with them. They were refused service only once. He then sent out a questionnaire to the owners of the establishments, asking them whether or not they would accept 'members of the Chinese race' as guests. The vast majority affirmed that they would not.

Stereotypes need not refer to a social reality, and they do not necessarily give accurate hints of what people actually do. Therefore, we must reflect on the causes and uses of stereotypes.

First of all, in Mauritius as well as in the Copperbelt, stereotypes help the individual to create order in an otherwise excruciatingly

**STEREOTYPES HELD BY OTHERS**

| Creoles | Lazy, merry, careless |
|---|---|
| Hindus | Stingy, dishonest, hardworking |
| Muslims | Religious fanatics, non-minglers |
| Sino-Mauritians | Greedy, industrious |
| Franco-Mauritians | Snobbish, decadent, undemocratic |
| Coloureds | Clever, conceited, too ambitious |

**STEREOTYPES OF SELF**

| Creoles | Fun-loving, compassionate, friendly |
|---|---|
| Hindus | Sensible, care for family |
| Muslims | Members of a proud, expanding culture |
| Sino-Mauritians | Clever, industrious |
| Franco-Mauritians | 'True Mauritian', dignified |
| Coloureds | 'True Mauritian', intelligent |

*Figure 2.1*   Mauritian ethnic stereotypes

Source: Eriksen, 1988.

complicated social universe. They make it possible to divide the social world into *kinds* of people, and they provide simple criteria for such a classification. They give the individual the impression that he or she understands society.

Second, stereotypes can justify privileges and differences in access to a society's resources. Conversely, negative stereotypes directed towards a ruling group may alleviate feelings of powerlessness and resignation: they can be seen as the symbolic revenge of the downtrodden.

Third, stereotypes are crucial in defining the boundaries of one's own group. They inform the individual of the virtues of his or her own group and the vices of the others, and they thereby serve to justify thinking that 'I am an X and not a Y.' In the vast majority of cases stereotypes imply, in some way or other, the superiority of one's own group. However, there are also minorities who have largely negative stereotypes of themselves and positive ones of the dominating group.

Stereotypes can sometimes function as self-fulfilling prophecies. A dominating group can stunt the intellectual development of a dominated group by systematically telling them that they are inferior. There are, of course, many stereotypes which have little or no truth, such as the ideas traditionally held by many African peoples and others to the effect that their neighbours are cannibals (Arens, 1978).

Finally, stereotypes can be morally ambiguous and contested by different parties. In Mauritius, it is often said that 'If a Creole has ten rupees, he will spend fifteen; but if a Hindu has ten rupees, he spends seven and invests the rest.' This saying is sometimes invoked by Creoles as well as Hindus as proof of their own community's moral superiority.

The moral character of stereotyping is not the main point here. Rather, it should be emphasised that stereotypes contribute to defining one's own group in relation to others by providing a tidy 'map' of the social world, and that they can be invoked in attempts to justify systematic inequalities in access to resources.

## FOLK TAXONOMIES AND SOCIAL DISTANCE

As noted above, informal groupings in the Copperbelt tended to be based on ethnic membership. For example, a vast majority of town-dwellers chose drinking companions from their own 'tribe' or ethnic category. In the barracks, they preferred to have room mates from their own group. However, if this was not possible they would rather share their room with people whom they perceived as close than with people they perceived as distant (Mitchell, 1974). Perceptions of distance, Mitchell notes, combined cultural and geographic criteria so that, for example, matrilineal peoples from the north would rank other matrilineal peoples from the north as those closest to themselves. In a large survey of townspeople (which was probably male-biased), Mitchell and his assistants used the following scale of 'stages of social distance or social nearness':

1. Would admit him to near kinship by marriage.
2. Would share a meal with him.
3. Would work together with him.
4. Would allow to live nearby in my village.
5. Would allow to settle in my tribal area.
6. Would allow as a visitor only in my tribal area.
7. Would exclude from my tribal area.

(Mitchell, 1956: 23)[2]

2. This categorisation is based on the Bogardus social distance scale, used in research on ethnicity in American cities by the Chicago School. The original categories were: (1) Would marry. (2) Would have as a regular friend. (3) Would work beside in an office. (4) Would have several families in my neighbourhood. (5) Would have merely as speaking acquaintances. (6) Would have live outside my neighbourhood. (7) Would have live outside my country.

On the basis of such perceptions of social distance, the town-dwellers developed – and reconfirmed, through interaction – a system of social classification where one did not just distinguish between Us and Them, but where there were various degrees of group inclusion and exclusion. In other words, there were different Us and Them groups. Depending on the situation, different levels of group membership could be activated. For instance, in local politics an individual would behave as a member of a larger group than he or she would concerning questions of marriage.

I have explored the functioning of ethnic classification in Mauritius, which officially has four ethnic 'communities'; that is to say, the Constitution of Mauritius acknowledges the existence of four communities: Hindus (52 per cent), Muslims (16 per cent), Sino-Mauritians or Chinese (3 per cent) and 'general population' (29 per cent). The general population is a residual category which encompasses people of African, European and mixed descent. Nearly all of them are Catholics, but they do not consider themselves, nor are they considered by others, an ethnic group. They rarely intermarry and do not vote together at elections. Moreover, it transpires that the 'Hindus' cannot be considered an ethnic group either, especially since this category includes both Biharis from north India (the most numerous segment) and a fair proportion of Tamils and Telugus, who do not identify themselves as members of the same ethnic group as the northerners, and who have periodically formed their own political parties.

It is impossible to tell straightforwardly how many ethnic groups exist in Mauritius. Cultural differences are communicated in a variety of situations, but they do not always refer to the same social distinctions. A Mauritian Hindu, for example, can be morally and socially compelled to marry at the caste level, but will usually vote for the party representing all (northern) Hindus. Further, distinctions are made between groups whose existence is ignored by other Mauritians, such as when Creoles distinguish between Rodriguais (from Mauritius' island dependency Rodrigues) and Mauritian Creoles. Similarly, Mauritian Tamils would distinguish between urban and rural Tamils, sometimes to the extent of discouraging intermarriage, but such a distinction is not widely known outside of the Tamil 'community'. To the question of 'How many ethnic groups exist in Mauritius?', therefore, we must reply that this depends on the situation.

As a general rule, ethnic folk taxonomies are at their most detailed closest to the actor. To a white Franco-Mauritian, it is of little consequence that Shi'ite and Sunni Muslims do not intermarry, or that there is little political loyalty between Marathis and Biharis (both of them Hindus). To the agents themselves, such distinctions may be of great importance in practical matters as well as in matters relating to identity and definition of self in relation to others.

## CONTRASTING AND MATCHING

Many studies of ethnicity have stressed the relative distinctiveness of ethnic groups. Very often it is taken for granted that the groups in a polyethnic social system remain apart and different in most regards, and a great number of studies focus on the ways in which the groups manage to remain discrete (see chapter 3). However, since ethnicity is an aspect of relationship, one may equally well stress the mutual contact and the integrative aspect. To some extent this was emphasised in Fredrik Barth's early study of ethnic 'niches' in Swat, where the biological metaphor of symbiosis was used to describe group relations (Barth, 1956), and it was a central point in the Chicago School (for example Wirth, 1956 [1928]) that the degree of isolation varied in interethnic relationships. Barth showed how the three ethnic groups of Swat valley (in north Pakistan), the Pathans, the Kohistanis and the Gujars, had adapted economically not only to the natural environment but also to the human aspect of their environment; that is to say, to each other. They had gradually developed mutual interdependencies through trade, exchanging necessities and services each of them had specialised in providing. The transhumant mountain Gujars, for example, depended on the lowland Pathans for fodder, while the Pathans bought dairy products from the Gujars.

In Harald Eidheim's (1971) studies of the Sami in northern Norway, processes of interethnic accommodation are described in great detail at the level of interaction. Eidheim shows how negative stereotyping can be interrelated with a shared cultural repertoire – indeed, that both aspects are probably necessary components of a stable system of interethnic relations.

Group membership and loyalties are confirmed and strengthened through stereotyping and the articulation of conflict or competition between Sami and Norwegians. This mutual demarcation process can be called contrasting, or in Eidheim's terms, 'dichotomisation'.

For interethnic interaction to take place at all, however, there must be some mutual recognition inherent in the process of communicating cultural differences. Otherwise, the ethnic identity of at least one of the parties will necessarily be neglected and undercommunicated in a situation of interaction. Such an acknowledgement of differences can be labelled matching (Eidheim uses the term 'complementarisation'). Here, the cultural differences communicated through ethnicity are considered a fact and frequently an asset. Whereas contrasting essentially expresses an Us–Them kind of relationship, matching can be described as a We–You kind of process. When one enters an interethnic relationship, it is necessary to establish a field of complementarity. This could be a shared language within which interaction can take place.

In relation to power, matching can lead to two opposite results. Indigenous and other minority movements which seek recognition by the majority may try to establish an ideology of complementarity in order to be able to negotiate on an equal footing with the majority. On the other hand, dominant groups may also speak of complementarity in order to justify exploitation of and discrimination against minorities. This may be particularly relevant in societies with an ethnic division of labour, where, for example, particular ethnic groups carry out most of the underpaid manual work. In such situations, dominant groups may emphasise that it is the 'nature' of the members of group X to do manual work; that they are 'unsuitable' – by nature or by culture – to carry out prestigious jobs. The former apartheid system of South Africa exemplifies this hierarchical kind of complementarity, as did race relations in the USA before the civil rights movement. The parallel with gender studies is obvious here; male-centred (or androcentric) ideologies of gender tend to justify the subjugation of women by referring to ideals of complementarity.

An important point demonstrated by the preceding discussion is that interethnic relations are not necessarily conflictual. Although there are frequently discrepancies of power (in Swat, the Pathans are clearly the dominant group), interethnic systems of communication and/or exchange may well be based on cooperation and mutual acknowledgement. Indeed, if there is little complementarisation in interethnic relations, there will usually be a tendency towards identity shift or assimilation among members of the weaker group. To sum up: ethnicity entails the establishment of both Us–Them differences (contrasting) *and* a shared field for interethnic discourse and interaction (matching).

## ETHNIC STIGMA

Although it has scarcely been accorded a central place in the anthropological study of ethnicity (as opposed to the sociological tradition of studying 'race relations'), it is a fact that many interethnic relations are highly asymmetrical regarding access to political power and economic resources. It therefore seems appropriate at this point to present an interethnic relationship which has for centuries been marked by clearly hierarchical aspects.

Unlike the transhumant Sami of the mountain tundra of northern Scandinavia, the Sami of the Norwegian Arctic coast are not reindeer herders. Like the Norwegians who live in the same area, they obtain their livelihood from fishing and marginal agriculture. The two populations have been in contact for many centuries. They occupy the same economic niche, they live in the same kinds of houses, wear the same kind of clothing and practise the same Protestant religion. Upon arriving in one of these mixed communities, Eidheim (1969, 1971) looked in vain for cultural traits distinguishing Sami from Norwegians. During the first months of his fieldwork, the locals took great pains to show off their Norwegianness. They always spoke the local Norwegian dialect. The housewives had what to Eidheim seemed 'a craze for cleanliness'. (Uncleanliness was considered a typical Sami vice by ethnic Norwegians.) On the face of it, there were no Sami in the community. However, although 'there is a conspicuous lack of "contrasting cultural traits" between ... [Sami] and Norwegians ... these ethnic labels are attached to communities as well as to families and individual persons, and are in daily use' (Eidheim, 1971: 51).

Gradually some of Eidheim's informants took him into their confidence, realising that he, a southerner and an unusual one at that, had no stake in the local interethnic system. As he grew to know them better, it turned out that many of the locals habitually spoke Sami (a Finno-Ugric language unrelated to Norwegian) at home. Indeed, a majority of the fjord population were Sami. However, it was impossible to engage people in conversations about ethnicity in public. In such situations, at the shop or at the quay for example, people would always act emphatically Norwegian. They would certainly speak Norwegian in such situations.

In this part of the country the Sami have traditionally been the weaker party in a patron–client relationship, and they had for centuries been considered primitive, backward, stupid and dirty by the dominant Norwegians. Therefore, Sami ethnic identity was consistently *undercommunicated* in public situations. Conversely, their command of modern Norwegian culture was strongly *over-communicated*; they presented themselves as Norwegians to others. Sami identity became a kind of secret. Still, everybody in the community knew who was 'really' a Sami and who was not. Thus a total identity change was nearly impossible in the short run (say, within an individual's lifetime), even if there were few 'objective cultural differences' between Sami and Norwegians. Since it was connected with undesirable and presumably immutable personality traits, Sami identity could be described as a stigmatised identity. Being recognised as a Sami entailed that one was considered inferior to Norwegians, and this, of course, was the main reason why Sami identity was being undercommunicated. Moreover, many Sami themselves shared the dominant, pejorative view of Sami culture, and refused to teach their children Sami. This kind of self-contempt is characteristic of powerless groups in polyethnic contexts.

Since the 1950s, the mountain Sami have gone through a process of ethnic *incorporation*: they have organised themselves politically on an ethnic basis. This coastal Sami population has rather moved towards *assimilation*, gradually losing their markers of distinctiveness and merging into the majority population. Eventually, it seemed at the time of Eidheim's fieldwork, the descendants of these Sami would become Norwegian, just like the inhabitants of many small fishing communities on this coast, which were formerly Sami but which are now – after generations of cultural 'Norwegianisation' – considered Norwegian. This kind of process is very common among discriminated minorities, but it presupposes that there is a real, practical possibility of removing the stigma imposed by the dominant population. If, for example, the Sami had been physically very different from the Norwegians, the process of assimilation would probably have been more difficult.

It should be noted, however, that many coastal Sami have remained 'split' between Norwegian and Sami identities in a sometimes problematic way (Hovland, 1996). Aware of their Sami ancestry and of the fact that their grandparents (and sometimes parents) had a way of life that was very distinct from the Norwegian one, many feel attached to their Sami identity despite its low public status. In other Sami areas there has actually been a strong Sami revitalisation movement in recent years, proclaiming the virtues of Sami identity in a manner reminiscent of the 'Black is beautiful' movement in the United States.

## NEGOTIATING IDENTITY

An important insight from the Copperbelt studies, foreshadowed in Robert Park's 'urban ecology', was that ethnicity and social identities in general are relative and to some extent situational. As Mitchell writes, an individual can behave as a 'tribal' in some situations and as a 'town-dweller' in others (Mitchell, 1966). This fact should remind us that even in typical polyethnic societies where cultural differences are pervasive, there are many situations where ethnicity does not matter. This holds good not only in intraethnic relationships, but also in interethnic ones. Mauritian Hindus and Creoles often meet without implicitly or explicitly referring to their respective ethnic identities, for instance where the situation is defined through their statuses as colleagues or business partners.

The material from the Copperbelt and Mauritius also indicates that the compass of the 'We' category may expand and contract according to the situation. At general elections in Mauritius an individual may identify him or herself with the Hindu community at large; when looking for a job the extended kin group may be the relevant category, and when abroad he or she may actually take on an identity as simply Mauritian, even to the extent of feeling closer to Christian and Muslim Mauritians than to Hindus from India (Eriksen, 1992a: chapter 9, 1998). Similarly, Scandinavian identity is at its strongest when a Scandinavian encounters people from the neighbouring Scandinavian countries abroad. In most other situations that particular identity is not activated; it does not seem relevant in the definition of social situations. In other words, individuals have many statuses and many possible identities, and it is an empirical question when and how ethnic identities become the most relevant ones.

This fluidity and relativity of identity can sometimes be studied in interaction as negotiation of identity. *The Kalela Dance* exemplifies such a negotiation, where the agents disagree about the definition of their relationship. Mitchell describes the situation in this way:

A man and three women are drinking beer together in a beer-hall. One of the women belongs to the Lozi tribe. The man is a Ngoni, while the two other women are Ndebele. Suddenly the Lozi woman snatches a coin from him, says, 'A foreigner has lost his money,' and buys herself a cup of beer. The man asks why she took the money and demands that she give it back. She replies that there is a joking relationship between their tribes and that she was therefore entitled to take the money. The man denies that such a relationship exists. It then turns out that there is a joking relationship between the Lozi and the Ndebele, and that the woman identifies the man as being 'more or less' a Ndebele. The Ngoni and Ndebele tribes are linguistically and geographically close. The man insists that he is not a Ndebele but a Ngoni, but the woman does not pay him back. (Mitchell, 1956: 39–40)

In this situation, the Lozi woman insisted that a Ngoni was for practical purposes 'the same' as a Ndebele and could therefore be dealt with in the standardised way, whereas the man insisted that he was certainly not Ndebele. He challenged the validity of her taxonomic extension including the Ngoni in the same general category as the Ndebele. Similarly, London Brahmins might feel offended if they were to be treated, by native English people, in the same standardised way as black Londoners of Jamaican origin. In such a situation the Brahmins would be challenging the English taxonomic category of 'immigrant' or 'minority', insisting that there were socially relevant differences between kinds of immigrants.

In other interethnic situations where identity is negotiated, the issue may rather be whether or not to make ethnic identity relevant. Although it may be difficult to neglect the ethnic dimension entirely in such situations, it can often effectively be over- or undercommunicated. Notably, members of stigmatised and powerless ethnic categories such as the coastal Sami would usually be prone to play down the importance of ethnicity in interaction with the dominant Norwegians – or they might try, in a negotiating approach, to present themselves as carriers of a Norwegian identity.

The point here is that ethnicity can be a fluid and ambiguous aspect of social life, and can, to a considerable degree, be manipulated by the agents themselves. Of course, ethnic identities cannot be manipulated indefinitely, and one cannot ascribe any identity to somebody by claiming, say, that an Irish person is 'really' a Jamaican. Ethnicity can be of varying importance in social situations, and it is often up to the agents themselves to decide upon its significance.

## ETHNICITY FROM THE INDIVIDUAL'S POINT OF VIEW

When does ethnicity matter? It has already been stated that ethnicity occurs in social contexts where cultural differences 'make a difference'. But what kind of difference? This is a very complex question which we can only begin to explore here.

In the mining towns of the Copperbelt in the 1940s and 1950s, ethnicity played a small but not insignificant role in the allocation of jobs. Although workers were hired by the mining companies, people could use their ethnic networks as sources of information and recommendations when looking for work. Ethnic distinctions still had a part to play in matters pertaining to marriage. Mitchell (1956) and Epstein (1958, 1978, 1992) also report the modest emergence of what we would today call ethnic politics, although ethnicity or 'tribalism' remained 'essentially a category of interaction in casual social intercourse' and did 'not form the basis for the organization of corporate groups' (Mitchell, 1956: 42). However, groups speaking the same language would, for example, protest that church services were conducted in a language unrelated to their own, and thus ethnic identity could function politically in certain contexts.

In Mauritius, which has a longer history as a plural society than the Copperbelt, ethnic membership can be important to individuals in a number of ways. Jobs have traditionally been allocated on an ethnic basis, usually through personal acquaintances or kinship. In many cases, religious associations and cults are also tightly linked with ethnic membership. Politics is thoroughly 'ethnified', and Mauritians tend to vote for parties which ostensibly represent the interests of their 'community'. Youth clubs tend to be ethnic or religious in character, and this is often where Mauritians make friends and meet prospective wives or husbands. Most families have traditionally insisted that their children marry within the 'community'. This means that in Mauritius, ethnic membership can provide people with their livelihoods, their spouses, their friends and their religion.[3] In addition, ethnic identity offers a sense of continuity with the past and personal dignity. This aspect of ethnicity will be looked at more closely from chapter 4 onwards.

For ethnic membership to have a personal importance, it must provide the individual with something he or she considers valuable. However, we must make one important reservation: in some cases, ethnic identities are imposed from the outside, by dominant groups, on those who do not themselves want membership in the group to which they are assigned.

For many years, sociology and social anthropology contended that modernisation would eventually level out and remove ethnic

3. To some extent, this has changed since Mauritius was industrialised and increasingly culturally globalised from the mid 1980s onwards. Some implications of these changes for ethnicity will be suggested in chapter 9.

distinctions. The general argument was that it would no longer be profitable to pay allegiance to ethnic groups in modern, individualistic and bureaucratic societies, and that the processes of modernisation would also remove the cultural differences between groups. This was Max Weber's view. Godfrey Wilson spoke of 'detribalisation', and in a later study of urbanisation in South Africa, Philip Mayer (1961) argued that 'trade unions transcend tribes', arguing along the same lines as Park, who described what he saw as melting-pot processes (see Bank, 2009, for an update of the South African ethnography).

Do trade unions transcend tribes? Ethnicity has not only proved resilient in situations of change; it has also often emerged in forceful ways during the very processes of change which many believed would do away with it. On the other hand, there is no doubt that the meaning as well as the organisational form of ethnicity changes with other aspects of society. In order to find out what actually happens to ethnicity in the context of social change, we must therefore pose the question in more accurate terms than merely asking whether it disappears or stays the same. Its relative social importance is highly variable, for one thing, and in this respect, Steve Fenton (1999) has proposed a useful distinction between *hot* and *cold* ethnicity, which refers to its varying degrees of social importance and emotional intensity. Obviously, the situation in Rwanda during the massacres of 1994, where survival was contingent on ethnic identity, has little in common with the situation in South Dakota, where farmers of Scandinavian ancestry occasionally celebrate their culture of origin.

## CRITERIA FOR ETHNICITY

Before we turn to look at ethnic group dynamics and processes of ethnic incorporation, we must enquire as to the substance of ethnic membership and classification. In other words, what is the stuff of ethnicity? How is it that some categories of people can be labelled ethnic while others cannot? Why is it that social classes, or the inhabitants of Somerset, or for that matter the members of a science-fiction club, are not considered ethnic groups, while the Sami, the Bisa and the Mauritian Creoles are? For a long time it was common to equate 'ethnic groups' with 'cultural groups'; any category of people who had 'a shared culture' was considered an ethnic group. As we have seen, this position has become difficult to justify. As Moerman discovered during fieldwork in Thailand (Moerman, 1965), the sharing of cultural traits frequently crosses group boundaries and, moreover, people do not always share all their relevant 'cultural traits' with the people who belong to their ethnic group. One may have the same language as some people, the same religion as some of those as well as of some others, and the same economic strategy as an altogether different category of people. In other words, cultural boundaries are not clear-cut, nor do they necessarily correspond with ethnic boundaries. As Eugeen Roosens remarks: 'There is more chance that the Flemish in Brussels, who always have to speak French, will become more "consciously" Flemish than their ethnic brothers and sisters in the rather isolated rural areas of West Flanders or Limburg' (1989: 12). With this observation, we are also reminded of the fact that ethnicity is an aspect of relationship, not a cultural property of a group. If a setting is wholly mono-ethnic, there is effectively no ethnicity, since there is nobody there to communicate cultural difference to.

It is also clear that the criteria which constitute ethnicity vary. It will simply not do to state that an ethnic group is marked by shared culture, or even to point at specific 'shared traits' such as shared religion, language and/or customs. The Mauritian case brings this out clearly. Of the four ethnic groups which legally exist in Mauritius, two are defined in relation to religion (Hindus and Muslims), one in relation to geographic origin (Chinese), and one is a residual category containing people with their origins in France, Africa and/or Madagascar (general population). Nearly all of the latter are Catholics, but this cannot be a distinguishing criterion since most of the Chinese are also Catholics. A few of those who are classified as Hindus are also Catholics.

Many anthropologists have grappled with the problem of criteria for what is and what is not ethnicity. Abner Cohen (1974b) has taken an extreme position in arguing that London stockbrokers may be said to constitute an ethnic group; they are largely endogamous (at least to the extent of marrying within their class) and have a shared identity. Many other anthropologists would wish to delimit ethnic status to groups with a more obvious permanence in time and a clearer cultural identity based on fictive kinship, and would perhaps emphasise that ethnic identity sticks to the individual, that one cannot entirely rid oneself of it (Barth, 1969a). The general problem remains, nevertheless: where should we draw the boundary between ethnic groups and other groups, such as social classes?

Manning Nash (1988) has proposed, as the lowest common denominators for all ethnic groups, the metaphors of 'bed, blood and cult'. By this he means that all ethnic groups consider themselves as biologically self-perpetuating and endogamous, that they have an ideology of shared ancestry, and that they have a shared religion. This kind of definition, whereby one denotes a number of presumedly objective criteria for ethnicity, has been challenged on many occasions (see chapter 3). Nonetheless, ethnic groups or categories generally have notions of common ancestry justifying their unity. But even this delineation can be contested within the group and from the outside, for how many generations does one have to go back in order to talk of shared ancestry?

Some ethnic groups use notions of 'race' or 'blood' in their ideology. Other groups rather emphasise criteria of cultural competence. Some groups do not allow outsiders to assimilate, whereas others do. However, they all have notions of shared culture in common; in this ethnic groups are distinct from classes.

The main problems which have been posed here deal with the relationship between ethnicity and culture, and the question of where an ethnic group ends and another begins. We shall return to both of these questions regularly in later chapters.

This chapter has argued that ethnicity is a product of contact and not of isolation, and it has also shown why the idea of an isolated ethnic group is meaningless. By implication, ethnicity entails both commonalities and differences between categories of people – both complementarisation and dichotomisation. The next chapter will show how social anthropologists conceptualise processes of ethnic incorporation and the maintenance of ethnic distinctions, or ethnic boundaries, through time.

## FURTHER READING

Epstein, A.L. (1992) *Scenes from African Urban Life: Collected Copperbelt Essays.* Edinburgh: Edinburgh University Press. Some of these essays were written in the 1950s, but they remain, with some of Mitchell's work, among the finest studies of ethnicity at the level of interpersonal relationships.

Hannerz, Ulf (1980) *Exploring the City: Inquiries Toward and Urban Anthropology.* New York: Columbia University Press. Excellent introduction to the main schools of urban anthropology, many of them concerned with ethnicity, up to the late 1970s.

# 3
# The Social Organisation of
# Cultural Distinctiveness

Cultural traits are not absolutes or simply intellectual categories, but are invoked to provide identities which legitimize claims to rights. They are strategies or weapons in competitions over scarce social goods.

Peter Worsley (1984: 249)

So far I have examined central aspects of ethnic processes at the interpersonal level, including stereotyping, under- and overcommunicating, contrasting and matching, and ethnic stigma. In this chapter I shall go one step further and ask how ethnic groups develop, what ends they serve and how they are reproduced through time. Although the emphasis remains on ethnic processes taking place at the interpersonal, individual level, some ways in which ethnicity may be present in other, more encompassing, social contexts will also be indicated.

## ASCRIPTION AS A DECISIVE FEATURE OF ETHNICITY

Towards the end of the last chapter, the question of the relationship between ethnicity and culture was briefly raised, and it was concluded that it would be misleading to state simply that ethnic groups are identical with cultural groups and that shared culture is the basis of ethnic identity. This problem has been addressed by many social anthropologists, and many of them have concluded that one ought to focus on social interaction and social organisation rather than 'cultural content'. Edmund Leach's classic monograph on the Kachin in northern Burma (Leach, 1954) analyses the Kachin–Shan relationship. Leach argues that social organisation is more fundamental than culture:

Culture provides the form, the 'dress' of the social situation. As far as I am concerned, the cultural situation is a given factor, it is a product and an accident of history. I do not know *why* Kachin women go hatless with bobbed hair before they are married, but

43

assume a turban afterwards, any more than I know *why* English women put on a ring on a particular finger to denote the same change in social status; all I am interested in is that in this Kachin context the assumption of a turban by a woman does have this symbolic significance. It is a statement about the [social] status of the woman. (Leach, 1954: 16)

In a later, highly influential essay, Fredrik Barth (1969a) develops a model for the study of ethnic relations which conforms to Leach's general perspective in that it displaces 'culture' from the front stage of ethnic studies and argues that the focus of research ought to be the *boundaries* which delimit the group and not the 'cultural stuff' it encloses. Although it has clear predecessors in the Chicago School, in Leach's work, the Copperbelt studies and in less known contributions by Soviet scholars (see Bromley, 1974), Barth's essay was remarkable for its clarity and conciseness, and it has played a pivotal part in delineating the field of enquiry in the anthropological study of ethnicity.

Arguing against those anthropologists who identify ethnic groups with cultural units, Barth stresses that such definitions of ethnic groups 'allows us to assume that boundary maintenance is unproblematic and follows from the isolation which the itemized characteristics imply: racial difference, cultural difference, social separation and language barriers, spontaneous and organized enmity' (Barth, 1969a: 11). This, in his view, is unfortunate for two main reasons.

First, a focus on the cultural uniqueness of ethnic groups wrongly presupposes that groups tend to be isolated. On the contrary, Barth suggests, a distinct, shared culture may profitably be seen as an implication or result of a long-term social process, rather than as a primordial feature of groups.

Second, definitions based on notions of shared culture wrongly imply that the maintenance of ethnic boundaries is unproblematic. In fact, Barth argues, the main task for the anthropological study of ethnicity consists in accounting for the maintenance and consequences of ethnic boundaries. As groups are in continuous contact with one another, the persistent fact of cultural variation needs to be accounted for, since this is not a fact of nature.

This approach to ethnicity advocates a focus on that which is *socially effective* in interethnic relations, and Barth regards the ethnic group chiefly in terms of social organisation. It follows that ethnic groups must be defined from within, from the perspective of their members. Instead of listing traits of 'objective culture', which members often share with non-members anyway, Barth defines ethnicity as categorical ascriptions which classify individuals in terms of their 'basic, most general identity'. Since ethnic membership must be acknowledged by the agents themselves in order to be socially effective, this is the crucial criterion for Barth. As he notes, it 'makes no difference how dissimilar members may be in their overt behaviour – if they say they are A, in contrast to another cognate category B ... they declare their allegiance to the shared culture of A's' (Barth, 1969a: 15). The discontinuity between ethnic groups is chiefly a social discontinuity, not a cultural one.

A different position would hold that ethnic identities and boundaries ought to be studied in relation to large-scale historical processes which the agents themselves can only influence to a negligible extent (see chapter 5). For now, we shall focus on the kinds of insight into ethnic processes which may emerge from a focus on ethnic boundary maintenance and interaction across these boundaries.

## BOUNDARY MAINTENANCE

In stressing that the focus of investigation ought to be the boundary that separates the ethnic groups from each other, Barth advocates a *relational* and *processual* approach to ethnicity. The ethnic group is defined through its relationship to others, highlighted through the boundary, and the boundary itself is a social product which may have variable importance and which may change through time. The group's culture, as well as forms of social organisation, may change without removing the ethnic boundary. In some cases, groups may actually become culturally more similar at the same time that boundaries are strengthened. This, it could be argued, has been the case in Trinidad, where a cultural 'Creolisation' of the population of Indian descent has taken place during the same period as a strong ethnic revitalisation and emphasis on boundary maintenance (Eriksen, 1992b, 2007c; Vertovec, 1992; see also chapter 5). Conversely, Jan-Petter Blom (1969) has shown that, due to peculiar ecological circumstances, Norwegian mountain farmers lead a very different life from lowland farmers, yet they are not considered a distinct ethnic group. It would therefore be misleading to argue that ethnic boundaries contain 'cultures'. Cultural differences relate to ethnicity if and only if such differences are made relevant in social interaction.

The outbreak of civil war in Yugoslavia in 1991, and the eventual fragmentation of the federation, exemplifies the relativity of ethnic boundaries. There had been peace between Serbs and Croats since 1945, and the rate of intermarriage between the groups had been high. Serbs and Croats spoke dialects of the same language. Perhaps the main cultural difference between the groups was the fact that they practised different variants of Christianity and that they used different scripts (the Serbs are Orthodox and use the Cyrillic alphabet, while the Croats are Catholic and use Latin script). Nonetheless, it was repeatedly stressed, following the outbreak of war in June 1991, that the groups were irreconcilable and culturally incompatible; Serbs claimed that the Croats were fascists and Croats claimed that the Serbs were imperialists.[1] Similar processes took place in the Bosnian countryside a couple of years later, where, as Tone Bringa has shown (Bringa, 1996), villagers of three religions had lived side by side for as long as anyone could remember. Ethnic boundaries, dormant for decades, were activated; presumed cultural differences which had been irrelevant for two generations were suddenly 'remembered' and invoked as proof that it was impossible for the two groups to live side by side. It is only when they *make a difference* in interaction that cultural differences are important in the creation of ethnic boundaries.

Barth further argues that cultural variation may indeed be an *effect* and not a *cause* of boundaries. Following the break-up of Yugoslavia and the creation of new Croat and Serb/Montenegrin states, not only did the national borders between the Croat and Serb states become permanent; a process is also under way which seems gradually to make their languages and other aspects of culture more distinctive.

## BOUNDARY TRANSCENDENCE AND FLUIDITY

Ethnic boundaries are not necessarily territorial boundaries, but social ones. They do not isolate groups entirely from each other;

1. Gellner (1983) wrote, years before violence erupted in the region, that the religious labels distinguishing the ethnic groups in polyethnic Bosnia refer to past, not present differences. 'What [the Bosnian Muslims] meant was that they could not describe themselves as Serb or as Croat (despite sharing a language with Serbs and Croats), because these identifications carried the implications of *having been* Orthodox or Catholic ... Nowadays, to be a Bosnian Muslim you need not believe that there is no God but God and that Mohamed is his Prophet, but you do need to have lost that faith' (Gellner, 1983: 71–2).

rather, there is a continuous flow of information, interaction, exchange and sometimes even people across them. The latter point needs to be exemplified, since it is normally assumed that people do not change ethnic membership.

An example cited by Barth is the flow of people across the Pathan–Baluch boundary in north-western Pakistan. Because of differences between the respective political systems, a male Pathan who has lost his position in Pathan society can be assimilated with his entire household as a client of a Baluch chief. Although clientship is despised among Pathans, it can be honourable enough among the Baluch. This change of identity is naturally two-sided: in assuming Baluch identity, one loses Pathan identity even if one's Pathan origins remain acknowledged. In this way, the boundaries are maintained despite a flow of persons across them.

Gunnar Haaland (1969) describes the mechanisms of boundary transcendence in Darfur, western Sudan in the mid 1960s (that is, well before the recent horrors in the region). Haaland describes the relationship between two groups, the Fur, who are sedentary cultivators, and the Baggara, who are pastoral nomads. Although they have been in contact for centuries, the two groups differ 'with regard to general style of life, subsistence pattern, overt cultural features like language, house type and weapons, and standards for evaluation of performance' (Haaland, 1969: 59). The ethnic boundary between the groups seems a rather impermeable one. Unlike the situation of the Lue and their neighbours, the ethnic segments of Chicago or the relationship between the tribal categories on the Copperbelt, the boundaries between the Fur and the Baggara are highly visible and are closely related to distinct cultural practices. Yet there are many examples of people who cross the boundary permanently.

The relationship between Fur and Baggara can be described as one based on economic complementarity. They exchange goods; notably, the Fur sell millet and receive milk and livestock in return. There is also some exchange of services between the groups. There is a clear contrasting of identities in interaction. The main reason that some Fur still choose to become Baggara, argues Haaland, is economic. For although Fur are chiefly growers of millet, many also own cows. When a Fur farming family has a certain number of cows, it is no longer profitable for it to remain sedentary. The family would then allocate its resources more efficiently by shifting to a semi-nomadic way of life. Such a shift is only the first step in the process of identity change. After a certain period of semi-nomadism when the household still cultivates some millet and stays close to the Fur village, it will eventually have a sufficient number of cattle to migrate to distant Baggara areas during the rainy season, and will no longer depend on millet cultivation. Then the household will attach itself to a camp of Arabic-speaking Baggara. The children will grow up speaking Arabic and will not learn the categories of Fur culture. They will consider themselves, and will be considered as, Baggara; 'they will constitute disappearing lines in local Fur genealogies' (Haaland, 1969: 65). Moreover, in interaction with sedentary Fur they will be treated as Baggara, since the same standardised statuses will be made relevant in the market-place and other arenas for interethnic encounters. Despite the fact that about 1 per cent of the Fur turn nomadic every year, the boundaries between the groups remain intact.

The rationale for the crossing of boundaries is in this case clearly economic. Nomadisation, it appeared, would most likely end in Darfur, since new investment opportunities were emerging for the sedentary population in the 1960s. Could this be stated as a general principle? Not unless we define 'economic' in a very wide sense, including non-tangible benefits. For a member of a stigmatised ethnic group, it may be worthwhile to assimilate even if it does not pay off economically, so long as it removes the stigma. Studies of caste-climbing in India (Bailey, 1968) have thus shown that low castes may be willing to invest considerable amounts of money in order to achieve a higher ritual status, and similar processes take place with ethnic groups. It should also be remembered that identity change is not always possible. Blacks in the United States, for example, cannot choose to become white, even if they spend several generations, or great sums of money on cosmetic surgery, on the attempt. In this regard, the boundaries between whites and blacks are more rigid than the boundaries were between Fur and Baggara. The violence of the Darfur region erupting in 2003, which involved Baggara tribes – Baggara being a term describing many nomadic groups in the eastern Sahel – and Fur fighting on different sides, is a reminder, incidentally, that long-term outcomes of interethnic relations cannot be predicted.

## DEGREES OF ETHNIC INCORPORATION

The concept of ethnic boundary places the focus of ethnic studies on the *relationship* between groups. The boundary is that invisible dividing line *between* them. Boundaries are generally two-way; that is to say, both groups in a relationship demarcate their identity and distinctiveness vis-à-vis the other. Concerning the character of the groups that the boundaries contain, Barth mentions their variable social importance. At one extreme, ethnicity can function merely as categorical ascriptions or labels used to classify people, which was to a great extent the case in the Copperbelt. At the other extreme, ethnic organisation may structure crucial aspects of the individual's life and have great importance at the level of society. As Abner Cohen has argued:

> There is ethnicity and ethnicity ... I think that it is common sense that the ethnicity of a collectivity that manifests itself in the form of an annual gathering of a few of its numbers to perform a dance or a ceremonial is different from the ethnicity manifested by, say, the Catholics in Northern Ireland. (A. Cohen, 1974a: xiv)

This variability in the organisational importance of ethnicity has been explored by Don Handelman (1977), who has constructed a useful typology of degrees of ethnic incorporation – from the very loose and socially almost insignificant category to the tight corporate group. He distinguishes between the ethnic category, the ethnic network, the ethnic association and the ethnic community. I will now show how this typology may shed light on ethnicity in Mauritius.

The least incorporated kind of ethnic collectivity is the *ethnic category*, which provides its members little in terms of tangible valuables. The ethnic category is constituted by the fact that contrastive categories are used to identify members and outsiders; its shared 'assets' could be described as 'categorical corporate holdings' (Handelman, 1977: 264). In other words, ethnic category membership teaches the individual appropriate behaviour vis-à-vis others, passes on knowledge about his or her (imputed) origins and legitimises the existence of the ethnic category. In a system of interaction where corporate ethnic groups do not exist, but where ethnic categorisation is used, ethnicity may still be highly important as a guiding principle for interaction. In Mauritius, the Creoles may be said to be an ethnic category (Boswell, 2006; Eriksen, 1986, 1988). They consider themselves, and are considered by others, as culturally distinctive. Yet they are politically fragmented and lack overarching organisations as well as effective interpersonal networks based on ethnicity.

The next degree of ethnic incorporation in Handelman's typology is the *ethnic network*. This concept 'suggests that people will regularly interact with one another in terms of an ethnic membership set' (Handelman, 1977: 269). Such a network, while based on principles of ethnic categorisation, creates enduring interpersonal ties between members of the same category and can also serve to organise contacts between strangers. The main difference between categories and networks consists in the latter's ability to distribute resources among group members. In situations where members of one's own group are preferred in the job market, ethnic networks are activated. However, the ethnic network is decentralised and can be broken down into dyadic relationships: it has no organisational nexus. In Mauritius, the Franco-Mauritians may be said to constitute an ethnic network. As they are a small numerical minority in a parliamentary democracy, they lack shared political organisation and do not function as a visible interest group, but there remains a strong sense of solidarity and cultural uniqueness. There are strong moral obligations for Franco-Mauritians to support each other on an individual basis (Salvierda, 2009).[2]

The ethnic category is constituted through the consistent application of mutually exclusive identity labels, and the ethnic network additionally channels a great deal of interaction along ethnic lines. When members of an ethnic category feel that they have shared interests, and develop an organisational apparatus to express them, it would be appropriate to talk of an *ethnic association*. Although Handelman describes this as a political pressure group encompassing only its members, one may usefully extend the notion to include ethnic categories where a larger or smaller segment of the members is active in such an organisation. The ethnic association, then, embodies the presumed shared interests of the ethnic category at a collective, corporative level. Mauritian Hindus may be mentioned as an example of an ethnic category incorporated in ethnic associations, which articulate the group's collective goals at the level of national society. Such organisations may be political parties, but they may also be Hindu youth clubs (*baitkas*) or religious associations.

2. During fieldwork in Mauritius, I have often been mistaken for a Franco-Mauritian on first encounter. Once a Franco-Mauritian gave me a lift while I was hitch-hiking, and he made a remark about Franco solidarity, adding that he would probably not have stopped if he had known I was foreign.

The highest degree of ethnic incorporation is that of the *ethnic community*. This kind of collectivity has, in addition to ethnic networks and shared political organisation, a territory with more or less permanent physical boundaries. Ethnic groups in political command of nation-states are eminent examples of ethnic communities in this meaning of the word. In a multi-ethnic island-state like Mauritius, no territorially located ethnic community exists, although the Sino-Mauritians or Chinese are close to meeting the requirements. They are linked through tight social networks based on kinship, affinity and friendship, and have pooled considerable economic and political resources in ethnic associations. About half of the category of 30,000 live in a clearly demarcated quarter, Chinatown, in Port-Louis. Handelman's main point, which is only partly true with respect to the Sino-Mauritians, is that the territorially based ethnic organisation places additional demands on its members: they are collectively responsible for guarding the boundaries and for ensuring the continued control of the territory.

As Figure 3.1 indicates, ethnic categorisation is logically prior to the other forms of incorporation.

|  | Category | Network | Association | Community |
|---|---|---|---|---|
| Standardised ethnic ascriptions | X | X | X | X |
| Interaction along ethnic lines |  | X | X | X |
| Goal-oriented corporate organisation |  |  | X | X |
| Territorial base |  |  |  | X |
| *e.g. in Mauritius* | *Creoles* | *Franco-M* | *Hindus* | *Sino-M* |

*Figure 3.1*   Degrees of ethnic incorporation

Source: after Handelman, 1977.

Handelman's typology can be read in a number of ways. It can be seen, as he suggests himself, as a *developmental framework* useful for the analysis of ethnogenesis or the emergence of ethnic corporate groups out of categories. There seems to be a clear development in time from the category through the network and the association to the community. It can nevertheless also be viewed, as my Mauritian examples suggest, as a non-developmental *typology of ethnic organisation*, where different types may coexist within the same polyethnic society. Finally, the typology may be interpreted as a model of *aspects of interethnic processes*. Thus one may through the course of a day pass from a situation where only one's categorical ascription is relevant, to a situation where one's ethnic network is activated, and later to situations where one's ethnic category appears as an association or an ethnic community. Even the Mauritian Creoles, who are usually a fragmented ethnic category lacking leadership and corporate organisation, have occasionally existed as an ethnic association. This has notably come about during election campaigns with politicians overtly representing Creole interests.

If Handelman's typology is read as an evolutionary schema, it should be kept in mind that not all ethnic categories undergo these transitions. In many cases, a very real alternative to ethnic incorporation can be assimilation. A great number of ethnic categories or groups have disappeared from the face of the earth in this way.

In a comparison between Hausa in Ibadan and Luo in Kampala, David Parkin (1974) makes a distinction which is similar to Handelman's typology. Parkin's main argument is that ethnicity is likely to take on corporative characteristics if a group is (i) economically self-sufficient, (ii) residentially segregated, (iii) insulated from the dominant values of greater society, and/or (iv) occupationally specialised (Parkin, 1974: 126–7). Parkin's distinction between 'interpersonal' and 'congregational' ethnicity also resembles the common distinction between 'private' and 'public' fields of interaction. Everything else being equal, an ethnic group operating in a public field will be more tightly integrated than one confined to private fields.

Such typologies of ethnic incorporation deal with ethnicity as a kind of social organisation, and they exemplify Barth's general point that the social content of ethnicity is highly variable. Seen from the individual actor's point of view, the main variable in the typology consists in the constraints and opportunities, or rights and duties, offered by ethnicity. However, the typology may also indicate circumstances under which ethnicity becomes a particularly important aspect of personal identity. It is evident that ethnic identity is normally more important to a member of an ethnic community than to a member of an ethnic category. In other words, the fact that an ethnic boundary exists does not necessarily imply that individuals form strong corporate groups (see also Brubaker, 2002; Jenkins, 2008: 22–3). The strength of group cohesion varies and must be studied empirically in each case.

## ETHNICITY AS RESOURCE COMPETITION

Abner Cohen's perspective on ethnicity, which is related to Barth's although it had its origins in a different school of British anthropology,[3] defines ethnic organisation essentially as a kind of political organisation. In Cohen's view, social interaction and organisation are essentially dual phenomena: they comprise aspects of utility and aspects of meaning. 'Political man is also symbolic man' (A. Cohen, 1974b: Preface). Ethnicity, he argues, is an organisational form which exploits this duality for particular ends, which may or may not be acknowledged by the agents themselves. Ethnic ideology has an immediate appeal because it offers answers to 'the perennial problems of life': the questions of origins, destiny and, ultimately, the meaning of life. However, Cohen adds, ethnicity must also have a practical function in order to be viable. Only by focusing on this aspect is it possible to explain why some ethnic groups thrive while others vanish, and why only some ethnic identifications assume great social importance. Two empirical studies by Cohen exemplify this approach (A. Cohen, 1969, 1981). Both depict ethnicity as an instrument for competition over scarce resources, which is nevertheless circumscribed by ideologies of shared culture, shared origins and metaphoric kinship.

The earlier of these monographs analyses the organisation of Hausa trade networks in the Yoruba city of Ibadan, western Nigeria (A. Cohen, 1969). Hausa migrants to Ibadan succeeded, in a relatively short space of time, in virtually monopolising cattle trade in the city. This was accomplished by way of ethnic organisation. Cattle were bought from Hausa traders in northern Nigeria. Drawing on ethnic solidarity expressed in the idiom of shared culture, and strengthening their group cohesion by joining the orthodox Muslim Tijaniyya order, the Hausa in Ibadan quickly

---

3. Cohen's intellectual lineage connects him to the Manchester School (who were students of Radcliffe-Brown and Evans-Pritchard), while Barth had studied with the Malinowskian Raymond Firth and Edmund Leach, a prominent critic of structural-functionalism.

established reliable trade links with the north. In Cohen's analysis, this was a principal function of ethnicity. Had it not been profitable to be a Hausa in Ibadan and to communicate one's ethnic identity to other Hausas and thereby strengthen ethnic boundaries, Hausa identity might well have disappeared in the Yoruba city.

The second monograph (A. Cohen, 1981) analyses the ways in which Creole[4] political interests were expressed in Sierra Leone during a period when ethnic politics were officially illegitimate. The Creoles were a professional elite, and the political elite, dominated by the numerically superiour Temne and Mende, aimed at reducing their dominance in white-collar professions. Cohen shows how the Creoles succeeded in retaining their privileges through becoming freemasons on a large scale and turning the Masonic lodges into unofficial Creole associations. Although the linkages thus developed might be described as ethnic networks rather than an ethnic association, the group succeeded in reproducing its boundaries and in keeping its 'corporate holdings' within the group. Information about available jobs, scholarships and so on was passed on inside the Masonic network, and the symbolic capital of the ethnic category was thereby kept inside the boundary. As in the Hausa monograph, Cohen argues that the identity tag 'Creole' would have been much less important (and might have vanished) if Creoledom did not have a clear function for its members.

## LEVELS OF ETHNIC INCORPORATION

Most of the anthropologists who have written about ethnic organisation have seen it in the context of competition for scarce resources. The focus has been on organisational forms reminiscent of Handelman's associations and communities rather than categories and networks. Many have seen ethnicity plainly as a possible instrument for pursuing particular interests, or for maximising values. In a book on contemporary ethnopolitics, Roosens (1989: 13) states

4. The term 'Creole' is not an analytic concept. In Mauritius, 'Creole' refers to people of largely African descent. In Sierra Leone it means people who are acknowledged to be descendants of liberated slaves. They are contrasted with 'tribals'. In Trinidad, 'Creole' means any Trinidadian of non-East Indian descent (which could be European, African, Chinese, Syrian/Lebanese or mixed), and in the French *département* of La Réunion, *créole* chiefly refers to whites born in the island (which, incidentally, corresponds to the original meaning of the Spanish *criollo*). See Stewart (2007) for a broad approach to the concept.

that '[m]any people change their ethnic identity only if they can profit by doing so'.

There are two common criticisms of this kind of perspective. First, it pays little attention to the symbolic aspect of ethnicity, ethnic identification, treating it either as irrelevant or as contingent on utility (see chapter 4). Second, through a focus on competition and interpersonal relationships, one will often fail to account for power differences in the society in question, even when these are crucial as a context for the competition (see e.g. B. Williams, 1989).

A focus on power relations may nevertheless divert attention from other important issues. In the Copperbelt, for example, there was scarcely any ethnically based division of labour (provided we exclude the few whites in the area, which the researchers did!). The relationships between the African groups could in this respect be described as *symmetrical*; they took part in the same social and economic system in roughly the same way. When there is an ethnic division of labour, a different pattern of ethnicity results. Very often, ethnicity then takes on a more strongly *hierarchical* character, where the groups are ranked according to their differential access to resources, and here the correlation between class and ethnicity is high.

In a study of ethnic resource competition in Guyana, Leo Despres (1975a) tries to integrate an analysis of societal power relations with an analysis of interpersonal ethnicity by distinguishing between three societal levels where ethnicity is articulated.

Guyanese society is polyethnic. The bulk of the population is divided between Africans (descendants of slaves) and East Indians (descendants of indentured labourers). At the 'level of the overall social system', that of Guyanese society as a whole, the economy is dominated by foreign interests. There is also an ethnic division of labour. The Indians tend to be rural and work in agriculture or small businesses, whereas most of the Africans are urban and do non-agricultural work. The Indians are more numerous than the Africans and have a higher birth rate, but the government is African-dominated. Thus the civil service also tends to be African-dominated. Since ethnicity functions as an ordering principle in interaction, competition for available resources 'has served to order categorically identified elements [ethnic categories] of the Guyanese population in an arrangement of unequal status and power' (Despres, 1975a: 99). This is a clear macro perspective, delineating the conditions, or structural parameters, for interethnic relations at the interpersonal level.

At the second level, that of 'organised ethnic group relations' (Handelman's 'associations' or Parkin's 'congregations'), Despres mentions a large number of organisations which more or less overtly represent the interest of a particular ethnic group. On the one hand, he describes how ethnic leaders pursue group political interests within organisations ostensibly devoted to religion or 'culture'; on the other, he describes the struggle for control over unions and parastatal bodies as interethnic competition. At this level, the ethnic categories themselves appear as corporate actors. Indians and Africans alike identify themselves with 'their own' leaders. Political parties are strongly ethnically based in Guyana, as in several other polyethnic countries. Ethnic differences, in other words, seem more important than other kinds of political differences.

The third level singled out by Despres is that of 'interpersonal encounters'. At this level, he finds much of that ambiguity, relativity and negotiation which was described in chapter 2. He finds many instances of contrasting, and notes that many informal social groupings are mono-ethnic. But he also stresses that Guyanese are flexible in switching situationally between identities. In interethnic situations, the typical mode of matching (the creation of We–You relationships) stresses *equality*. The nation-building ideology of independent Guyana has officially emphasised the irrelevance of ethnicity in relation to citizenship and participation in civil society, even if Guyanese society remains *de facto* ethnically divided. Despres, however, notes that in relation to foreigners, people tend to take on an identity as Guyanese (in contrast to Trinidadian, Jamaican, American, or whatever) rather than as Africans or East Indians. Since ethnic identities are situationally defined, they are imperative only under particular circumstances. In a society like Guyana, where ethnic incorporation is discouraged by the state and where there is great social tension between the groups (there have been numerous 'race riots' since the 1950s), it makes sense that ethnicity should be undercommunicated in daily interethnic encounters.

A main theoretical point in Despres' analysis is that in order to understand ethnicity at the interpersonal level it is necessary to know something about the societal conditions which structure interethnic encounters. Although this perspective incorporates Barth's emphasis on the ethnic group as an organisational vessel based on subjective self-ascription, it introduces an additional element in the account of ethnicity, namely the institutional framework of society. Before considering the relationship between social class and ethnicity, I shall present a perspective on polyethnic societies where the focus is almost entirely on the institutional arrangements of society.

## THE THEORY OF PLURAL SOCIETIES

The theory of plural societies may be compatible with the Barthian model of ethnic differentiation and boundary maintenance, but it does not focus on the acting individual or on the competitive advantages of ethnic organisation. Rather, it deals with the *integration of societies* and is historically linked with the tradition from Durkheim and Radcliffe-Brown in social anthropology: that is, structural-functionalism.

The theory of pluralism is usually associated with the geographer J.S. Furnivall, who wrote extensively on the Dutch and British colonies of South-East Asia (Furnivall, 1948). He regarded these 'plural' societies as being composed of groups which were socially and culturally discrete, which were integrated through economic symbiosis (or mutual interdependence) and the political domination of one group (the colonial masters), but which were otherwise socially discrete, as well as being distinctive concerning language, religion and customs. There were no shared values in these societies, argued Furnivall, and so the groups were held together in a political system by the coercive force of the state, the police and the military. Such societies were, in his view, deeply divided.

A later proponent of pluralist theory is M.G. Smith. His principal work deals with the West Indies before and immediately after independence (M.G. Smith, 1965, 1984). Smith has defined his unit of study as 'the plural society as a unit of disparate parts which owes its existence to external factors, and lacks a common social will' (1965: vii). In a typical plural society, the constituent groups will be differentially integrated: there will be a wide array of ethnically discrete fields of activity, so that extensive contact and mutual influence are kept at a low level. In Smith's view, plural societies are notoriously unstable precisely because they lack 'a common social will'.

Although Smith has been severely criticised for regarding ethnic groups as static, as well as for reifying culture (seeing cultures as fixed and closed systems), notions similar to Smith's remain implicit in many later studies of ethnicity. If the focus of the investigation is on the ethnic boundary that keeps ethnic groups discrete, then one is led to regard the total system as a 'unit of disparate parts', even if the analysis focuses on the contact between members of different ethnic categories. How much contact across ethnic boundaries is necessary for a society to cease to be a volatile plural society composed of discrete groups with no shared values? Conversely, one might say that virtually every society is a unit of disparate parts in so far as it consists of competing interest groups (Jenkins, 1986; cf. also Grillo, 1998: chapter 1).

The theory of social and cultural pluralism is a clear example of what can be called an objectivist approach in ethnicity studies. According to Smith, a chief cause of ethnic differentiation is objective differences of culture. Whereas Barth sees cultural differentiation as a long-term effect of ethnic differentiation and Cohen would regard the cultural aspect of ethnicity as subordinate to its social functioning, Smith sees culture largely as an independent variable. According to this view, ethnicity and ethnic identity cannot be chosen, situationally or otherwise, since there is an intrinsic link between ethnicity and language, custom and social organisation. Since cultural discontinuity is a readily observable fact, this perspective may represent a challenge to ethnicity studies, which have largely been concerned with the social organisational and political aspects of ethnicity while disregarding the cultural dimension (see Bentley, 1987; Eriksen, 1991a, 2000; Haaland, 1992). Below, and in later chapters, we shall pursue some of the difficult questions concerning the relationship between ethnicity and culture further.

## ETHNICITY AND HIERARCHY

Some writers distinguish between 'ranked' and 'unranked' polyethnic systems (for example, Horowitz, 1985; see also Tambiah, 1989). This distinction suggests that in some societies, ethnic groups compete for scarce resources on an equal footing, whereas others are based on systematically unequal access to resources. From an anthropological point of view, such a distinction is unfortunate because it classifies entire societies on the basis of a single principle which is far from unambiguous. Therefore, it may be a better solution to assume that ethnicity may, in different contexts in societies, appear as either horizontal or vertical aspects of social classification. If we regard ethnicity in its horizontal aspect, it may be relevant to focus on competition for scarce resources and/or processes of dichotomisation and boundary maintenance. If, on the other hand, we focus on the vertical aspects of ethnicity, it will be more relevant to focus on power relations. Both the vertical and the horizontal aspects of ethnicity vary in importance: situationally, historically and between societies.

Ethnic ideologies may justify social hierarchies. It is therefore necessary to clarify the relationship between ethnicity and other criteria for hierarchisation.

There is never a simple one-to-one relationship between ethnic membership and rank in a society. The reason is that there are always additional criteria for rank. Gender, class membership, age and other criteria – which vary from society to society – all contribute to defining a person's rank. To illustrate this complexity, we may ask who has the highest rank in British society: a female black surgeon or a male white gardener? It would not be possible to arrive at a simple, unambiguous answer to this question.

In many polyethnic societies, there is nevertheless a high *correlation* between ethnic identity and class membership. In colonial plantation societies (in the Caribbean, in South America and elsewhere), the division of labour was strongly correlated with ethnic identifications; in industrial European societies, non-European immigrants generally occupy the lowest-ranking jobs. It must nevertheless be emphasised that, although ethnicity and class may be linked, they refer to different categorisations. Even in strongly ethnically ranked societies, like South Africa and Namibia during apartheid, there are great variations in class membership within any ethnic categories – there are black capitalists as well as white manual workers.

'Doxic' stereotyping ('doxa' is Bourdieu's, 1977, term for the unquestionable, taken-for-granted aspects of culture) is very powerful in many polyethnic societies and can often function as self-fulfilling prophecies: the negative stereotype created by a dominant group may become part of a group's view of itself. Such stereotyping in turn usually feeds on differences in the respective positions of ethnic groups in the economy and the political system. Peter Worsley (1984: 236) thus notes that 'whole peoples ... are perceived as being naturally suited for distinctive roles in the division of labour, and these "natural" differences often include cultural as well as physical characteristics'.

Worsley further criticises those theorists who assume that there is an 'invariant relationship' between the two criteria for social differentiation; that is, that ethnic groups tend to be congruent with classes in polyethnic class societies. Rather, he continues, class divisions may be related to ethnic divisions in three main ways:

They may *overlap*, reinforcing each other in a congruent or isomorphic manner (as when all workers in a given factory, industry, town or region are of the same ethnic background). If the employer is of a different ethnic background, this solidarity is further reinforced. Ethnicity may, however, cut *across* class, vertically, when members of the same ethnic group are to be found at various levels as workers, clerks or managers, and the employer may also be of the same ethnic group. Thirdly, classes may be *segmented* by ethnicity with skilled workers drawn from one ethnic group, unskilled from another, and so forth: one segment may be of the same ethnic affiliation as management; others may not. (Worsley, 1984: 240)

In Mauritian society, all three kinds of relationship between ethnicity and class can be identified. The mutually reinforcing and localised variety can be found in some coastal villages where the majority of inhabitants are Creoles engaged in fishing, and in some agricultural villages where the majority of the population are Hindu smallholders, labourers or sharecroppers.

Worsley's second type, where ethnicity cuts across class, can be observed in Mauritian towns and in the textile industry, the bureaucracy and in tourism. Members of most ethnic groups may be found at most class levels, although they are not equally represented at each level.

The third variety, perhaps most characteristic of colonial Mauritian society (before 1968), can still be identified in the many villages associated with the large sugar estates. The estates themselves are owned by Franco-Mauritians. The Creoles of these villages tend to work at the factory as skilled workers, whereas the Hindus and Muslims tend to be field labourers. In these villages there is often a single grocery which is run by a Sino-Mauritian family. In some of them there is virtually a one-to-one relationship between ethnic membership and occupation.

Folk taxonomies tend to link ethnic categorisation with occupational categories as well as 'cultural traits'. In a study of the relationship between ethnicity and class in highland Peru, Pierre van den Berghe states:

Ethnicity and class are interrelated but *analytically distinct* phenomena. The fact that different social classes most commonly show subcultural differences and, conversely, that ethnic groups living under a common government are more often than not ordered in a hierarchy of power, wealth and status does not make class reducible to ethnicity, or ethnicity to class. (1975: 73; see also Wade, 1997)

The main social hierarchies in Peru can be described as several partly overlapping systems of domination. In geographic terms, the countryside is dominated by the town, the town by the regional centre, the regional centre by the capital city and the capital by international metropolises. The class system, the administrative or political hierarchy and the linguistic hierarchies are similarly constituted as relationships of domination. Finally, in the ethnic hierarchy, the 'Mestizos' (mixed Indian–European descent) dominate the *cholos* (mixed Mestizo–Indian descent), who in turn dominate the Indians. (There are few Peruvians of European descent.) There is a high correlation between ethnic membership, area of residence, education and linguistic abilities, and class membership. At one end of the continuum there is the cosmopolitan elite, and a typical member of this group is a Mestizo who is trilingual in Spanish, English and French, university-educated, lives in Lima and is a member of a wealthy family with business interests. At the other end of the continuum we find the marginal peasants, who are Indians, largely monolingual in one of the low-status languages (Quechua or Aymara), illiterate and propertyless.

## THE INTERRELATIONSHIP BETWEEN CRITERIA

Despite this high correlation between class membership and ethnic membership, van den Berghe emphasises that the two principles for differentiation function in different ways and ought to be distinguished from each other analytically. He outlines two typical kinds of situation marked by different relationships between class and ethnicity. The first is the colonial African variety, where, to use Worsley's term, the social classes are 'segmented' by ethnicity. Movement of individuals across the ethnic boundaries, which are highly correlated with class and are often codified as 'race', is extremely difficult, although considerable cultural assimilation may take place.

In the other kind of situation, of which Peru is a characteristic example, the 'ethnic groups are clearly hierarchical, but the culturally dominant group is relatively open to members of other ethnic groups' (van den Berghe, 1975: 78). Movement across the ethnic boundary is possible, provided the people in question succeed in acquiring cultural characteristics and class membership associated with the higher-ranking ethnic category. (Downward mobility along these lines is also possible.) Many individuals are ethnically ambiguous; indeed, the largest ethnic category in highland Peru, the *cholo* category, is seen as a fuzzy intermediate category between the 'poles' of Mestizo and Indian. Designation of *cholo*-ness is largely situational in that Mestizos tend to describe their social inferiors as *cholos*. The inhabitants of a highland town would be *cholos* seen from Lima, but they would be regarded as Mestizos from the perspective of the countryside, by virtue of their urban way of life, their dress code and so on. Despite this social transference of class characteristics to ethnic classifications and the high correlation between the two criteria for differentiation, it would be misleading to claim that there is a one-to-one relationship between class and ethnicity. Although class membership is partly determined by a person's command of languages and acquisition of particular cultural markers, class is also determined by several non-ethnic factors. Conversely, there are many aspects of ethnic identity and boundary maintenance which are unrelated to class.

The example from Peru nevertheless shows that there is a certain *contagious* effect of class on ethnicity and vice versa. Etienne Balibar (1991), writing about 'class racism', has argued that ethnic discrimination in France derives from a widely held assumption to the effect that classes are 'natural', and that the idea of superior and inferior races has replaced the aristocratic–commoner dichotomy in French society (see also Wieviorka, 1991). A Mauritian Creole who becomes a member of the middle class and thereby acquires Coloured ethnic characteristics, may change ethnic membership and effectively *become* a Coloured or *gen de couleur*. Further, as M.G. Smith (1965) has noted for the West Indies, people in this kind of society often believe that they classify others by virtue of skin colour, whereas the actual classification relates to class or other criteria of socio-economic status.

Many light-skinned Mauritians are classified as Creoles or *ti-kreol* ('small Creoles'), since they live in a way considered typical of Creoles – they are manual workers or fisherfolk, poor and have many children. Similarly, many dark-skinned Mauritians are considered *gens de couleur* by virtue of their education, use of French language at home and middle-class suburban place of residence. Actual colour is not unimportant in social classification (successful male Creoles tend to marry women with lighter skins than themselves), but in practical classification it functions together with other criteria.

It is widely seen as 'unnatural' that a Franco-Mauritian should be poor or that a Creole should be rich. In the case of one poor Franco-Mauritian in a Mauritian town, some of his acquaintances argued that he was 'really' a 'Mulatto' – they claimed that there were 'negroes' in his ancestry. However, although the relationship between class and ethnicity is sometimes evident and although ethnic classification is sometimes contingent on class membership, we should keep in mind that the relationship varies between societies, and also within societies. Although 'Creole' connotes working class in Mauritius, there are people who are acknowledged as, and regard themselves as Creoles, who belong to the middle class.

## INSTRUMENTALISM AND ITS CRITICS

Disagreements between anthropologists who study ethnicity sometimes reflect fundamental theoretical differences. At this stage some such disagreements will only be outlined, and I shall return to them later.

First, it is common to distinguish between 'primordialist' and 'instrumentalist' perspectives on ethnicity. Barth describes ethnic categories as 'organisational vessels that may be given varying amounts and forms of content in different sociocultural systems' (1969a: 14). Implicitly, he seems to say that despite the contact across boundaries and the change in cultural content of the groups, the ethnic categories as such are constants which may be called upon when the need arises, as in a competitive situation. Barth explicitly defines ethnic ascriptions as categorical ascriptions which classify 'a person in terms of his basic, most general identity, presumptively determined by his origin and background' (1969a: 13). Abner Cohen has argued against this view, which he sees as a 'primordialist' position since it defines ethnic identity as an imperative status, as a more or less immutable aspect of the social person. Although Barth argued against cultural determinism in ethnic studies and stressed the need for investigating the social enactment of ethnicity through flexible and negotiable boundary processes, Cohen accuses him of promoting a static view on ethnicity (A. Cohen, 1974a: xii–xv). In Cohen's view, ethnic identities develop in response to functional organisational requirements. He defines ethnicity simply as a particular form of informal political organisation where cultural boundaries are invoked so that the group's resources or 'symbolic capital' can be secured. In this way, Cohen goes even further than Barth in severing the tie between ethnicity and culture. Indeed, as mentioned above, he regards London stockbrokers as an ethnic group (A. Cohen, 1974a, 1974b).

Cohen's reorientation both widens and narrows the scope of ethnic studies. Unlike Barth, who remains interested in cultural variation, Cohen delimits the field to political processes involving informal corporate groups. In order to obtain the support of their potential followers, the leaders of these groups use 'primordial' symbols in their political strategy. As Cohen himself admits, the very term 'ethnicity' may be unfortunate here. Cohen's position, opposed to the primordialism he attributes to Barth, can be described as an instrumentalist view, where the sole *raison d'être* of ethnicity and ethnic organisation lies in its political functioning. In this view, ethnicity needs no historical or cultural explanation: it arises entirely from contemporary social conditions (see chapter 5).

A critic of Cohen's position might ask why it is that certain symbols are effective and certain ethnic configurations are possible, while others are not. If ethnic identities are created wholly through political processes, then it should have been possible to create any identity at all. Then it would have been possible, for example, to persuade members of the Maasai ethnic category in Kenya that they were really Kikuyus. Since such a feat is evidently not possible, ethnicity must have a non-instrumental, non-political element. However, to be fair, Cohen's main argument is that it is the formation and functioning of ethnic corporate groups that matters sociologically and should provide the focus for research. In this regard, he is on safe ground in arguing that such groups, far from being 'primordial', are results of processes of change – frequently urbanisation and migration. What he does not discuss is the nature of the stuff on which these groups feed. So, it seems, the shared identity of the individuals who eventually form an ethnic group is taken for granted after all in Cohen's model.

Whether Barth is a primordialist or not is a debatable point – he is usually described as an instrumentalist. The distinction between primordialist and instrumentalist views of ethnicity can be useful chiefly because it highlights a crucial duality in ethnicity (see Geertz, 1973 [1963]; Shils, 1980 for positions that might credibly be described as primordialist). The 'organisational vessels' referred to by Barth must have some kind of purpose in order to operate, and they must simultaneously have some kind of appeal to their target group that justifies group allegiance. This point is elegantly driven home by Cohen in his *Two-Dimensional Man* (A. Cohen, 1974b), where the main argument is that ethnic organisation must simultaneously serve political ends *and* satisfy psychological needs for belongingness and meaning.

A second controversy can be described as the relationship between 'subjectivist' and 'objectivist' views on ethnicity. Barth's perspective, where ethnicity is defined as categorical ascriptions undertaken by the agents themselves, is usually regarded as a subjectivist position. An opposing view would hold that ethnic distinctions, ethnic organisation or even ethnic stratification may well exist without the acquiescence or even the awareness of the agents themselves. Typical objectivist perspectives either approach ethnicity as observable characteristics of social organisation, rejecting subjective ascription as an important criterion of ethnicity (A. Cohen's approach), or stress large-scale historical processes and power differences inherent in the social structure as determinants of ethnicity, rather than strategic action (see chapter 5). To some anthropologists, a focus on self-ascription, social classification and strategic action may represent either an unwanted intrusion of psychology into what is essentially a sociological discipline, or a neglect of large-scale historical processes which may be instrumental in determining ethnic relations at the interpersonal level.

A related controversy concerns the notion of 'situational selection', which seems to presuppose that agents are free to choose their actions and whether to under- or overcommunicate ethnic identity. Can ethnicity simultaneously be an imperative status *and* subject to situational selection and choice, or are the two views mutually exclusive? In a major review article, Jonathan Okamura (1981) notes that the anthropologists who have written about situational ethnicity tend to emphasise either the *cognitive* aspect (choice and strategy) or the *structural* aspect (constraints imposed upon actors) of interethnic situations.

This difference in emphasis, as well as the difference between subjectivist and objectivist views of ethnicity, pertains to a fundamental duality in the social disciplines; the distinction, as Holy and Stuchlik (1983: 1) succinctly put it, between 'approaches that study how societies, social systems, or structures function, and approaches that study why people do the things they do'. This difference in perspective is sometimes described as the distinction between a Weberian and a Durkheimian view of social life. Anthony Giddens is an important spokesman for the fusion of the two perspectives. In his theory of structuration (Giddens, 1979, 1984), social life is seen as fundamentally dual, comprising both agency and structure simultaneously; both freedom and constraint, if one prefers.

Studies of ethnicity highlight the interrelationship between choice and constraint. A Pathan may under certain circumstances choose to become a Baluch, but this deprives him of rights in Pathan society and gives him new obligations to a Baluch chief. A Mauritian Creole may choose to undercommunicate her ethnic identity situationally, but she cannot eliminate it altogether. In a plural society such as Guyana, Indo-Guyanese, who are largely smallholders, can choose how they would like to allocate their resources and may even climb socially to a white-collar job, but they cannot choose away the ethnic division of labour and the Afro-Guyanese political hegemony. In a friendly critique of Barth's emphasis on individual choice, Sandra Wallman concludes: 'The ultimate constraint must lie in the fact that no one can take up an option which is not there' (1986: 233). In a more polemical vein, Worsley has written:

> Many interactionist studies of ethnicity at the level of the community are vitiated by a liberal metaphysic developed in open societies, where a degree of choice exists for the individual to consciously decide whether to assimilate or not, and where social mobility is permitted and significant. The individual is thus taken as the jumping-off point in the analysis, and choice is assumed to be the crucial social fact. Life, it would seem, is a market, or a cafeteria. (1984: 246)

Ethnic identities are neither ascribed nor achieved: they are both. They are wedged between situational selection and imperatives imposed from without. I have up to now emphasised the cognitive and voluntary aspects of ethnicity. From now on we shall oscillate somewhat between the two perspectives, trying to show how, as Marx wrote, people make history, but not under circumstances of their own choosing.

## A PROBLEM OF CULTURE

One of the deepest controversies in ethnicity studies concerns the role of culture. As the above discussion indicates, the extremes in this debate are defined through, on the one hand, a position which holds that ethnic groups are simply culturally defined and determined groups; and on the other hand, a position which argues that culture enters ethnicity only in so far as it can be exploited politically. Four decades after *Ethnic Groups and Boundaries*, the debate still goes on. In an exploration of the Protestant–Catholic conflict in Northern Ireland, Jenkins (2008) concludes that 'the cultural stuff' is indeed important, and that 'being a Catholic or a Protestant *really means something*' to the people in question. A similar view was developed earlier by A.P. Cohen (1985) in his book on the symbolic construction of community, where it becomes apparent that the production of boundary maintenance and the production of 'cultural stuff' merge in the creation of symbols. Cohen has also expressed misgivings about the Barthian boundary concept (1994: esp. 121), suggesting that more vaguely defined *frontier areas* frequently occur in intergroup relationships (see chapter 8 for examples).

The relationship between ethnicity and culture is sometimes discussed in the context of *social constructivism* (Bader, 2001; Baumann, 2001). In an extensive critique of Gerd Baumann's study of multi-ethnic Southall (Baumann, 1996; see chapter 8), Veit Bader argues that Baumann's constructivist view of culture reduces it to discourse and self-identifications, thus discarding the objective, often unacknowledged and implicit, aspects of culture. The anthropology of ethnicity thus may be restricted to studying people's *perceptions* of their own culture and their actions, instead of studying their culture. Baumann (2001) responds by distancing himself from cultural determinism and essentialism, emphasising agency and flexibility in identification strategies. The debate reveals important differences; I have elsewhere (Eriksen, 2000) argued that the orthodox positions on ethnicity and nationalism are deeply informed by empiricist, analytical philosophy; while an alternative approach (represented here by Bader) would take its cue from Continental rationalist philosophy, with a resulting difference in emphasis. The Belgian anthropologist Luc de Heusch, in a strong critique of the dominant school of ethnicity studies, accuses his colleague Eugeen Roosens (see chapter 7) of 'a blatant confusion between two levels: the cultural and the political' (de Heusch, 2000: 104), before moving to a detailed discussion of sacred kingship in African societies and its importance for intergroup relations. De Heusch, a structuralist, is concerned with understanding the patterns underlying cultural variation and insists on seeing the *ethnie* 'as a cultural unit and ... a basic anthropological element' (2000: 113). It is nevertheless a fact that very few studies of ethnicity have been undertaken within this tradition in anthropology.

It is also clear that the criticisms – friendly in the case of Jenkins, more hostile in the case of de Heusch – of the instrumentalist bias in ethnicity studies need to be taken seriously. A one-sided emphasis on the manipulation of symbols, the situational selection of identity, and the fleeting and indefinite character of culture seems to suggest that nothing really endures, that the social world is continuously re-created, and that constructivist analytical approaches may tell the whole story about human identification. This kind of view, which is rarely far away in contemporary studies of ethnicity and nationalism, would not just be methodologically individualist, but also a rather strong expression of voluntarism. Such a view would imply, to the social scientist, that he or she would have to unlearn everything he or she has learnt about socialisation, the transmission of knowledge and skills from one generation to the next, the power of norms, the unconscious importance of religion and language for identity and a sense of community. For how are societies integrated, if not through culture, which cannot be seen merely as a socially constructed common heritage but rather as a shared system of communication? In Tim Allen and John Eade's words, 'there is a fine line between trying to describe the value system of minorities (or any ethnicity) and suggesting that those values determine identity' (1998: 33).

Although the differences discussed above may be important and sometimes reflect fundamental theoretical differences, it seems appropriate to end this chapter by noting some of the many similarities between the research strategies which have been presented so far (with the possible exception of pluralist theory). Most social anthropologists who study ethnicity agree on certain vital points developed, inter alia, by Barth and his associates, although there is disagreement on where to place the emphasis, and although the relationships between culture and ethnicity, between identification and politics, between collective *habitus* and individual choice, remains contentious and to a great extent refers to questions which can only be answered empirically.

- Even if ethnicity may be widely believed to express cultural differences, there is a variable and complex relationship between ethnicity and culture; and there is no one-to-one relationship between ethnic differences and cultural ones.
- Ethnicity is a relationship between two or several groups, not a property of a group; it exists *between* and not *within* groups.

- Ethnicity is the enduring and systematic communication of cultural differences between groups considering themselves to be distinct. It appears whenever cultural differences are made relevant in social interaction, and it should thus be studied at the level of social life, not at the level of symbolic culture.
- Ethnicity is thus relational, and also situational: The ethnic character of a social encounter is contingent on the situation. It is not, in other words, absolute.

The studies discussed in this chapter have focused on the social organisational or political aspect of ethnicity; its potential for organising the interests of groups, often in situations of group competition. In the following chapters I shall indicate how the anthropological study of ethnicity has branched off in various directions, now paying greater attention to the identity side of ethnicity, ideology, the historical emergence of ethnicity and the ethnic constructions of history, and power relations.

## FURTHER READING

Allen, Tim and John Eade, eds (1998) *Divided Europeans: Understanding Ethnicities in Conflict*. The Hague: Kluwer. A diverse collection of essays drawing extensively on the social anthropological approach to ethnicity, applying it to European case studies.

Fenton, Steve (1999) *Ethnicity: Racism, Class and Culture*. London: Macmillan. A sociologist's comparative bird's eye view on the current resurgence of ethnicity. Analytically clear, many empirical examples.

# 4
# Ethnic Identification and Ideology

[I]f we are to understand ... 'the persisting facts of ethnicity', then I believe that we need to supplement conventional sociological perspectives by paying greater attention to the nature of ethnic identity.

A.L. Epstein (1978: 5)

The North African mule talks always of his mother's brother, the horse, but never of his father, the donkey, in favor of others supposedly more reputable.

Clifford Geertz (1988: 8)

In the two previous chapters, we have considered aspects of ethnicity from a largely behaviourist point of view. Processes of social inclusion and exclusion, and forms of ethnic incorporation have been described in relation to interaction and social integration. Such a perspective does allow for an investigation of the symbolic aspect of ethnicity – the ethnic identity – yet this dimension is generally seen as a concomitant, or even an effect, of social process, individual utility or social functionality. This chapter will discuss how ethnic identification may assume fundamental importance for the individual; how attachment and loyalty to ethnic categories or groups is created and maintained. In order to deal with this topic, we need to understand how individuals perceive and classify their social surroundings, and also how the past is used to make sense of the present. Notions of shared origins are usually crucial for ethnic identity, and interpretations of history are therefore important to ideologies seeking to justify, strengthen and maintain particular ethnic identities.

Approaches focusing on the identity aspect of ethnicity were for a long time met with scepticism in social anthropology (but not to the same extent in American cultural anthropology; cf. Romanucci-Ross and DeVos, 1995). Since social anthropology deals with processes taking place *between* people, and since identity has conventionally been held to exist *inside* each individual, the study of personal identity was for a long time neglected by anthropologists. Nonetheless, in recent years there have been considerable advances in the social anthropological study of identity or identification, which is strictly speaking the more accurate term, since 'identity' gives an impression of being a fixed thing. For now, I use the two terms interchangeably.

It has been shown that aspects of the person which have conventionally been held to be unchangeable, inner and private, may fruitfully be studied as symbolic aspects of social processes. In other words, what was formerly considered private and fixed is now increasingly held to be public and negotiable. In cross-cultural studies of emotions, it has been argued that emotions, far from being innate, are socially created (Howell and Willis, 1989; Rosaldo, 1984). Similarly, studies of ethnicity have demonstrated that there is a close, but variable relationship between social processes and personal identities (for example A.P. Cohen, 1994; Epstein, 1978, 1992; Jenkins, 2008). At the same time, it has also been argued convincingly that the act of classification is in fact based on an innate capacity (just as human beings doubtless have inborn capacities for a variety of emotions), but that the actual form of classification into, say, 'kinds of human beings', varies with the circumstances (Hirschfeld, 1998). Distinctions between us and them exist everywhere, but they can take on a number of forms and be based on a variety of criteria.

In anthropological discourse, identity means *being the same as oneself* as well as *being different*. In Jean-Marie Benoist's words, the study of identity must 'oscillate between the poles of disconnected singularity and globalising unity' (1977: 15). When we talk of identity in social anthropology, we refer to social identity, not the depths of the individual mind – although A.P. Cohen, in a challenging and complex book on self-consciousness (A.P. Cohen, 1994), has argued the need to understand just that.[1] It would nonetheless be prudent to begin by looking at social relations and social organisation.

If we want to understand ethnic identity, we cannot a priori assume that ethnic categories exist by virtue of certain 'functions'. This implies that in order to come to grips with ethnic identity, we must try to understand what it is about ethnic classification and categorical belonging that makes sense to the people involved.

---

1. For example, A.P. Cohen states (1994: 71): 'Societies do *not* determine the selves of their members. They may construct models of personhood; they may ... *attempt* to reconcile selfhood to personhood. But they have no absolute powers in this regard.'

## ORDER IN THE SOCIAL UNIVERSE

Since the publication of Durkheim and Mauss's *Primitive Classification* (1964 [1903]), the study of classification has been a central concern in anthropology. Claude Lévi-Strauss (1962), Mary Douglas (1966, 1970), Gregory Bateson (1972b), Scott Atran (1990) and many others have demonstrated that humans are classifying beings who create order at the symbolic and social levels by distinguishing between kinds or classes of phenomena. Classification is a kind of native theory whereby the infinite complexity of the experienced world is reduced to a finite number of categories. Social classification usually expresses power asymmetries.

The kinds of classification developed in any society are necessarily related to that society's organisation and way of life. Thus the Nuer have more than 15 words for different colour patterns of cattle (Evans-Pritchard, 1940), and some Inuit groups have 25 words for different kinds of snow. The classifications of plants and animals are not objective, but rather social constructions. Thus, while Europeans classify the cassowary as a bird, the Karam of New Guinea do not. For them, it cannot be a bird since birds fly and the cassowary does not. However, bats are classified together with birds (Bulmer, 1967).

Ethnic classifications are also social and cultural products related to the requirements of the classifiers. They serve to order the social world and to create standardised cognitive maps over categories of relevant others.

Taking as his point of departure the Copperbelt studies undertaken by himself and his colleagues in the 1950s, Epstein (1978) asks how it could be that the hundreds of ethnic categories present in the larger towns on the Copperbelt could be reduced to a handful of groups in actual, ongoing social classification. People who belonged to different 'tribes' were lumped together in general categories. The reason is that ethnic taxonomies tend to become less detailed with increasing perceived social distance from oneself. In Europe it is therefore common to think of 'Africans' or 'North American Indians' as ethnic categories, although each of these 'groups' comprises hundreds of mutually exclusive ethnic categories. Clearly, it would have been impractical (and in most cases impossible) to make hundreds of fine distinctions between categories of people: usually, one will limit oneself to making those distinctions which are socially relevant (see chapter 2).

Ethnic classification can thus be seen as a practical way of creating order in the social universe. Racial theory, which was a respectable branch of physical anthropology in the nineteenth century and well into the twentieth, endeavoured to divide humanity into four mutually exclusive 'races', and it can retrospectively be seen as a typical attempt to classify the bewildering variety of humans into a few unambiguous categories. In a similar way (but with much less devastating effects), the townspeople of the Copperbelt divided their neighbours into a few standardised categories.

In Britain, the ethnic category 'West Indians' has been applied for decades to immigrants from dozens of different islands and territories: Guyanese, Trinidadians, Jamaicans, Barbadians and 'small-islanders' are considered members of the same ethnic group, although they regard themselves as members of different groups. Eventually, the British ascriptive category 'West Indian' may become an integral part of their own self-identification: they may start to regard themselves as West Indians, even if such a label was scarcely relevant in their country of origin. Eventually, they may even classify themselves with descendants of Africans as Black British (cf. Gilroy, 1987, 2000). In extreme cases, even a categorical ascription like 'immigrant' may be applied to people belonging to a dominant group – and it may include people with highly different cultural backgrounds, say, from Chile to Vietnam.

The creation of loyalty to nations follows a similar logic. With the emergence of nationalist ideology and nation-states, people are being taught that they are not primarily from Paris, Savoie, Languedoc or wherever, but that they should instead define themselves as French (E. Weber, 1976). If such an ideological pressure is successful, the compass of one's community thereby increases many times.

Apart from illustrating the general point that social identities are relational, these examples suggest that there is a close relationship between identities and external circumstances, including pressure and often coercion from powerful groups which are socially dominant. Identities may change as society changes, and they are certainly not as 'inner', as private and immutable, as common sense may sometimes take for granted. Systems of social classification and principles of inclusion and exclusion always create order, but the kind of order created is related to aspects of the wider social system, including relations of power and possibilities of social mobility.

## ANOMALIES

Every social community or identity is exclusive in the sense that not everybody can take part. Groups and collectivities are always constituted in relation to *others*. A shared European identity, for example, would have to define itself in contrast to Muslim, Middle Eastern or Arab identity, possibly also in relation to African, East Asian and North American identities – depending on the social situation.

The boundaries of ethnic groups, we have seen in chapters 2 and 3, are relative and vary situationally in significance. There are situations where ethnicity is relatively unimportant, and there are situations where it provides a decisive mechanism for exclusion and inclusion, as well as clear guidelines for behaviour. However, there are also contexts where it may be difficult to ascribe a definite ethnic identity to an individual. If your father is a Cree Indian and your mother a Francophone Canadian, or vice versa, what about yourself? What is likely to be the religion of the children of an Indian Muslim and a Hindu? In what ways is the answer influenced by class and gender? People who are 'betwixt and between', to use Victor Turner's (1967) famous phrase, can be numerous and tend to mess up any neat system of contrasts in ethnic classification. I shall propose, inspired by Mary Douglas (1966), to call them *ethnic anomalies*. They can be considered as 'neither-nor' or 'both-and', depending on the situation and/or the wider context.

A typical 'anomalous' ethnic category is that made up by second- and third-generation immigrants in Europe, or rather, the children and children's children of immigrants. They may consider themselves, and may be considered by others, as members of the same ethnic group as their parents; yet they may also consider themselves as having 'adapted' to the majority culture. They are often bilingual in their mother-tongue and the national language of the host country. Some of them have double citizenship, and many experience conflicting loyalties. In some situations, they are expected to be individualistic and independent-minded; in others, they are expected to be obedient and loyal. Typically, children of Pakistani immigrants to Norway may claim that they do not properly feel at home either in Norway or in Pakistan (see Barth, 1994), although recent studies show that they increasingly identify with Norway. Provided that these groups are permanent minorities, there are two likely outcomes of this situation: assimilation to the dominant group or ethnic incorporation. The former option presupposes that the dominant group allows new members (which is not always the case). The latter option has two varieties: the anomalous group may branch off and declare itself an ethnic category; or its members may continue to be loyal to their grandparents' ethnic category, although they are conscious of being culturally different. A third option would entail a solution where 'hybridity' and ambiguous identities were allowed; this will be looked at in some detail in chapters 7 and 8.

An illustration of the first alternative could be the development of 'Black British' as an ethnic category. Black British are neither African nor Caribbean, although their ancestors were either African or Caribbean. They have no country other than Britain and no vernacular other than that classified by linguists as English, possibly with the qualifier 'Black British English'. They have clubs, informal associations and frequently a sense of solidarity, and may in effect be considered an ethnic category native to Britain.

The other alternative consists of insisting that one is still an X, even if one has taken on some of the habits of the Ys. In this way, the considerable population of Indian origin in Britain has managed to develop and maintain Indo-British identities, although there is great cultural variation within the category and considerable change. Some British citizens of subcontinental origin have adapted to British ways of life in important respects, whereas others try to stick to tradition, and new, flexible, intermediate or innovative forms of identification develop (Baumann, 1996; Rushdie, 1991: chapter 1; Werbner, 1997).[2] This does not have to be more difficult than maintaining English identity, which is normally unproblematic, despite great cultural variation within the category of people whose members define themselves, and are defined by others, as English (see also chapter 7).

For the kind of ethnic anomaly described here, problems arise chiefly in relation to *gatekeeping*. If one is simultaneously a member of two groups which are partly defined through mutual contrasting, difficult situations are inevitable. Drawing on earlier discussions of culture and identity, we may argue that this is not necessarily because the 'cultures' are incompatible, but because the ethnic ideologies hold that they are, and because certain resources flow within groups, but not across boundaries. In a social environment where one is expected to have a well-defined ethnic identity, it may be psychologically and socially difficult to 'bet on two horses'.

2. Consider author and Nobel laureate V.S. Naipaul's situation for an extreme case. He is an 'East Indian from the West Indies' (Naipaul, 1973), a Trinidadian descendant of indentured labourers from India in a region where 'Indian' usually means 'native American'. Imagine his attempts to explain his ethnic identity to foreigners! But then again, Naipaul all but abandoned ethnic identity relatively early in his life.

The offspring of 'mixed' couples are a different kind of ethnic anomaly, although their identity problems may be similar to those of the children or grandchildren of immigrants. In colonial Haiti, an extremely detailed taxonomic system was developed in order to distinguish between people with varying 'racial' origins. An individual with 127 parts 'white' and one part 'black' was actually defined as a *sang-mêlé* (of mixed blood)! In other societies, people are less scientifically inclined and distinctions tend to be less meticulous.

In some societies, 'mixed' people are very numerous. Sometimes, separate labels are invented for them, such as 'Eurasian' in some South-East Asian societies, or *gens de couleur* in the former French sugar colonies. In some cases, they become distinctive ethnic categories with tendencies towards ethnic incorporation. In Mauritius, the 'Mulattoes' or *gens de couleur* have traditionally occupied a distinct place in the division of labour (white-collar and middle-managerial jobs); they have their own clubs and informal associations, and may be considered an ethnic category. Some of them might even argue that they are the only true Mauritians, since they are the only group that grew out of Mauritian soil – the only people who are not descendants of immigrants. Stable 'mixed' ethnic categories have also developed elsewhere. In certain societies in South and Central America, for example, people considered as 'racially mixed', notably Mestizos, have gradually become permanent ethnic categories with more or less clear boundaries, external symbols communicating their cultural distinctiveness, and rules of endogamy. In other societies, such as urban Brazil, skin colour represents a continuum with no clear boundaries or corporate groupings; it does not express ethnicity, but denotes racial distinctions which are correlated with rank (Wade, 1997).

Ethnic anomalies are often lumped with one of the groups, usually the lowest-ranking one. This has happened to North American 'Mulattoes', who are defined as blacks following the 'one-drop principle'. Others may find themselves in uncomfortable 'betwixt-and-between' situations, such as the Trinidadian *douglas*. *Dougla* is a somewhat pejorative Bhojpuri word meaning 'bastard', and the *douglas* are Trinidadians with one Indian and one African parent. It almost goes without saying that their identity problem can be severe in a society where the main classificatory principle contrasts Africans and Indians.

In modern state societies, it may be socially necessary to develop unambiguous delineations of ethnic identity. Particularly in situations where certain ethnic groups are granted special rights, 'objective' definitions of ethnicity have been created. In Norway, one has the right to consider oneself Sami, and has political rights as a Sami, if at least one grandparent used Sami as his or her first language; the criterion is in other words linguistic, not racial or genetic. According to Jewish ideology, anybody with a Jewish mother has the right to consider him- or herself a Jew. In Canadian legislation, Roosens (1989) explains, the criteria for Indian identity have changed at several points in modern history. With the relatively recent introduction of special rights for Indians and the rise of powerful Indian interest groups, it has become important to decide on clear criteria for inclusion and exclusion. Whereas the Norwegian state decided on a linguistic criterion for Sami identity, the Canadian state decided, in a law passed in 1951, on a pseudo-biological criterion. If one's father was an Indian, one had the right to be considered an Indian. In terms of genetics, this is an arbitrary distinction (given the extent of mixing in the past); in terms of culture, it is probably even more so, and the example is interesting in indicating how biology and 'race' are culturally constructed. In other words, although contrasting ethnic classifications and bounded identities may seem tidy on paper (and in native theory, including national statistics!), they are more complicated and knotty in actual societies.

## ENTREPRENEURS

Do people, when all is said and done, create their identities, or do they inadvertently express aspects of their society through their social selves? To put it differently: should anthropology stress the voluntary, chosen and strategic aspects of agency and social identity, or should it rather concentrate on showing the ways in which humans are products of culture and society? There is no definite answer to these questions, but the choice of perspective can make for important differences in the resulting analyses. In describing *douglas*, second-generation immigrants and Indian 'half-castes' as anomalies, I have essentially viewed them as creations of society. They become anomalies by virtue of pre-existing classificatory categories which they can do little to change. In this way, the Barthian view of ethnicity as a system of mutually exclusive self-ascriptions must be slightly modified: the ascriptions attributed by *others* also contribute to creating ethnicity, and may be of paramount importance. A common criticism of multicultural ideology is that it virtually forces people to take on an ethnic identity, even if they would have preferred not to have this aspect of their personal identity highlighted (see Lock,

1990); in its least benign form, this kind of practice may become extremely rigid and alienating, especially in societies which are ethnically stratified (see Eriksen, 2001c; see also chapter 8).

An actor-centred perspective on 'anomalous' ethnic categories might lead to a different conclusion. For just as it can be shown that individuals who fall between acknowledged categories are defined 'by the system' as anomalous, sometimes morally suspect outsiders, they may also exploit this ambiguity to their own advantage. Instead of seeing these individuals as anomalies, one may regard them as entrepreneurs or cultural brokers who turn the classificatory ambiguities to their own advantage. A Mauritian friend, who is of partly Tamil, partly mixed (*personne de couleur*) origin and who has a Catholic first name and a Tamil surname, sometimes exploits this ambiguity in such a way. When dealing with Tamils or Hindus he stresses his Tamil aspect, but if he does business with Catholics he overcommunicates his Creole aspect.

Whether one regards this kind of fuzzy ethnic category as anomalous or as an entrepreneurial category is partly a matter of theoretical perspective, but it also depends on the empirical context. In some societies, for some individuals and in some situations, it may be more or less difficult or profitable to be a 'between and betwixt' person. And we should not a priori assume that having an ambiguous ethnic identity implies having no roots and no culture and is therefore unbearable. An assumption to this effect is perhaps neither more nor less than an expression of English native theory; and before assuming that ethnic anomalies are by default unhappy, we ought to look into their actual lives.

There is no doubt that societies differ strongly on this score. In some societies, identities are to a greater extent chosen than in others. In this context, Ernest Gellner (1991) once introduced what he calls 'the potato principle', referring to the strongly territorial identity and feeling of 'rootedness' which he assumes to be prevalent among peasants. In such societies, there is little social mobility, and people are tied to a place and rank through webs of kinship and patron–client relationships. Gellner contrasts this kind of identity with the more fluid identities typical of industrial societies, where social mobility is considerable and individual choice is a major value. The contrast may be simplistic. We should nevertheless keep in mind that ethnic identities are flexible to a highly varying degree. The fact that they are socially constructed does not imply that they are not real and can thus easily be done away with. Money is a social construction too, as is language.

## ANALOG AND DIGITAL; WE AND US

Ethnic categorisations can be analysed as attempts to create order in, and make sense of, a bewildering chaos of different 'kinds' of people. And, as we have just seen, this kind of map creates its own problems because the territory it describes is more complex than itself. Both natives and anthropologists therefore quickly run into paradoxes and contradictions when they try to apply a stylised ethnic taxonomy consistently.

In the discussions of ethnicity in the Copperbelt and Mauritius in chapter 2, I pointed out that people classify others not only along the axis of identity versus difference (the basic Us–Them mechanism), but also according to perceived *degrees* of difference. For a Kamba in Kenya, the Kikuyu and other Bantu-speaking peoples are perceived as closer than Luo and others who speak Nilotic languages. To a Swede, a Dane is considered closer than a German, who is in turn considered closer than a Hungarian. Bogardus-type scales of perceived social distance can be helpful here in mapping out such differences, although we should keep in mind that actual behaviour does not necessarily correspond to expectations which may arise from interviews.

In a complex multi-ethnic environment, people will thus develop different standardised forms of behaviour vis-à-vis different categories of others. Some are perceived as 'almost like ourselves'; others are perceived as 'extremely different from us'. When such principles of exclusion and inclusion allow for differences of degree, we may call them *analog*. They do not encourage the formation of unambiguous, clear-cut boundaries. The children of Polish immigrants to a Scandinavian country, for example, are rarely thought of as immigrants, while their parents are. When, on the contrary, systems of classification operate on an unambiguous inclusion/exclusion basis, where boundaries are fixed and all outsiders of certain kinds are regarded as 'more or less the same', they may be spoken of as *digital*.

Further, the communities whose existence is postulated by ethnic ideologies may be seen as expressions of different aspects of community. Here we can distinguish between two modalities of group solidarity, which we may, following the philosopher Jean-Paul Sartre (1943), call *we-hood* and *us-hood*, respectively.[3] Being *us*,

3. French has no word for 'us', and Sartre therefore distinguishes between 'we-as-subject' and 'we-as-object'.

people are loyal and socially integrated chiefly in relation to *the other*; through competition, enmity, symbiosis or the contrastive use of stereotypes and boundary symbols. Being *we*, on the other hand, entails being integrated because of shared activities within the collectivity.

Although ethnicity, being relational, is by definition a phenomenon of us-hood, the ethnic category or group must additionally have an element of we-hood in order to be viable – a shared language or religion, a division of labour which creates interdependence, or a notion of shared origins.

It is often remarked that assumed cultural differences tend to be magnified and distorted in stereotyping, in intergroup competition and during ethnic conflicts, through contrasting and dichotomisation. However, intergroup similarities may also be perceived as threatening. Simon Harrison (1999) has argued that, in fact, the cultural practices and notions associated with a group may be regarded as scarce resources – indeed as *inalienable possessions* (Weiner, 1992) which cannot be bartered with, traded or exchanged. Harrison's point is that all symbolic practices 'are capable of being *copied*, either with or without the consent and cooperation of their possessors' (1999: 241). He gives several examples of this – from the perceived piracy of Australian Aboriginal art by commercial agents, to a more subtle and less obvious case from New Zealand (Aotearoa in Maori), where white farmers have developed notions of spiritual relatedness to the land. These notions are reminiscent of Maori notions, and seem to give an ideological justification for their claims to land. Advocates for Maori rights have protested against this 'cultural borrowing', arguing that it is a form of cultural piracy. Harrison thus concludes that communities may see themselves as under threat not only from those who differ from them, but also from those 'ethnic Others who resemble them, or who seem to identify with them too closely' (1999: 250).

Let us now turn to an exploration of some ways in which ethnic ideologies use notions of shared culture to define and delimit ethnic identity.

## THE EMERGENCE OF ETHNIC IDENTITIES

Epstein (1978) noted more than thirty years ago that many of the societies traditionally studied by anthropologists were undergoing rapid processes of social and cultural change, yet ethnicity – contrary to many expectations – did not vanish as a result, but instead emerged in new, often more powerful and more clearly articulated form. Epstein states:

> [S]ince ethnicity arises so often in circumstances of social upheaval and transformation, which are frequently accompanied by severe cultural erosion and the disappearance of many customs that might serve as marks of distinctiveness, a critical issue is *how that identity is to be maintained* over a number of generations. (1978: xiii, my emphasis)

Ethnic symbolism referring to the ancient language, religion, kinship system or way of life is crucial for the maintenance of ethnic identity through periods of change. Generally speaking, social identity becomes most important the moment it seems threatened. Several factors may constitute such a perceived threat, but they are always related to some kind of change – migration, change in the demographic situation, industrialisation or other economic change, or integration into or encapsulation by a larger political system (see chapter 5).

Conspicuous forms of boundary maintenance become important when the boundaries are under pressure. Ethnic identities, which embody a perceived continuity with the past, may in this way function in a psychologically reassuring way for the individual in times of upheaval; they seem to tell people that although 'all that is solid melts into air' (Marx and Engels; cf. Berman, 1982), there is an unchanging, stable core of ethnic belongingness which assures the individual of a continuity with the past, which can be an important source of self-respect and personal authenticity in the modern world, which is often perceived as a world of flux and make-believe. If one can claim to 'have a culture', it proves that one is faithful to one's ancestors and to the past. Religion may or may not play an important part here. Many ethnic movements are religious in character and stress the importance of religious conformity to their members, but other movements may be just as efficient, with respect to both politics and identity, without such a component.

Ethnic identities can be seen as expressions of metaphoric kinship. Some notion of shared descent may be a universal element in ethnic ideologies (Nash, 1988; Yelvington, 1991). Notions of 'race' are sometimes, but not always, part of such ideologies. Sometimes ethnic ideologies, like kin genealogies, trace common descent back to a known ancestor, although the actual linkages are unknown.

The formation of new ethnic categories, which presupposes the formation of new identities, generally follows one of two possible paths. First, it may come about through an extension of existing identifications; it may thus be argued that all Aymara (a category of Andes Indians) are descendants of a particular pre-Columbian people, and that all Aymara should therefore be loyal to the Aymara group as a whole and not just to their extended lineage, clan or village. Similarly, in the creation of a Norwegian ethnic identity in the nineteenth century, an imputed genealogical continuity with early medieval Viking chieftains was stressed as an argument for the uniqueness of Norwegians in relation to Swedes and Danes, who were culturally and linguistically close.

The second possibility is the reverse: it consists in reducing the size of the group with presumed shared ancestry. A common sociological term for this kind of process is 'fission'. At the levels of ideology and personal identity, it can be expressed through a shallowing of genealogies. Instead of tracing one's group origins back to, say, Adam or Noah, one may thus trace it back to one of their respective sons (or to a more recent ancestor, as in the case of the 'twelve tribes of Israel') and thereby argue the validity of present ethnic boundaries.

Both of these possibilities for the delineation of ethnic identities require creative reinterpretations of the past. The notion of ancestry is itself ambiguous. For if a shared ethnic identity presupposes a notion of shared ancestry, how many generations should one feel compelled to go back in order to find a starting point for one's present ethnic identity? And how many of one's ancestors does one need to take into account? There is no objective answer to that question: the answer is conditional on the social context. When the African-American author Alex Haley wrote his fictionalised autobiography *Roots* (1998 [1976]), he traced his ancestry back to the Gambian coast. However, had he followed his father's lineage rather than that of his mother, he would have ended up in Scotland.

This aspect of ethnic identity also indicates that there is no simple one-to-one relationship between ideology and social practices. For although Jews justify their ethnic identity by referring to shared ancestry, it is evident that all Jews do not have the same ancestry. Jews from Eastern Europe tend to look like East Europeans, and Jews from North Africa tend to look like North Africans. Despite an ideology of endogamy, there has been considerable *de facto* mixing with the surrounding populations.

Finally, the criterion of imputed shared origins seriously reduces the possible number of ethnic categories in any society. It is true that ethnicity is a social creation and not a fact of nature, and ethnic variation does not correspond to cultural variation. But ethnic identities must seem convincing to their members in order to function – and they must also be acknowledged as legitimate by non-members of the group. If a group of London punks insist that they have a unique culture with origins in a mythical and misty past, their potential for becoming an ethnic category depends on the recognition of others. Similarly, if someone claims that Indians and Africans have the same origins and should therefore be considered an ethnic group, he or she will probably not be successful, since most Africans and Indians would disagree.

In recent years, anthropologists have been concerned with the ways in which history and cultural symbols are manipulated in the creation of ethnic identities and organisations. Such a focus implies an interest in the ways in which ethnic identities are being constructed, and we will now consider a few examples indicating how this may take place.

## THE CREATION OF AN ANCESTRAL IDENTITY

The Huron Indians of Québec (Wyandots) are today a respected Canadian tribe (Roosens, 1989). Unlike many other indigenous peoples, they have succeeded in presenting themselves to society at large as an oppressed people with a unique, if vanishing, culture, who have for centuries been harassed, massacred and deprived of civil and territorial rights by the colonialists and the Canadian authorities. A comparison between the ethnic leaders' presentation of their case and other, historical sources shows that it is possible to go very far in the reinterpretation of history in order to create collective identity and political cohesion.

Historical monographs dealing with the Hurons indicate that their contacts with the colonisers were for centuries both voluntary and profitable. They were sedentary and acted as intermediaries between French fur traders and the nomadic hunters who provided the furs in the sixteenth and early seventeenth centuries. Later, they were in regular contact with Jesuit missionaries, who were nevertheless unsuccessful in their attempts to convert them.

The Hurons' main enemies were the Iroquois. In the mid-seventeenth century the Iroquois began to attack Huron villages with unprecedented intensity, and the survivors were dispersed. Most of them were assimilated into Iroquois groups, and some fled to Québec. It was during this period that traditional Huron culture, as well as their language, vanished. Later, they collaborated with the French and were for this reason granted a hunting area to which they had no aboriginal claim.

An influential Huron version of their history differs from this version on a number of points. It is presented in a book by their Chief Max Gros-Louis, *Le Premier des Hurons* (1981; reference in Roosens, 1989). The book does not acknowledge that there were traditional enmities between Indian tribes in general and between the Hurons and neighbouring Iroquois in particular. It is also suggested that such enmities, if ever they occurred, were incited by the colonialists. According to Roosens, the book also depicts 'a kind of pan-Indian culture', which 'unites all Indians against all outsiders and primarily against the whites'. This 'culture', as described and reified in Gros-Louis' book, is composed of elements which conform to widespread positive stereotypes of Indians in Euro-Canadian society. The Indians are depicted as being close to nature and respectful of plants and animals; they are spontaneously hospitable, patently honest, incorruptible and have great personal integrity; they are tolerant and mild-mannered, and are open-minded in respect to foreign cultures. In brief, 'Indian culture' is depicted as superior to the 'white' one in a number of ways.

Roosens' rather uncharitable conclusion is that this 'Indian culture' is an invention which may be politically efficient but which is one-sided, 'to put it mildly'. That the Hurons have achieved their present position is, he argues, through the deliberate creation of an *ethnic counterculture*, including a rendering of their history and presentation of their ancestral culture which may be described as very inventive. Roosens concludes:

> When I compared the characteristics of this neo-Huron culture with the culture depicted in the historical records, most of the modern traits, virtually everything, were 'counterfeit': the folklore articles, the hair style, the mocassins, the 'Indian' parade costumes, the canoes, the pottery, the language, the music. (1989: 47)

## HISTORY AND IDEOLOGY

Selective renderings of history are not confined to ethnic minorities such as the Hurons. Historians working in modern European nation-states have taken great pains to demonstrate that their nations are really very old, although they were usually created in the nineteenth century (Anderson, 1991 [1983]). This may be a feature of modernity. In his book about the Hurons, Chief Gros-Louis effectively turned 'Indian culture' into *an object*, regarding it from the outside, as something existing independently of whatever activities the actual Hurons might be involved in. When culture is reified in this way, it can be manipulated. Thus, several Hurons have in recent years taken Indian names and have begun to wear Indian clothing, as self-conscious ways of communicating that they 'have a culture'. In the years following the publication of Roosens' book, Hurons/Wyandots have also begun to learn the Wyandot language. This kind of personal identity politics is characteristic of modern societies.

Imputed aboriginality and continuity with the past can be sources of political legitimacy. Simultaneously, knowledge of one's own history (whether fabricated or not) can be highly important in the fashioning of ethnic identity. Genealogies, both personal and cultural ones, are always written in selective ways – both for political and other reasons. Thus many white North Americans who have traced their origins have found English nobility among their ancestors. The fact that their family trees probably contain prostitutes and manual workers as well, is undercommunicated. Similarly, Hurons and other Indian groups in North America would today undercommunicate the fact that many of their ancestors were in fact Europeans; that mixed marriages have been common for a very long time.

At this juncture, many anthropologists would part company with professional historians in the study of ethnogenesis. While many historians tend to try to find out what *really* happened – some even distinguish between 'invented' traditions and 'real' traditions (Hobsbawm, 1983; cf. chapter 5) – most anthropologists would rather concentrate on showing the ways in which particular historical accounts are used as tools in the *contemporary* creation of identities and in politics. Anthropologists would stress that history is not a product of the past but a response to requirements of the present. For that reason, this discussion of history relates not to the past but to the present. In the next chapter, I shall look into the past itself and as such.

An example of a reconstructed history which has been only partly successful concerns the Muslims in Mauritius (Eriksen, 1988, 1998). Comprising 16–17 per cent of the Mauritian population, all Mauritian Muslims are descendants of merchants and indentured labourers who came from British India in the eighteenth and nineteenth centuries. Their languages were Bhojpuri, Sindhi and Gujarati; a few were literate in Urdu. At the 1972 population census, virtually all of the Muslims stated that their ancestral language was an Indian language. (Urdu, being a prestige language, was over-represented.) By the next census ten years later, however, more than half of the Muslims stated that their ancestral language was Arabic. During the 1970s a powerful pan-Arabic movement had emerged, and with the oil crisis culminating in 1973 it became evident that the Arabs represented a considerable force in world politics. It became more interesting to be a part of this movement than to trace one's roots back towards Pakistan or India. Thus, Mauritian Muslims redefined their ancestral culture. In the capital, Port-Louis, Muslim women began to wear hijabs and the men started to wear long white robes and to grow beards. They tried, effectively, to become descendants of Arabs instead of being descendants of Indian labourers. However, this turn towards the Arab world was generally not acknowledged by other Mauritians, and many pointed out that, really, the Muslims were just as Indian as the Hindus. The new identity was, in other words, a contested one. During the 1980s the orientation towards the Arab world was lessened somewhat, but it should be noted that many Mauritian Muslims supported Iraq during the Gulf War, although both Mauritius and Pakistan were on the Allied side; and that the subsequent 'war on terror', beginning with the terrorist attacks on the USA in 2001 has led to political repercussions in Mauritius as in other countries with substantial Muslim populations.

These two examples, the Hurons and the Mauritian Muslims, may appear almost as parodies of ethnic groups, but they are more typical than they may seem. Interpretations of the past are important to every ethnic identity, and the relationship between such interpretations and 'objective history' is necessarily contestable. As Lévi-Strauss has argued in a comparison between myth and history (1962: chapter 8), historical accounts include only a minute fraction of all the events that have taken place in a certain time-span, and they necessarily involve interpretation and selection. There is always an element of creativity in history writing (Lowenthal, 1985), and identity always has an important element of subjective *identification*.

Since it is not 'objective culture' that shapes ethnicity, it makes sense to state that ethnic identities can be maintained despite cultural change. However, such an identity maintenance may seem paradoxical, since ethnic ideologies stress the continuity of that very cultural content as a justification for the continued existence and cohesion of the group. An important point in Leach's (1954) study of Kachin politics is that there is never a perfect fit between ideology and social practices. Leach shows that the same Kachin myths and cosmology can be used to justify two highly different ideal social orders, *gumlao* and *gumsa*, which are egalitarian and hierarchical, respectively (Leach, 1954: chapter 3). This ambiguity or 'multivocality' of symbols (V. Turner, 1967) makes it possible to manipulate them politically. Thus, in Sri Lanka Tamils and Sinhalese have slightly different versions of the same myths: both of them have created versions tailored to fit their respective political projects (Kapferer, 1988). Just as individuals can romanticise their childhoods, it seems, ethnic groups can acquire a tragic and heroic history. And, as the Comaroffs state, 'while ethnicity is the product of specific historical processes, it tends to take on the "natural" appearance of an autonomous force, a "principle" capable of determining the course of social life' (Comaroff and Comaroff, 1992: 60). What we are looking at here is thus not the past, but present-day *constructions* of the past.

## GENETICS, KINSHIP AND ETHNICITY

Increasingly, the middle classes of the world are becoming aware of the ambiguous, multifaceted character of their own origins. Since ethnicity is related to kinship as a form of metaphorical or even literal, extended kinship, research into family origins can have important implications for ethnicity. With the development of sophisticated techniques for mapping the DNA of individuals towards the end of the twentieth century, it has become possible – increasingly so for anyone willing to pay – to ascertain one's exact genetic origins. Private companies have been set up to accommodate and stimulate demand to this effect, and anthropologists have begun to do research on this and related practices reflecting, simultaneously, the mixed heritage of most living humans and the ongoing discourses about 'real' identities. In Ben Campbell's words: 'DNA is seen as offering added narrative value in relation to stories of race, ethnicity and nation' (2007: 169). Yet which stories one tells depends on circumstances. A Jamaican-British man featured in British news in 2003 discovered 'to his delight' that in addition to having genes from 15 different ethnic groups in Africa, he had white male ancestry. (To anyone who has worked with the history of slavery, this is anything but surprising.) This man saw the results as evidence that Afro-Caribbeans had 'the right to claim a heritage in [the UK]' (Campbell, 2007: 171). Another newspaper article referred to by Campbell describes another Jamaican-British person, a woman this time, as being 'really a Nubian princess'.

The use of the term 'really' is highly significant in this context. DNA tests tend to reveal mixed origins, and can thus be interpreted in a number of ways. A third newspaper story discussed by Campbell describes the ancient Britons (that is, those who inhabited the islands before the Celts, the Romans and the Anglo-Saxons) as 'a very civilized lot' since parts of their DNA has survived up to the present (albeit mixed with Celtic, Roman, etc. DNA). In this way, a story of genetic and territorial continuity is being told by using available material selectively.

It may not seem obvious at the outset, but it is clear that research into DNA testing, as well as new reproductive technologies and new forms of kinship, may shed new light on ethnicity. Since ethnic identity always contains an element of imputed ancestry, the facts of mixed origins may both reflect and affect popular thought on the matter. In a study from Norway, Howell and Melhuus (2007) discuss both adoption of non-European children and sperm donation in this context, showing that although Norwegian discourses of nationhood (and Norwegian ethnic identity) tend to be racialised and essentialist, adopted children can bypass these constraints on group membership through the 'kinning' process taking place from a very early age in the adoptive family. It would probably be fair to say that Norwegian nationalism, like most European nationalisms, has an ethnic element, but that nationhood can also transcend ethnicity. This question will be discussed in greater detail in chapters 6 to 8.

## SOCIAL FACTORS IN IDENTITY PROCESSES

Culture is in a sense invented, and the relationship between culture as ideology and culture as fact is tenuous. Yet it is evident that anything will not function equally well in the social legitimation of ethnic identities. If the agents themselves hold that a certain description of their culture is obviously false, it cannot provide them with a powerful ethnic identity. If a group's version of its cultural history is seriously contested by other groups, as was the case with the Mauritian Muslims, it may also be problematic to maintain the identity postulated by that account of history. So we cannot conclude that anything goes and that everything about ethnic identity is deception and make-believe. A principal point throughout this chapter has rather been that identities are ambiguous, and that this ambiguity is connected with a negotiable history and a negotiable cultural content. Even when the biological history of a person is scientifically documented, it is open to varying interpretations.

Many scholars have regarded *utility* as the master variable in accounting for the maintenance of ethnic identity, regarding identity as contingent on ethnic political organisation which is formed in situations of competition over scarce resources. However, notions of utility are themselves cultural creations, and so the boundary between that which is useful and that which is meaningful becomes blurred. It is therefore difficult to predict which ethnic or other identities will be dominant for any given population in the future. The rise of a global Muslim identity in the last decades, often overruling ethnic and national identities, is one example of a form of identity politics which had not been predicted by most scholars.

In addition, it has been shown that a number of ethnic categories reproduce their identity even if it actually reduces their chances of attaining prosperity and political power. I have myself written of Mauritian Creole identity along these lines (Eriksen, 1986, 1988): the features of Creole identity which are used internally and externally as identity markers emphasise values which are incompatible with social mobility and political organisation. Individual freedom is seen as a typical Creole 'cultural trait', and it is expressed in ways which make formal political organisation and long-term planning extremely difficult.

It has been argued, along similar lines, that the maintenance of Roma (Gypsy) identity in Europe should be seen as a cultural and symbolic phenomenon rather than as a competitive strategy. Roma society displays different values from mainstream society, and the goals pursued by Roma are different from those of the sedentary population (Okely, 1983; Stewart, 1991). For this reason, there is no real competition between the groups. Roma identity is thus better viewed as a cultural fact than as an aspect of group competition.

## IS A EUROPEAN IDENTITY CONCEIVABLE?

In order to arrive at a better understanding (if not necessarily an explanation) of the development of the various forms of social identification, it may be instructive to look at the historical junctures where new overarching identities are being presented, and the processes which lead to their acceptance or rejection. The long-standing attempts to create tighter political, economic and cultural integration in the European Union (EU), and the widespread counter-reactions to such attempts, offer interesting material in this regard, and may also suggest what is at stake in attempted redefinitions of identity.

The EU may be regarded as a coordinating organ, an economic market-place and an alliance between sovereign states. That was how it began in 1957. However, since the late 1980s, it has been an expressed policy of the EU to strengthen integration in important respects. Notably, the transfer of political power from the national capitals to Brussels which took place during the 1990s entailed attempts at redefining loyalties and attachments. A possible consequence of this shift could be that political parties in the European Parliament eventually align themselves along political, not national, lines, so that, say, Greens and Social Democrats will form blocs with Greens and Social Democrats from other European countries, respectively, instead of aligning themselves with other parties from their own countries. This has not come about yet in a significant way, but the EU of the early twenty-first century has been invested with more power than it had a couple of decades earlier. The common currency, the euro, finally introduced in January 2002, is one indication, as were the admissions of new member states from Central and Eastern Europe in the first decade of the twenty-first century. The attempted coordination of asylum and immigration policies is a third example, the Schengen Act allowing citizens from most membership countries to travel freely without a passport a fourth. The immense popularity of the pan-European Champions' League in football, often trumping both national leagues and international matches in spectator numbers, could also indicate the growth of shared collective emotions at the European level. Legislation has progressively been standardised among the member countries (and their satellites). A main issue of contention has been the issue of citizenship. As Cris Shore shows (2000: chapter 3), however, there is no common agreement concerning the substantial content of a European citizenship, what it should entail in terms of rights and obligations; and the failure to ratify the European Constitution in 2005 signals that many inhabitants in Europe prefer to be citizens of a European country rather than being European citizens.

The economic effects of European integration may also be formidable in that, for example, French peasants increasingly produce *for Europe* and not for France or their own region. This kind of economic integration may serve as an encouragement for the formation of a European identification at the subjective level.

Will economic and political developments towards European integration lead to the development of a shared European identity overruling national ones? This question has at least three interesting aspects. First, it seems that enthusiasm for European integration is greatest in the poorest regions, and among the political and economic elites, which may for different reasons reap the greatest economic and political benefits. In other words, in this regard it seems that identity formation is conditional on perceptions of utility.

Second, economic and political processes are not in themselves sufficient for the development of identity, although they serve as an incentive. Ideology production – notably, the creation of a shared history – is also crucial. Several European history books have thus attempted to redraw the past. The most influential one in the 1990s was Jean-Baptiste Duroselle's *Europe – A History of its Peoples* (1990), where the author concludes that 'it should be possible ... to build a united Europe' (1990: 414). The book was published simultaneously in several of the European languages. Whereas many earlier history books had stressed the emergence of nation-states and have written history largely from the perspective of the nation, this book explicitly intended to play down the role of individual nations, instead emphasising the shared European heritage as well as the local and regional communities. The outcome was, bluntly phrased, a history of Europe where Greece ostensibly had the same history as Ireland, but not the same history as Turkey.[4] This illustrates the general point that history is open to a variety of interpretations, which may be contested. There are political and economic reasons why nobody endeavours to create a Levantine identity encompassing all the peoples in the eastern Mediterranean, although such an identity might have as much to recommend it in terms of 'objective history' as a European one.

As Shore shows (2000: 52), the 'new repertoire of Euro-symbols' tried to neutralise national differences. A clear example, which shows both the inventiveness and perhaps fragility of contemporary European 'identity engineering', is the symbolism of Euro

4. Neumann and Welsh (1991) have described how 'the Turk' for centuries served as the significant Other for European identity, in other words how ideas of European identity have depended on contrasting and negative stereotyping of non-Europeans, particularly Turks (and, it must be added, 'pseudo-Europeans', particularly Jews and Gypsies). Perhaps this factor in European identity may partly explain why Turkey is unlikely to be admitted to the EU in the near future.

banknotes. Instead of using the notes to depict actually existing European buildings, landscapes and so on (at the risk of alienating Euro-citizens from other countries), the banknotes depict imaginary buildings, classic as well as modernist, none of which exist in reality but all of which may appear as European in character, almost like so many Platonic ideal types.

Third, a European identity is not necessarily incompatible with national or ethnic identities. Social identities are segmentary in character, following the general formula described in Evans-Pritchard's (1940) study of Nuer political organisation. Being a member of a family does not preclude being a member of an ethnic group; and being a member of an ethnic group does not necessarily preclude being a member of a more encompassing category. However, for that more encompassing group to exist, it must be *socially relevant*. It must have some goods to deliver – material, political or symbolic – and those goods must be perceived as valuable by the target group.

The question of whether a common, supranational European identity will be widespread in the near future cannot be answered straightforwardly. All we can say is that it would have to be conditional on *both* symbolic justification and political organisation.[5] Many observers do not believe that this can come about. A.D. Smith (1995: 143) thus argues that 'to transfer the loyalties and identifications of the [European] populations ... and attach them to a new set of shared European myths, memories, values and symbols' will involve an impossible feat of sociocultural engineering. Others are more optimistic, but also more modest in their ambitions, which have been thwarted several times since the immense pan-European optimism of the early 1990s.

## WHAT DO IDENTITIES DO?

Ethnic identity becomes crucially important the moment it is perceived as being under threat. Since ethnicity is an aspect of relationship, the importance of boundaries may thus be said to be conditional on the pressure exerted on them. On the other hand, we have seen that expressions of ethnic identity may also

---

5. Salman Rushdie, incidentally, has identified a kind of proposed identity which, apparently, does not work; namely, that linked with the Commonwealth. Being interviewed as a 'Commonwealth writer' by the British press, he had to admit that he found 'this strange term, "Commonwealth literature", unhelpful and even a little distasteful' (Rushdie, 1991: 61).

be regarded, not as psychological responses to threats from the outside or attempts to create order in the social universe, but rather as symbolic tools in political struggles. The social importance of ethnic identities is greatest when the two conditions are fulfilled simultaneously in enacted ethnic ideologies. We shall return to this important point in later chapters.

It must also be stressed that the rigidity and boundedness of ethnic groups is much less clear on the ground than commonly assumed. As Gerd Baumann puts it: 'all identities are identifications, all identifications are dialogical' (1999: 140) and identity formation is dynamic and many-sided. Add to this A.P. Cohen's critique of the boundary concept (chapter 3; see also A.P. Cohen, 2000), and it becomes clear that one should not, as a student or scholar, enter an ethnically complex situation, which may seem clear-cut enough from afar, with the prior assumption that all members of a category are culturally similar, relate in the same way to their ethnic label, and allow ethnicity to be the overriding concern in their lives. In all this, there is very considerable variation, as later chapters will show in detail.

Identity processes are fundamentally dual and comprise aspects of meaning as well as politics in a wide sense. Functionalist or actor-centred accounts of ethnicity may provide good analyses of ethnic incorporation at the level of interaction and group competition, but they usually decline to ask why it is that ethnic identities are so pervasive and fundamental to people; why, as Benedict Anderson (1991 [1983]) puts it, people are willing to die for their nation (or ethnic community) but usually not for their social class or city. Nor do they delve into the 'cultural intimacy' experienced by members of a group (Herzfeld, 1997), which enables them to trust each other (but not outsiders), and the ways in which primary groups offer a sense of security which is necessarily socially exclusive. I have deliberately not given a simple answer to these very complex questions here, but have instead shown a few ways in which they can meaningfully be asked without recourse to pure speculation.

The next chapter will approach the questions of ethnic identity and group formation from a perspective which is complementary to those developed so far. We now turn to assessing the importance of historical and societal macro processes for the development of ethnic groups and identities. Eventually, it will also be indicated how social anthropology, despite (or perhaps because of) its bias in favour of small-scale societies and interpersonal relations, can be instrumental in creating an understanding of global processes in the contemporary world.

## FURTHER READING

Cohen, A.P. (1985) *The Symbolic Construction of Community*. London: Routledge. Very influential and consistent argument for the importance of symbolic meaning in communal identity.

Fitzgerald, Thomas K. (1993) *Metaphors of Identity: A Culture–Communication Dialogue*. New York: SUNY Press. Textbook rich in ethnographic examples, combining perspectives from psychological and social anthropology.

Romanucci-Ross, Lola and George DeVos, eds (1995) *Ethnic Identity: Creation, Conflict and Accommodation*, 3rd edn. Walnut Creek, CA: AltaMira Press. Written chiefly by American scholars, most of the chapters present a psychosocial perspective on ethnic identity, emphasising the significance of symbolic meaning.

# 5
# Ethnicity in History

We no longer believe that there are 'people without history'. The contemporary ethnographic challenge is how to enter into and understand those ongoing histories from the vantage point of everyday life.

Richard Jenkins (2008: 5)

Where are your parents from? And your grandparents? Your great-grandparents? Eventually, if the questioner persists, he will find a transplanted root. The 100 per cent American is, after all, 100 per cent something else.

Motto for the Bicentennial Exhibition (1976) at
the Smithsonian Institute, Washington, DC

The argument and material presented so far seem to suggest that although ethnicity is not confined to modern societies, there are aspects of many interethnic processes which are less likely to come about in non-modern than in modern contexts. In particular, this could be true of reflexive self-identity and that reification of culture which seems to presuppose widespread literacy. The contemporary phenomena of nationalism and minority issues are clearly confined to the modern world or at least, in the case of indigenous peoples, the interface between modernity and a traditional way of life. It could be argued that pre-colonial notions of cultural differences refer to different kinds of phenomena altogether from those engendered by capitalism and the state (Comaroff and Comaroff, 1992; Fardon, 1987; Southall, 1970). On the other hand, it should also be kept in mind that the various ethnic processes analysed in Barth (1969b) largely take place in non-modern settings.

This chapter will analyse the process of 'ethnogenesis' – the emergence of ethnic relations and ethnic identities – from the perspective of historical change. Several of the theoretical problems discussed in previous chapters will be further illuminated here, notably the relationships between ethnicity and modernity, culture and ethnicity, and agency and structure.

## THE HISTORICAL DEVELOPMENT OF ETHNIC RELATIONS

In his seminal 'Introduction', Barth (1969a) criticised a then widespread view on ethnicity for assuming that ethnic phenomena come about due to contact between groups which are already culturally distinctive, often in a colonial setting. Rather, Barth reasons, we should 'ask ourselves what is needed to make ethnic distinctions *emerge* in an area' (1969a: 17). What he seems to call for here is an historical perspective on ethnicity. However, neither the book edited by Barth nor most other anthropological studies of ethnicity really undertake the task of showing how ethnic distinctions develop and unfold in an area; how initially homogeneous groups are historically split into two or several distinctive ethnic groups. Barth argues, largely on logical grounds, that occupational specialisation, and the development of some form of group complementarity, will gradually encourage the creation and enactment of distinguishing signs and, eventually, the emergence of distinctive groups, with separate genealogies, each of which considers the others to be culturally distinctive from themselves.

Cultural discontinuities are likely to have developed roughly in this way in a number of settings. In situations where groups simply split and no complementarity develops, cultural variation without ethnicity (defined as the systematic communication of cultural difference) will eventually develop. There are nevertheless great difficulties involved in studying this process empirically, since very long and largely unknown time-spans are normally involved. The development of ethnically based political organisation, as well as mass movements based on ethnic identity, is nevertheless recent (and related to modernisation processes), and that may be a reason why anthropologists have focused on these aspects of 'ethnogenesis'. The political context for the emergence of such ethnic movements has in nearly all cases been a colonial situation or a nation-state.

## EXPANSIONS OF SYSTEM BOUNDARIES

Ethnicity must by definition arise either from a process of social differentiation within a population, which eventually leads to the division of that population into two distinctive groups, through migration, or by an expansion of system boundaries bringing formerly discrete groups into contact with each other. Years ago, Eric Wolf (1982) showed that interconnections between societies have been far more widespread than has commonly been assumed by anthropologists working in the Malinowskian tradition, and he demonstrates the importance of such, ultimately global, interconnections from around AD 1400. These connections, Wolf emphasises, cannot all be subsumed under the labels of 'colonialism' or 'the emergence of the capitalist world-system'. In fact, there were important and often wide-reaching regional links of trade, warfare and migration connecting 'tribes' and bands in most parts of the world. Such links also often involved societies which anthropologists have tended to regard as 'cold', after Lévi-Strauss (1962) – slowly changing societies which see themselves as essentially timeless and unchanging, in contrast to the 'hot' modern societies which change fast and whose inhabitants have reconciled themselves with change, often to the point of believing in notions of 'progress' etc. Wolf's point is that it is misleading to regard the world as an 'archipelago of cultures' (see also Eriksen, 1993b); that seemingly discrete societies have always been partly reproduced by virtue of their mutual, 'symbiotic' contacts. However, Wolf shows, the intensity and range of these contacts increased greatly with the 'great discoveries' and European colonialism from the fifteenth century onwards. Many ethnic categorisations and ethnic hierarchies still functioning today were the intended or unintended results of European colonialism in North and South America, the Caribbean, Africa, South Asia, East Asia, Australia and the Pacific. Notably, the extent of complementarity and resource competition increased many times over through wagework, capitalism and the incorporation of various peoples within a colonial, then independent state formation.

For the sake of clarity, I shall distinguish between four aspects of these processes of change, which have proceeded with uneven pace and in different ways in different societies up to the present. First, we shall look at the consequences of slavery and capitalism for the development of ethnic relations in the New World. Second, the importance of labour migration will be discussed. Third, the importance of naming and semantics – the relationship between language and the non-linguistic world – for the formation of ethnic identities in Africa will be discussed. Fourth, I shall deal with the consequences of social change for identity formation and group organisation. The empirical examples in this chapter are chosen with a view to depicting some of the variation as well as some of the similarities in different kinds of colonial and post-colonial ethnic relationships. The focus in this chapter is largely on non-European settings, as recent and current European cases will be discussed extensively in later chapters.

## CAPITALISM AND INDIVIDUALISATION

If by ethnicity we refer to the social organisation of communicated cultural differences, ethnicity appeared together with capitalism in many parts of the world. As Epstein (1978, 1992) has shown, 'tribal' relationships in the Copperbelt area were qualitatively different before and after colonial pacification, monetarisation and the introduction of labour migrancy and wagework. Before their exodus the migrants were integrated largely on the village level – politically through the kin group and economically through subsistence farming on the ancestral land. They then became political subjects under the British and participants in a uniform capitalist economic system based on the individual labour contract and monetary exchange. The boundaries of the relevant systems expanded enormously. The migrants entered into horizontal competitive relationships with each other, and were ranked in an occupational hierarchy with an important ethnic element: the managerial positions were held by expatriate Europeans. Where the relevant boundary of the social system formerly had been, in many respects, the boundary of the village, it now became a non-physical boundary, based on the classification of others rather than their place of residence, their kinship system or their customs. Interaction across linguistic boundaries increased many times over (often turning languages such as Bemba or English into *linguas francas*), and as a consequence people became more self-conscious concerning their origins and cultural identity: they acquired an ethnic identity with an everyday relevance. Further, as I have argued in chapters 2 and 3, the urban setting offered new opportunities for informal and formal organisation. The beer-halls, unions and later the political parties created new possibilities for group organisation. Thus in some parts of the Copperbelt, the 'tribes' re-emerged as interest groups organised on the basis of ethnic identity; language, kinship, ancestral territory and myths of origin. This form of ethnic organisation was, of course, unknown in pre-colonial times. In this setting, it was intrinsically linked to capitalism. Furthermore, in such a situation it became imperative to establish clear criteria for group membership.

A similar development took place with Canadian Indians because of their increased integration into the nation-state. From the moment Indian identity became a possible vehicle for the acquisition of particular rights, Indian identity became relevant as an abstract 'umbrella' identity; at the same time, it became important to find clear criteria for distinguishing between Indians and non-Indians (see chapter 7).

In plantation societies, the introduction of ethnic or 'racial' elements in the division of labour was perhaps even more apparent. In some societies, such as Malaysia and Guyana, different categories of labourers were systematically recruited from distinctive 'races' or 'groups'. After the abolition of slavery in the British and French colonies (1835–9), thousands of East Indians were recruited to many of these societies as indentured labourers, to replace the former slaves on the sugar plantations. In these societies, divisions of labour based on colonial ethnic categorisations emerged.

In Mauritius, Indians were recruited as labourers on the canefields, and the Brahmins among them were hired as *sirdars*, foremen. Many Creoles (the descendants of slaves) now worked as skilled workers and artisans at the sugar factories. The middle managerial positions were held by Chinese and 'Mulattoes', whereas the estate managers were always Franco-Mauritian (white). In Trinidad, Guyana and Fiji, the pattern was different; in Trinidad, the foremen were blacks. The idea that particular categories of people were particularly well equipped to carry out particular kinds of work gradually became part and parcel of colonial ideology and practice. Members of different ascribed groups had different political rights; individuals were ranked in the economic and political systems according to which category they were placed in.

Ethnicity, which is today a major social preoccupation and a chief principle for political organisation in many of these societies (see Nash, 1988 and Watson, 2000, for Malaysia; B. Williams, 1991, for Guyana; Klass, 1991 and Vertovec, 1992, for Trinidad; Eriksen, 1998, for Mauritius; Grillo, 1998, for comparisons), must therefore be understood in relation to the colonial division of labour.

## THE LABEL 'BLACK IDENTITY'

Scientific racism arose in the late eighteenth century, largely as a response to calls for the abolition of slavery (Banton, 1987; Todorov, 1989; Wade, 2002). Although most scientists had abandoned the concept of race by the 1920s, cultural notions of race continue to exist in folk taxonomies. Personality traits and cultural distinctiveness are in many societies still attributed to people on the basis of 'race', and it is in this way that 'race' overlaps with, and sometimes becomes, ethnic categorisation. The physical appearance of a person may in this sort of society serve as a convenient shorthand way of telling other members of the society what 'kind of person' he or she is. Such categorisations, and their accompanying evaluations and stereotypes, are the work of colonial history and a particular division of labour and political power; they are no more natural than the ethnic distinctions differentiating Finns from Swedes.

The African slaves who were transported to the New World and to the plantation islands in the Indian Ocean from the early sixteenth century onwards belonged to many different groups who spoke mutually unintelligible and often unrelated languages, had different kinship systems and so on. Under different economic and political circumstances they might well have reproduced their distinctiveness after migrating, or they might have merged into other new groups than those they actually did form. As it happened, strict measures were introduced in order to prevent the slaves from retaining a sense of group identity. Families were split up and persons who spoke different languages were compelled to live and work together. As a result, strict legislation dividing people into occupational categories and kinds of political subjects on the basis of colour emerged. Distinctive ethnic categories based on colour became more salient than place of origin or ancestral language. As slaves, and later as an underpaid working class, they were collectively stigmatised by the rulers. By virtue of their identical treatment, they also had shared political interests in promoting their rights and, later, contesting the hegemonic world views represented by the colonial or white American hegemonic groups. In the Caribbean, the United States and the Indian Ocean, a distinctive 'black' ethnic category thus developed, and it is sometimes politically incorporated.

Under different economic and political circumstances such an ethnic identity would not have been viable: it is far from evident that people of Wolof, Ibo and Ashanti origin should consider themselves members of the same group. In other words, slavery led to a de-ethnification of African identities, while liberation and subsequent developments, notably the Civil Rights Movement in the USA and independence in the colonies, encouraged a re-ethnification of the slaves' descendants, leading to the formation of black ethnic identities based on notions of origins (in Africa as such), sociolects, religious practices and/or other traits seen as essential (Collins, 2004). The fact of their being defined by the hegemonic white groups as black also contributed to their internal cohesiveness.

'Black' ethnic identity is relative to social context. In the Caribbean, distinctions are conventionally drawn – and are socially relevant – between blacks and browns. Historically, browns have been a relatively privileged group. Originating as the illicit offspring of white settlers and slave women, those in the category of 'Mulattoes' were rarely allowed to inherit from their fathers but, in return, they were often liberated and educated. Up to this day, browns are associated with the liberal professions in these societies; in Jamaica, 'brown' is virtually a synonym for 'middle-class'. In the United States, on the contrary, the category of the Mulatto disappeared during the nineteenth century. Today, any individual who has the slightest phenotypical trace of African origin is classified as 'black' (the 'one drop principle'). So when a famous American professor in black history came to Trinidad in 1989 to give a lecture commemorating the 150th anniversary of the abolition of slavery, the Trinidadian audience was startled to discover that the man was 'nearly white'. In the US, of course, he would have had no other choice than to define himself as black, being attributed a fixed place in the black/white binary system of the USA.

## INDIANS IN NEW WORLDS

With the arrival of Indian indentured labourers in some of the plantation colonies in the second half of the nineteenth century, a new kind of ethnic complexity developed. First, it is interesting to note that the basis for the development of (East) Indian ethnic identity was different from that of black identity. Although their economic and political situation was scarcely better than that of the slaves (Tinker, 1974), the Indians were free to form their own communities after migrating. As a result, important cultural practices and social forms were retained in their new worlds. Exaggerating somewhat, the famous Indo-Trinidadian author V.S. Naipaul (1969) has described rural Trinidad as a replication of rural Bihar (a state in north India). In some of these societies, notably in Mauritius, caste has continued to play an important part in social and political life. Linguistic and cultural subdivisions which had been relevant in India, notably the Muslim–Hindu division and the division between speakers of Indo-European languages (such as Hindi) and speakers of Dravidian languages (such as Tamil), were to some extent reproduced or refashioned. The latter distinction continues to be socially relevant in Mauritius, but not in Trinidad and Guyana.

There are two complementary explanations for this. In Mauritius, unlike in the other societies which received indentured Indian labourers, a certain number of Tamils had already arrived as free merchants during the period of slavery. There was thus a Tamil elite in place before indentureship. Second, the Tamils were sufficiently numerous in Mauritius to be able to form effective career networks based on kinship and shared ethnic identity, and by the same token they were able to remain more or less endogamous.

In several of the societies which received large numbers of Indians, the blacks responded by strengthening their identity and ethnic boundaries. They developed stereotypes of Indians as backward, illiterate and pagan, and as a consequence many blacks began to reify and overcommunicate their own culture as more sophisticated, more up-to-date and sometimes more 'Europeanised' than that of the Indians, who were then at the bottom of the social hierarchy. This kind of dynamic is common in hierarchical polyethnic systems. A group which is powerless undercommunicates its distinctiveness, but when the same group is in a superior position, its members will overcommunicate it. This switch is frequently situational. The coloured middle class of nineteenth-century Trinidad, it has been said (Brereton, 1979), tended to be anti-racist upwards (vis-à-vis the whites) and racist downwards (vis-à-vis the blacks).

In order to understand the historical emergence of a particular ethnic configuration, we have seen repeatedly that it would be misleading to start from an assumption of 'primordial characteristics' of groups or categories. The formation of different categories of 'Indians' in Mauritius and Trinidad, respectively, clearly shows this. Not only are the ethnic subdivisions within the 'Indian' category different in the two societies, but so too are the stereotypical assumptions about 'Indian culture'. Indians in Mauritius, where they are in a majority and dominate the state bureaucracy, often complain that they are good politicians but 'have little talent for business'. In Trinidad, Indians have a smaller stake in the state bureaucracy and many Indians have gone into business. Here, the common stereotype of self is exactly the opposite in this respect.

When we try to understand how and why particular forms of ethnic organisation have emerged in different societies, we must therefore ask not 'What are these people *really* like?', but rather 'How have ethnic identifications developed in a particular political and economic setting, and what purposes do they serve?' Seen in this perspective, ethnicity as it can be identified in colonial and post-colonial societies with a capitalist mode of production must necessarily be very different from the kinds of categorisations which existed in pre-colonial times. The goals pursued by individuals are different, the relevant means for their achievement are different, and the encompassing social system is different. This brief description of plantation societies also indicates that ethnicity can be studied both as a phenomenon created by economic and political circumstances, and as a reaction to such circumstances. I shall now consider some further historical aspects of ethnogenesis in contexts of social and cultural change.

## ETHNIC REVITALISATION: FROM PEOPLE TO *A PEOPLE*

Following the integration of so-called traditional peoples into modern nation-states, symbolic universes merge in many respects. People become more similar as regards practices and representations; increasing segments of their learnt capabilities for communication, their taken-for-granted structures of relevance – simply put, their *culture* – become shared. Under these circumstances, people are more liable than before to reflect upon and objectify their way of life as *a* culture or as *a tradition*, and in this way they may become *a people* with an abstract sense of community and a presumed shared history. This kind of process has taken place among Trinidadians of Indian origin since the 1950s, but particularly since the economic growth associated with the oil boom of the 1970s (Vertovec, 1991, 1992). Formerly, the 'East Indians' or Indo-Trinidadians were politically fragmented and had a poorly developed shared identity. They were villagers living off the land, with their extended kin group and their village as the most important foci for social organisation. In later years, education, the spread of modern mass media and social mobility have simultaneously integrated the mass of Indo-Trinidadians into a social system of larger scale than before, *and* increased their knowledge of the outside world. They have become consciously concerned with the preservation of 'their culture' and have formed organisations intended to pursue their cultural and political interests. Although the majority of Indo-Trinidadians no longer speak an Indian language, they are strongly oriented towards India in their search for roots and 'authentic culture'. Many middle-class Hindus in Trinidad began, in the 1980s, to associate themselves with the charismatic Hindu Sai Baba movement, which helped them to see their history as that of a dignified culture (Klass, 1991). The spread of the Internet in the 1990s, further facilitated the integration of Trinidadian Hindus into a much larger world of diasporic Hinduism (Miller and Slater, 2000).

Most of the Indians who arrived in Trinidad as indentured labourers in the second half of the nineteenth century were rural low-caste people. The culture their descendants seek to 're-create', however, is largely Brahminic in character. Their ancestors in Bihar and Uttar Pradesh were villagers with no collective organisation and no social identity as 'Indians'. In other words, the presumed revitalisation of a half-forgotten ancestral culture turns out to be something qualitatively new – even if it is presented as old and time-honoured. The concept of 'Indian', as it is used in Trinidad, is a Trinidadian product, or rather, a modern identity fashioned from traditional materials.

It was formerly common to view contemporary ethnicity and 'tribalism' in Africa and elsewhere either as vestiges of the past or as forms of revitalisation, that is the re-emergence of identities and forms of organisation which had existed formerly, but which had been on the verge of disappearance. More recent research has shown that this view, while it conforms to ethnic ideologies themselves (which are primordialist in that they stress continuity with the past as a *raison-d'être* for the unity of the ethnic group), tends to be misleading. Important aspects of such 'revitalisation movements' are entirely new, although they imagine themselves as old and glorify presumably ancient handicrafts, rituals or other cultural practices. The next example will illustrate this point clearly.

## COLONIALISM AND MIGRATION

The creation of plantation societies and the slave trade are well known aspects of colonialism. Somewhat less studied are the processes of social upheaval which took place in large parts of Africa in a later phase of colonialism, caused by the introduction of centralised state administration and a capitalist system of production. The state has integrated different groups into social systems of unprecedented scale. In many cases, this integration had only a superficial influence on people's daily lives. There are still, in the early twenty-first century, many Africans who are for most practical purposes socially and culturally integrated at the village level. In many other cases, however, capitalism and the state represented new systemic parameters with profound consequences for social organisation and individual life-paths. It is by virtue of these kinds of processes, many scholars have argued (for example A. Cohen, 1969; Peel, 1989; Worsley, 1984), that the contemporary ethnic identifications and boundaries were created. Categorical distinctions certainly existed before colonialism and capitalism, but perhaps 'the pocket in which they properly belong is part of a garment of an altogether different cut' (Fardon, 1987: 178). Notably, such categorisations were segmentary, fluid and less institutionalised than modern ethnic distinctions.

Drawing extensively on historical material as well as original fieldwork, Jay O'Brien (1986) has analysed the emergence of ethnic categorisations and groups in the Gezira area of east-central Sudan. The area was opened for irrigated cotton production in 1925, and it required the recruitment of large numbers of seasonal labourers during the peak season. The various groups or 'tribes' that recruited such labourers were integrated into the capitalist system of production in different ways because of differences in social organisation. However, the new ethnic categorisations, O'Brien argues, did not emerge from cultural differences but rather from variations in the form of integration in the capitalist system. Two examples illustrate this.

People from a variety of West African groups were recruited as cotton workers. They were all Muslims, and most could speak Hausa, but in other respects they were – and considered themselves as – culturally distinctive. These immigrants were accustomed to wagework and adapted easily to the conditions on the Gezira scheme, and the British frequently used them to replace locals who did not fulfil their obligations. Locally, the settlers were known under the generic term 'Fellata', which took on a basically pejorative meaning, with connotations of 'hard-working and slavish'. The settlers responded through a process of 'cultural realignment'. They began, collectively, to emphasise their distinctiveness vis-à-vis the locals, turning it into a virtue, and became Islamic fundamentalists in contrast to the less pious Muslims of the other categories. Gradually, they began to use the term 'Takari' for themselves, which is a respectful term for religious pilgrims from West Africa. In conclusion, O'Brien finds that 'partly in defensive adaptation to circumstances of discrimination and lumping together by others, these diverse cultural groups have drawn on commonalities of their past heritage and contemporary circumstances to forge a more or less coherent ethnic identity' (1986: 903).

A different process of ethnic incorporation in the same area concerns the people now known as Joama'. They are Arabic-speakers, Muslims and claim Arab origins. They had a reputation as reliable and hard-working labourers and were in high demand at the Gezira scheme, particularly from the 1950s. Their area of settlement became a prime recruiting ground for the cotton estates. Many job-seekers who were not Joama' thus began to settle near the Joama' area to facilitate their access to the labour market. Some of them would work as sharecroppers for the Joama' outside the cotton-picking season, and thus were gradually integrated into the Joama' social system. During fieldwork in 1977, O'Brien found that many families of non-Joama' origins were about to become assimilated. Some, who stated that they 'used to be Fellata', were already recognised as Joama', whereas others, in an earlier phase of assimilation, were seen as good workers who were 'just like the Joama".

These analyses of different processes of ethnic incorporation show that the formation of ethnic identities in the Gezira came about through a specific intersection of existing local character-istics and the introduction of a capitalist system of production. Generalising further, O'Brien concludes that 'ethnicity as it has been encountered in the contemporary Third World ... has been constituted by the same world-historical process that has produced modern capitalism, wage labor, and class structures' (1986: 905). Contemporary ethnicity, or 'tribalism', is not, in other words, a relic of the past but a product of modernisation processes leading up to the present. This point is supported further by a look at the semantics of ethnicity in contemporary Africa.

## THE POWER OF NAMING

It has frequently been remarked that many of the 'tribes' anthro-pologists have written about had no empirical existence outside the mind of the ethnographer (Kuper, 2005; Southall, 1976). Abstract loyalty to, and identification with, entities such as 'the Nuer' or 'the Dinka' were in many cases unthinkable for the persons in question themselves, whose main principles of organisation were kinship and locality. In many cases, even the actual names of 'tribes' were simply labels used by the colonial administration and were rarely or never used by the 'tribals' themselves. Thus the 'Yoruba', a major Nigerian tribe or ethnic group today, is a twentieth-century phenomenon. Categorical labels with no social significance are likely to be unimportant, and in pre-colonial times many groups were politically organised along lines of kinship and personal loyalties and usually did not require categorical labels of greater scope. Epstein sees this when he writes, referring to Copperbelt material, that 'the term "tribe" did not carry the same meaning in the towns as it did in the rural areas; "tribalism" in urban and rural contexts related to phenomena of quite different orders' (1978: 10).

This means that although ethnicity existed in pre-colonial times in Southern Africa, it took on a very different form from that which it does today. Complex modern societies seem to imply processes of identity and boundary maintenance which are much more acutely felt, and more self-consciously fashioned, than has been the case in other kinds of societies.

In a critique of the most generalising uses of the term 'ethnicity', Richard Fardon (1987) gives an account of the development of Chamba ethnicity which shows that today's ethnic categorisations can have historical precedents which were quite different in their social functioning.

The Chamba are presently considered, and consider themselves, a people or an ethnic group. They number around a quarter of a million and live on both sides of the Nigeria–Cameroon border. The western and eastern Chamba speak different languages, which may belong to different classes, while the central Chamba 'were formed by the fusion of speakers of the two languages' (Fardon, 1987: 179). It seems likely that intermingling between the groups, followed by the formation of Chamba chiefdoms in the nineteenth century, account for the present distributions of Chamba peoples.

Even today, different categories of Chamba, and members of the same categories in different situations, use four different terms of self-identification which distinguish them from different categories of others, both within and outside of 'the Chamba group'. The word Chamba itself derives from one of these four categorisations, Sama or Samba, and as an identity tag it 'became ... absolute only after the establishment of the colonial and then the national state' (Fardon, 1987: 181). Further, there were formerly important distinctions based on contrasts between chiefly and priestly sections in the communities, as well as the ubiquitous distinctions based on lineage.

Fardon's conclusion is that 'the Chamba did not exist in the nineteenth century, not just because [the term] Chamba describes people whose origins, languages and cultures are diverse ... but because ethnic entities which have the form of the modern Chamba ethnicity are modern inventions' (1987: 182).

A related but more general point concerning the historical emergence of ethnic labels is stated forcefully in Edwin Ardener's short essay 'Language, ethnicity and population' (1989a [1972]). In this rather dense and pyrotechnic exposition, Ardener first relativises the significance of contemporary and colonial ethnic labels by showing that they scarcely correspond to pre-colonial identities. He then argues that they function in a recursive way, since the labels used by colonisers, missionaries and foreign scholars were returned to and appropriated by the people in question. Finally, Ardener divorces ethnicity from demography altogether by showing that there does not have to be biological continuity among the carriers of a particular ethnic label. The linguistic and ethnic category of 'Kole', he argues, 'may have been filled according to different criteria at different times' (Ardener, 1989a [1972]: 69) – in other words, people classified as 'Kole' were recruited from other groups according to varying principles.

Ardener's theoretical points concerning ethnic labelling are as follows:

1. The ethnic classification is a reflex of self-identification.
2. Onomastic (or naming) propensities are closely involved in this, and thus have more than a purely linguistic interest.
3. Identification by others is an important feature in the establishment of self-identification.
4. The taxonomic space in which self-identification occurs is of overriding importance.
5. The effect of foreign classification, 'scientific' and lay, is far from neutral in the establishment of such a space. (1989a [1972]: 68)

Fardon, Southall and Ardener are all concerned with the semantics of ethnicity – with the introduction of and use of names in the conceptual reification of groups. A shared assumption is that groups tend to be fluid and segmentary in character and that boundaries between them are fuzzy, ambiguous and situational. The establishment of clear labels for large categories of people may thus have a conceptually, but also socially reifying effect on groups, as they become official names and their members start using them in their self-identification. As we shall see in the next chapter, the same kinds of processes are at work in nationalist movements.

The mere act of naming a smaller or larger cluster of clans, villages or lineages using a collective label is not, of course, sufficient to turn the discrete and fluid groups into ethnic categories. Fardon connects the emergence of Chamba ethnicity with the development of centralised (colonial) state administration, but also notes that other writers have 'given prominence to the economic conditions associated with the spread of capitalist organization of production and marketing'. He attributes this difference to variations between societies: his material deals with 'an economically underdeveloped area of west Africa, whereas emphasis upon economic factors occurs in analyses of southern Africa' (Fardon, 1987: 178).

Studies of changes in the semantics of ethnicity are thus complementary to studies of more general processes of social and cultural change such as those discussed earlier in this chapter. Their importance should not be underestimated. There is power in naming and, more specifically, there is political power inherent in the ability to make a system of social classification relevant. As Grillo (1998: 100) notes, in colonial times, the subject populations were amalgamated 'into a few, broad, hierarchically ordered groups'. Labels accorded to people as tools of domination would sometimes stick and linger after the initial conditions of domination had been transformed, creating an often hierarchical classificatory grid with particular connotations of 'race', 'character' and so on, again forming the basis for contemporary ethnopolitics and stereotyping.

## MODERN EDUCATION AND ETHNIC IDENTITY

Technology can be essential in generating opportunities and constraints for culture and social organisation. Most of the complex, large-scale societies we know would probably have been less effectively integrated without effective communication technology. Mass education, which entails the spreading of books and other texts which describe and reify history and culture, plays an important part in this respect.

Uniform educational systems covering large areas greatly facilitate the development of abstract identifications with a category of people whom one will never meet – who are neither kinsfolk, nor affines nor neighbours (for example 'the Chamba' or 'the Kole'). It enables a large number of people to learn, simultaneously, which ethnic group they belong to and what are the cultural characteristics of that group. Standardised mass education can therefore be an extremely powerful machine for the creation of abstract identifications. Literacy enables people to create 'authorised' versions of their history, and in view of the 'objective' status granted written accounts of history in most literate societies (see Lévi-Strauss, 1962: chapter 9, for a depiction of history as myth), the manipulation, selection or reinterpretation of history for political or other purposes becomes an important activity in the creation and re-creation of ethnic allegiances.

In this way, mass education can be an efficient aid in the establishment of standardised reifications of culture, which are essential in the legitimation of ethnic identities. Mass-produced accounts of 'our people' or 'our culture' are important tools in the fashioning of an ethnic identity with a presumed cultural continuity in time.

As Lévi-Strauss has emphasised, illiterate people are no less capable of forming abstractions than the literate, but the kinds of abstraction created in nonliterate societies are of a different order: they can be described as the 'science of the concrete' (Lévi-Strauss, 1962: chapter 1; cf. Comaroff and Comaroff, 1992: chapter 2). Similarly, Benedict Anderson would argue two decades later, all communities beyond the size of a closed village are abstractly imagined by their members, but the *style* of imagination differs. Anderson singles out modern imagined communities, in particular nations, as distinctive and unique – largely because they have arisen in the age of 'print-capitalism' (Anderson, 1991 [1983]; cf. Goody, 1977; see also chapter 6). Distinctions between us and them can be found in every human society, but the form, relevance and reach of such distinctions vary hugely. In order to understand the causes of these variations, historical knowledge is necessary – the snapshots of conventional anthropological fieldwork can give a profound understanding of the contemporary functioning of ethnicity or other categorical distinctions, but not of their emergence.

## ETHNICITY, HISTORY AND CULTURE

Several of the anthropological perspectives on ethnicity discussed in this book deliberately ignore the possible ways in which *cultural* peculiarities may give shape to ethnicity. In fact, many important studies of ethnicity – from the contributions to Barth (1969b), Abner Cohen (1974b) and Despres (1975b) to Rex and Mason (1986), Nash (1988), Vermeulen and Govers (1994), May *et al.* (2004) and others, seem to argue that culture and cultural variation as such should be bracketed in analyses of ethnicity. What is usually the focus of enquiry is the way in which 'real or imagined' cultural differences assume social, political and economic importance, and it has become a standard procedure for anthropologists to polemicise against the misplaced concreteness involved in reifications of culture, whether they are undertaken by natives or by anthropologists. It has been stressed repeatedly that ethnic identities, groups and beliefs of shared culture and history are *creations* – whether they are created by historical circumstances, through strategic agency or as unintended consequences of political projects. Ethnic identities based on assumptions of shared culture may thus appear as 'accidents of history' (Leach's phrase) and little more. As Ardener has so eloquently argued, ethnic groups can profitably be regarded as self-defining entities: 'Ethnicities demand to be viewed from the inside. They have no imperative relationship with particular "objective" criteria' (1989b [1974]: 111). As numerous studies have shown, history, including 'emic' ethnohistory of the kind discussed in chapter 4, is written in the present and expresses present concerns (see Tonkin *et al.*, 1989). Thus the work of historians, lay or professional, may ultimately be equated with informants' statements by this kind of anthropological perspective.

An extreme version of this argument would lead to radical constructivism (see the discussion at the end of chapter 3). Granted that ethnic categorisations and group formations are the results of historical contingencies, and granted that the history documenting the existence of a certain ethnic group can be written in virtually any way, regardless of what really happened in the past, one seems forced to conclude that 'anything goes' – that *any* ethnic identity is imaginable, regardless of actual cultural variation or proveable distinctive origins. The fact that ethnic categories like Chamba, Joama' and Afro-Caribbean have come into being, according to this way of reasoning, has no intrinsic relationship to any shared cultural characteristics initially possessed by the members of these categories. In sum, one may conclude, with Ernest Renan, that nationhood (or ethnic identity) involves shared memories, but also a great deal of shared forgetting (Renan 1992 [1882]).

This kind of argument has clearly been indispensable (and it pervades much of the Anglophone anthropological literature on ethnicity), but it leaves important questions unanswered. Obviously, it would have been impossible to persuade Chamba that they were really Yoruba, or to convince English people that they belonged to the same ethnic category as Chinese. At the least, such categorisations seem very, very far off. It seems clear, therefore, that the construction of ethnic categories takes place within a defined space and that some new categorisations may be viable while others are not. The question is: can such a space be defined in terms of cultural variation at all? The answer is, probably, that this is sometimes possible, but not always.

In a series of books on nationalism, A.D. Smith (see in particular A.D. Smith, 1986, 1995; cf. also Guiberneau, 2004) argues that modern ethnic ideologies, notably nationalisms, have identifiable 'objective' cultural roots in historically stable *ethnies*. He claims that the cultural continuity with the past which is emphasised by ethnic ideologists and national historians is not all make-believe and a manipulative invention of the past. In effect, he argues that there *is* such a cultural continuity with the past, although the nations and ethnic movements themselves are modern creations. In many cases it is clear that group history has been fashioned so as to serve present needs, but this does not imply that anything goes. There are only so many plausible versions of history.

Concerning the construction of national ethnic identity in Norway, for example (see chapter 6), the number of options available in the mid-nineteenth century for western Norwegian nationalists were limited: they could effectively choose between a western Norwegian, a Norwegian, a Dano-Norwegian, and a Scandinavian identity. This was partly due to political circumstances, but also to the fact that the people involved would scarcely identify themselves as members of an ethnic nation containing people to whom they felt culturally unrelated.

Twentieth-century anthropology had a strong bias towards studying the present, and in their dealings with the past many anthropologists tended to regard it as neither more nor less than present-day constructions of the past. Some anthropologists, among them Wolf and Worsley, did stress the need to understand the past in order to understand the present – and by this they meant understanding what really took place, not what present-day informants or historians claim took place. O'Brien's work in the Sudan, summarised above, exemplifies the importance of studying history *as such*, and not just as a present-day rationalisation or part of an ideological justification for would-be ethnic leaders, although the latter aspect is also highly relevant, but for other ends.

## HISTORY AND MYTH

Arguing explicitly against those studies of ethnicity which ignore cultural history and cultural factors generally, John Peel (1989; see also Peel, 2000) offers an interpretation of Yoruba ethnicity in historical perspective. He admits, referring to Abner Cohen's work in Ibadan, that there may be compelling political reasons for ethnic mobilisation. He also concedes, referring to Maryon McDonald's work in Brittany (1989; cf. chapter 6), that the creative fashioning (or invention) of 'ethnohistory' among intellectuals has been an important technique for the creation of that abstract group consciousness among the masses which we think of as ethnic identity.

However, Peel says: 'despite the "invention of tradition" that [the writing of ethnohistory] may involve, unless it also makes genuine contact with people's actual experience, that is with *a history that happened*, it is not likely to be effective' (1989: 200, my emphasis). Nothing comes out of nothing, in other words (see also Eriksen, 2000; Jenkins, 2002).

Along with the Hausa and the Igbo, the Yoruba is one of Nigeria's 'mega-tribal' groupings, with more members than there are citizens in many nation-states. As such it is entirely a modern category, since the great-grandparents of most of the people who today identify themselves as Yoruba did not identify themselves in such a way. In other words, the parallel with the other African examples discussed in this chapter is evident. At the beginning of the twentieth century, the Yoruba were identical with what is today one Yoruba grouping, the Oyo. Like the Joama' of the Sudan, this ethnic category was vastly expanded as other groups took on Yoruba identity from the 1920s onwards, following migration, cash-cropping, education and conversion to world religions, creating a Nigeria-wide system of communication and exchange. From the late 1930s, modern Yoruba political organisation, contrasted against a similar Igbo organisation, began to develop. Thus Peel is in accord with the constructivist argument on the modern character of ethnicity by admitting that administrative units (regions and states) have in important ways contributed to shaping ethnic organisation. However, he also stresses that this has been a two-way process, mediated by politics, where the ethnic groups themselves have also played an important part. It is certainly no accident that the main divisions in Nigerian politics follow ethnic boundaries, and Peel connects this to cultural differences and identifications that were intrinsically related to pre-colonial experiences. In order to document this connection with the past, he draws extensively on historical accounts.

The peoples who would later come to know themselves as Yoruba would in pre-colonial times recognise their affinity with others through shared language and/or shared customs. Since customs were to a great extent shared with members of other groups, language eventually became the most important vessel for Yoruba identity. This language-based identity was codified and spread in two principal ways: through liberated Yoruba slaves in diasporas (particularly in Sierra Leone) and through the work of missions, which played a pivotal part in creating a written Yoruba language. The missions were successful in this part of Nigeria and, during the latter half of the nineteenth century, Yoruba identity came to be associated with Christianity. A local scholar called Samuel Johnson even fashioned a version of Yoruba history, completed in 1899 but published only in 1921, which claimed that the Yoruba were descendants of Coptic Christians from Upper Egypt. In this way, the recent paganism was depicted as an unfortunate interlude. In addition, wars with other groups, notably the Fulani, strengthened the feeling of a shared destiny and sharpened boundaries.

Paradoxically, Ibadan, the main Yoruba city, was to become a predominantly Muslim city. Although Yoruba cultural history is strongly associated with early conversion to Christianity, the modern Yoruba ethnic group is divided between Christianity and Islam. Moreover, the Muslim Yoruba are identified as the 'Yoruba proper' (the Oyo), whereas the Christians are regarded as 'adopted Yoruba'. Due to this 'faultline' dividing the community (and several other Nigerian ethnic categories) along religious lines, religion cannot be used as a marker of ethnic identity. This ethnic 'pan-Yoruba' identity is nevertheless evident in both groups, although they do not always function as a political corporation. Yoruba segments, whether Christian or Muslim, or in alliances with Igbo or Hausa, remain Yoruba by virtue of their cultural identity.

The material presented by Peel is reminiscent of Fardon's and Ardener's accounts of ethnogenesis in neighbouring areas, as he links the development of contemporary ethnic identity and organisation to the same kind of modernisation processes that the other authors cite. However, Peel's conclusions are different in that he emphasises not the ways in which the present has shaped the past, but the ways in which the past has shaped the present. Arguing rather pointedly against the 'presentism' dominating social anthropology, he targets in particular Abner Cohen's contention that ethnicity requires neither a cultural nor a historical explanation, but can be reduced to politics and contemporary 'structural conditions'. Against Cohen, Peel argues the need to take historical accounts seriously – both as sources documenting actual events more or less accurately, and as serious attempts by 'natives' to come to terms with their past. Ethnohistory should not, in his view, simply be regarded as a technique to generate a particular present, but can also be taken seriously at its face value – as an expression of an interest in the past.

This point is important. Together with the kind of history Wolf, Worsley and O'Brien recommend for scrutiny – economic and political history – the cultural histories of peoples may certainly shed light on the origins of contemporary ethnicity, and should not be seen merely as aspects of the present. Two main concerns in the anthropological study of ethnic identity and organisation have been to reveal ethnohistory as ideology fashioned to satisfy contemporary needs (as discussed in chapter 4), and to point out that there is no necessary fit between ethnic discontinuities and discontinuities of 'objective culture', respectively. This kind of argument leaves important questions unanswered. We may nevertheless ask, with Peel, whether anthropologists are really trained to ask questions relating to history seen as the past and not just as justifications for present concerns. Peel writes:

> The present has often been treated by anthropologists as a kind of temporal plateau, coterminous with the duration of their fieldwork, inhabited by structures and categories; but it is much more evanescent than that, no sooner come than gone, really no more than the hinge between the past and future. (1989: 213)

The issue he takes on is much too vast for us to go into here. Many anthropologists would be inclined to argue against claims to the effect that identities *are* continuous through time. Perhaps they only *seem* continuous and our analytical task consists in showing that they are not, and that the very notion that people ought to be concerned with the past is an ideological child of the age of nationalism. In this perspective, one might argue that while trees have roots, humans don't – and that any claim to the effect that humans need roots is ideological. On the other hand, there is no doubt that the past shapes the present in objective ways and not merely through present reconstructions, and since Peel wrote his article in the late 1980s, many anthropologists have taken the study of history much more seriously than was common at the time. As a way of examining this and related questions in greater detail, we now turn to a closer investigation of nationalism, thereby bringing the anthropological study of ethnicity even closer to home than we have done so far.

## FURTHER READING

Comaroff, John L. and Jean Comaroff (1992) *Ethnography and the Historical Imagination*. Boulder, CO: Westview Press. Combining ethnographic and historical methods in a series of case studies from Southern Africa, the authors show why an anthropology without historical depth ultimately becomes myopic and limited.

Hobsbawm, Eric J. and Terence Ranger, eds (1983) *The Invention of Tradition*. Cambridge: Cambridge University Press. A standard reference on the instrumental, often imperial motivations for reifying certain views of the past and embedding them in public displays.

Tonkin, Elizabeth, Maryon McDonald and Malcolm Chapman, eds (1989) *History and Ethnicity*. London: Routledge. A collection of seminal articles which explore the ways in which anthropologists may deal with history – as strategic reconstructions of the past or as events shaping the present.

# 6
# Nationalism

Nationalism is not the awakening of nations to self-consciousness: it invents nations where they do not exist.

Ernest Gellner (1964: 169)

—But do you know what a nation means? says John Wyse.
—Yes, says Bloom.
—What is it? says John Wyse.
—A nation? says Bloom. A nation is the same people living in the same place.
—By God, then, says Ned, laughing, if that's so I'm a nation for I'm living in the same place for the past five years.
So of course everyone had a laugh at Bloom and says he, trying to muck out of it:
—Or also living in different places.
—That covers my case, says Joe.

James Joyce (1984: 329–30)

## THE RACE TO NATION[1]

For years, social anthropological studies of ethnicity concentrated on relationships between groups which were of such a size that they could be studied through traditional field methods: participant observation, personal interviews and surveys. The empirical focus of anthropological studies was almost by default a local community. If the state was given consideration, it would usually be as a part of the wider context, for instance as an external agent influencing local conditions. Besides, anthropology was traditionally biased towards the study of 'remote others'. As argued earlier, the general shift in terminology from 'tribe' to 'ethnic group' relativises such an Us/Them dichotomy, since ethnic groups, unlike 'tribes', obviously exist among 'ourselves' as well as among the 'others'. The boundary mechanisms that keep ethnic groups more or less discrete have the same formal characteristics in a London suburb as in the New Guinea highlands, and the development of ethnic identity can be

---

1. The pun is stolen from Brackette Williams' essay 'A class act: anthropology and the race to nation across ethnic terrain' (1989).

studied with largely the same conceptual tools in New Zealand as in Central Europe – although the empirical contexts are distinctive and ultimately unique. This has today been acknowledged in social anthropology, where a majority of researchers now study complex 'unbounded' systems rather than supposedly isolated communities.

Nationalism is a relatively recent topic for anthropology. The study of nationalism – the ideology of the modern nation-state – was for many years left to political scientists, sociologists and historians. Nations and nationalist ideologies are modern large-scale phenomena *par excellence*. However, although the study of nationalism raises methodological problems relating to scale and the impossibility of isolating the unit of study, these problems inevitably arise in relation to other empirical foci as well. Since the beginning of modern fieldwork, social changes have taken place in the heartlands of anthropological research, integrating millions of people into markets and states. Like ourselves, our informants are citizens (while formerly they might have been colonial subjects). Further, 'primitive societies' probably never were as isolated as was formerly held, and they were no more 'pristine' and 'original' than our own societies (Wolf, 1982). Indeed, as Adam Kuper (2005) has shown, the very idea of primitive society was a European invention which emerged under particular historical circumstances.

An early, but largely neglected, venture into the anthropological study of nation-states, was Lloyd Fallers' (1974) research in Uganda and Turkey, where he explicitly tried to link data from both micro and macro levels in his analyses (cf. also Gluckman, 1961; Grønhaug, 1974; for a later, influential work, see Scott, 1998). However, the study of nationalism truly became a topic within anthropology only during the 1980s.

In the classic terminology of social anthropology, the term 'nation' was used in an inaccurate way to designate large categories of people or societies with more or less uniform culture. In his introductory textbook, I.M. Lewis (1985: 287) states: 'By the term nation, following the best anthropological authority we understand, of course, a culture-unit.' Later, Lewis makes it clear that he sees no reason for distinguishing between 'tribes', 'ethnic groups' and 'nations', since the difference appears to be one of size, not of structural composition or functioning. Comparing groups of several million with smaller segments, he asks: 'Are these smaller segments significantly different? My answer is that they are not: that they are simply smaller units of the same kind ...' (Lewis, 1985: 358).

In this chapter, I shall argue that it can indeed be worthwhile to distinguish nations from ethnic categories, largely because of their relationship to a modern state. It will also be shown that an anthropological perspective is essential for a full understanding of nationalism. An analytical and empirical focus on nationalism can further be illuminating in research on modernisation and social change, as well as being highly relevant for the wider fields of political anthropology and the study of social identification.

## WHAT IS NATIONALISM?

Ernest Gellner begins his highly influential book on nationalism by defining the concept like this:

> Nationalism is primarily a political principle, which holds that the political and the national unit should be congruent.
>
> Nationalism as a sentiment, or as a movement, can best be defined in terms of this principle. Nationalist *sentiment* is the feeling of anger aroused by the violation of the principle, or the feeling of satisfaction aroused by its fulfilment. A nationalist *movement* is one actuated by sentiment of this kind. (Gellner, 1983: 1; cf. Gellner, 1978: 134)

While this definition at first glance may seem a straightforward one, it turns out to be circular. For what is the 'national unit'? Gellner goes on to explain that he sees it as synonymous with an ethnic group – or at least an ethnic group which the nationalists claim exists: 'In brief, nationalism is a theory of political legitimacy, which requires that ethnic boundaries should not cut across political ones' (Gellner, 1983: 1; cf. also Gellner, 1997). In other words, nationalism, the way the term is used by Gellner and other contemporary social scientists, explicitly or implicitly refers to a peculiar link between ethnicity and the state. Nationalisms are, according to this view, ethnic ideologies which hold that their group should dominate a state. A nation-state, therefore, is a state dominated by an ethnic group, whose markers of identity (such as language or religion) are frequently embedded in its official symbolism and legislation. There is a drive towards the integration and assimilation of citizens, although Gellner concedes that nations may contain 'non-meltable' people, what he calls *entropy-resistant groups*. More of them later.

In another important theoretical study of nationalism, the South-East Asianist and political theorist Benedict Anderson proposes the following definition of the nation: 'it is an imagined political community – and imagined as both inherently limited and sovereign' (1991 [1983]: 6). By 'imagined', he does not mean 'imaginary', but rather that people who define themselves as members of a nation 'will never know most of their fellow-members, meet them, or even hear of them, yet in the minds of each lives the image of their communion' (1991 [1983]: 6). Unlike Gellner and many others, who concentrate on the political aspects of nationalism, Anderson is concerned to understand the force and persistence of national identification and sentiment. The fact that people are willing to die for their nation, he notes, indicates its extraordinary force.

Despite these differences in emphasis, Anderson's perspective is largely compatible with Gellner's. Both stress that nations are ideological constructions seeking to forge a link between (self-defined) cultural group and state, and that they create abstract communities of a different order from those dynastic states or kinship-based communities which pre-dated them.

The main task Anderson sets himself is to provide an explanation for what he calls the 'anomaly of nationalism'. According to both Marxist and liberal social theories of modernisation, nationalism should not have been viable in an individualist post-Enlightenment world, referring as it does to 'primordial loyalties' and solidarity based on common origins and culture (see Nimni, 1991). In particular, Anderson notes with a certain puzzlement that socialist states tend to be nationalist in character. 'The reality is quite plain,' he writes, 'the "end of the era of nationalism", so long prophesied, is not remotely in sight. Indeed, nation-ness is the most universally legitimate value in the political life of our time' (1991 [1983]: 3).

Anthropological research on ethnic boundaries and identity processes could help to illuminate Anderson's *problématique*. Anderson does not himself discuss ethnicity, and some of his main examples – the Philippines and Indonesia – are indeed polyethnic countries fraught with internal tensions and separatist movements based on both ethnic identity and religion. Research on ethnic identity formation and boundary maintenance has indicated that ethnic identities tend to attain their greatest importance in situations of flux, change, resource competition and threats against boundaries. It is not surprising, therefore, that political movements based on cultural identity are strong in societies undergoing modernisation, although this does not account for the fact that these movements become *nationalist* movements.

The remarkable congruence between theories of nationalism and anthropological theories of ethnicity seems unrecognised (or at least unacknowledged) by Gellner and Anderson. Since the two bodies of theory have largely developed independently of each other, I shall point out the main parallels.

Both studies of ethnicity at the local community level and studies of nationalism at the state level stress that ethnic or national identities are constructions; they are not 'natural'. Moreover, the link between a particular identity and the 'culture' it seeks to reify is not a one-to-one relationship. Widespread assumptions of congruence between ethnicity and 'objective culture' are in both cases shown to be cultural constructions themselves. *Talk about culture* and *culture* can here, perhaps, be distinguished in roughly the same way as one distinguishes between the menu and the food. They are social facts of different orders, but the former is no less real than the latter.

When we look at nationalism, the link between ethnic organisation and ethnic identity discussed earlier becomes crystal clear. According to most nationalist ideologies, the political organisation should be ethnic in character in that it represents the interests of a particular ethnic group. Conversely, the nation-state draws an important aspect of its political legitimacy from convincing the popular masses that it really does represent them as a cultural unit.

An emphasis on the duality of meaning and politics, common in ethnicity studies as well as research on nationalism, can also be related to anthropological theory on ritual symbols. In his work on the Ndembu, Victor Turner (1967, 1969) has showed that these symbols are multivocal and that they have an 'instrumental' and a 'sensory' (or meaningful) pole. In a remarkably parallel way, Anderson argues that nationalism derives its force from its combination of political legitimation and emotional power. Abner Cohen (1974b) has argued along similar lines when he states that politics cannot be purely instrumental, but must always involve symbols which have the power of creating loyalty and a feeling of belonging. More recently, studies of national flags (Eriksen and Jenkins, 2007) show how these symbols of nationality can both divide populations (if substantial numbers feel no loyalty towards the state and see the flag as a symbol of oppression) and unite them, precisely by being multivocal symbols that are amenable to different interpretations, thereby giving people who otherwise see each other as different a sense of unity.

Anthropologists who have written about nationalism have generally seen it as a variant of ethnicity. I shall also do this at the outset; later on, however, I shall raise the question of whether *non-ethnic nationalisms* are imaginable.

## THE NATION AS A CULTURAL COMMUNITY

Both Gellner and Anderson emphasise that although nations tend to imagine themselves as old, they are modern. Nationalist ideology was first developed in Europe and in European diaspora (particularly in the New World; see Anderson, 1991 [1983]; Handler and Segal, 1992) in the period around the French Revolution. Here we must distinguish between *tradition* and *traditionalism*. Nationalism, which is frequently a traditionalistic ideology, may glorify and re-codify an ostensibly ancient tradition shared by the ancestors of the members of the nation, but it does not thereby re-create that tradition. It *reifies* it in the same way that the Hurons reified their supposed tradition (see chapter 4).

Since nationalism is a modern phenomenon which has unfolded in the full light of recorded history, the 'ethnogenesis' of nations lends itself more easily to investigation than the history of non-modern peoples. Thus, the creation of Norwegian national identity took place throughout the nineteenth century, which was a period of modernisation and urbanisation. The country peacefully moved to full independence, leaving the union with Sweden, in 1905.

Early Norwegian nationalism mainly derived its support from the urban middle classes. Members of the city bourgeoisie travelled to remote valleys in search of 'authentic Norwegian culture', brought elements from it back to the city and presented them as the authentic expression of Norwegianness. Folk costumes, painted floral patterns (*rosemaling*), traditional music and peasant food became national symbols even to people who had not grown up with such customs. Actually it was the city dwellers, not the peasants, who decided that reified aspects of peasant culture should be 'the national culture'. A national heroic history was established. The creation of 'national arts', which were markers of uniqueness and sophistication, was also an important part of the nationalist project in Norway as elsewhere. Typical representatives of this project were the composer Edvard Grieg, who incorporated local folk tunes into his Romantic scores, and the author Bjørnstjerne Bjørnson (who, unlike Henrik Ibsen, was awarded a Nobel Prize), whose peasant tales were widely read.

Certain aspects of peasant culture were thus reinterpreted and placed into an urban political context as evidence that Norwegian culture was distinctive, that Norwegians were a people on a par with other European peoples, and that they therefore ought to have their own state. This national symbolism was efficient in raising ethnic boundaries between them and the culturally similar Swedes and Danes, and simultaneously it emphasised that urban and rural Norwegians belonged to the same culture and had shared political interests. This idea of urban–rural solidarity, characteristic of nationalism, was, as Gellner has pointed out, a political innovation. Before the age of nationalism, the ruling classes were usually cosmopolitan in character. Anderson writes with a certain glee (1991 [1983]: 83n) that up to the First World War no 'English' dynasty had ruled England since the mid-eleventh century. Furthermore, the idea that the aristocracy belonged to the same culture as the peasants must have seemed abominable to the former and incomprehensible to the latter before nationalism.

Nationalism stresses solidarity between the poor and the rich, between the propertyless and the capitalists. According to nationalist ideology, the sole principle of political exclusion and inclusion follows the boundaries of the nation – that category of people defined as members of the same culture.

Large-scale processes such as industrialisation, the Enlightenment and its Romantic counter-reactions, standardised educational systems and the growth of bourgeois elite culture are often mentioned in connection with the development of nationalism. It may therefore be relevant to mention that the nation is not just reproduced through state social engineering and major upheavals such as war, but also through everyday practices. For one thing, *sport* is a ubiquitous presence in most contemporary societies, and it often has a nationalist focus. Moreover, as Michael Billig (1995) has shown, 'small words, rather than grand memorable phrases', make up the stuff of national belonging for a great number of people: coins, stamps, turns of phrase, unwaved flags, televised weather forecasts; in brief, the *banal nationalism* continuously strengthens and reproduces people's sense of national belonging.

## THE POLITICAL USE OF CULTURAL SYMBOLS

The example of Norwegian nationalism is suggestive of the 'inventedness' of the nation. Until the late nineteenth century, Norway's main written language had been Danish. It was partly replaced by a new literary language, *Nynorsk* or 'New Norwegian', based on Norwegian dialects. Vernacularisation is an important aspect of many nationalist movements, since a shared language can be a powerful symbol of cultural unity as well as a convenient tool in the administration of a nation-state. When it comes to culture, it could be argued that urban Norwegians in Christiania (today's Oslo) and Bergen had more in common with urban Swedes and Danes than with rural Norwegians. Indeed, the spoken language in these cities is still, in the 1990s, closer to standard Danish than to some rural dialects. Further, the selection of symbols to be used in the nation's representation of itself was highly politically motivated. In many cases, the so-called ancient, typically Norwegian customs, folk tales, handicrafts and so on were neither ancient, nor typical, nor Norwegian. The painted floral patterns depict grapevines from the Mediterranean. The Hardanger fiddle music and most of the folk tales had their origin in Central Europe, and many of the 'typical folk costumes' which are worn at public celebrations such as Constitution Day were designed by nationalists early in the twentieth century (and have, incidentally, grown hugely in popularity during the era of globalisation, see Eriksen, 2004a). Most of the customs depicted as typical came from specific mountain valleys in southern Norway.

When such practices are reified as symbols and transferred to a nationalist discourse, their meaning changes. The use of presumedly typical ethnic symbols in nationalism is intended to stimulate reflection on one's own cultural distinctiveness and thereby to create a feeling of nationhood. Nationalism reifies culture in the sense that it enables people to talk about their culture as though it were a constant. In Richard Handler's accurate phrase, nationalist discourses are 'attempts to construct bounded cultural objects' (1988: 27). The ethnic boundary mechanisms discussed earlier are evident here, as well as inventive uses of history which create an impression of continuity. When Norway became independent, its first king was Prince Carl from the Danish royal family. He was nevertheless rebaptised Haakon VII as a way of creating a sense of continuity with the dynasty of kings that ruled Norway before the collapse of the medieval Norwegian state around 1350.

The discrepancy between national ideology (comprising symbols, stereotypes and the like) and social practice is no less apparent in the case of nations than with respect to other ethnic groups. However, as Anderson diplomatically remarks, every community based on wider links than face-to-face contact is imagined, and nations are neither more nor less 'fraudulent' than other communities. We have earlier seen similar identity processes in discussions of other ethnic groups; what is peculiar to nationalism is its relationship to the state. With the help of the powers of the nation-state, nations can be invented where they do not exist, to paraphrase Gellner (1964). Standardi-sation of language, the creation of national labour markets based on individual labour contracts and compulsory schooling, which presuppose the prior existence of a nation-state, gradually forge nations out of diverse human material. Thus, while it would have been impossible 150 years ago to state exactly where Norwegian dialects merged into Swedish dialects, this linguistic boundary is now more clear-cut and follows the political one. As is sometimes said: a language is a dialect backed by an army.[2]

The earlier, dynastic states in Europe placed few demands on the majority of their citizens (Birch, 1989), and they did not require cultural uniformity in society. It did not matter that the serfs spoke a different language from that of the rulers, or that the serfs in one region spoke a different language from those in another region. Why is the standardisation of culture so important in modern nation-states?

## NATIONALISM AND INDUSTRIAL SOCIETY

Gellner, Grillo (1980) and others have argued that nationalist ideology emerged as a reaction to industrialisation and the uprooting of people from their local communities. Industrialisation entailed great geographic mobility, and a vast number of people became participants in the same economic (and later the same political) system. Kinship ideology, feudalism and religion were no longer capable of organising people efficiently.

In addition, the new industrial system of production required the facility to replace workers on a large scale. Thus workers had to have many of the same skills and capabilities. Industrialisation implied the need for a standardisation of skills, a kind of process which can also be described as 'cultural homogenisation'. Mass education is instrumental in this homogenising process. By introducing national

2. Swedish, Danish and the two varieties of Norwegian are closely related languages. We owe to nationalism the fact that they are considered three or four distinctive ones and not variants of a shared Scandinavian language – a fact still bemoaned by small but dedicated groups of Scandinavianists.

consciousness to every nook and cranny of the country, it turns 'peasants into Frenchmen' (Weber, 1976).

In this historical context, a need arises for a new kind of ideology capable of creating cohesion and loyalty among individuals participating in social systems on a huge scale. Nationalism was able to satisfy these requirements. It postulated the existence of an imagined community based on shared culture and embedded in the state, where people's loyalty and attachment should be directed towards the state and the legislative system rather than towards members of their kin group or village. In this way, nationalist ideology is functional for the state. At the same time, it must be remarked, the drive to homogenisation also creates stigmatised others; the external boundaries towards foreigners become frozen, and 'unmeltable' minorities within the country (Jews, Gypsies – but also, say, Bretons, Occitans and immigrants in the case of France) are made to stand out through their 'Otherness' and thereby confirm the integrity of the nation through contrast. In a period such as the present, when claims to cultural rights challenge hegemonies, this means trouble (see chapters 7–8). There is no inclusion without exclusion.

Its political effectiveness is one condition for nationalist ideology to be viable; it must refer to a nation which can be embodied in a nation-state and effectively ruled. An additional condition is popular support. What, then, does nationalism have to offer? As some of the examples below will suggest, nationalism offers security and perceived stability at a time when life-worlds are fragmented and people are being uprooted. An important aim of nationalist ideology is thus to re-create a sentiment of wholeness and continuity with the past; to transcend that alienation or rupture between individual and society that modernity has brought about.

At the level of personal identification, nationhood is a matter of belief. The nation, that is the *Volk* imagined by nationalists, is a product of nationalist ideology; it is not the other way around. A nation exists from the moment a handful of influential people decide that it should be so, and it starts, in most cases, as an urban elite phenomenon. In order to be an efficient political tool, it must nevertheless eventually achieve mass appeal.

## COMMUNICATION TECHNOLOGY AND NATIONHOOD

One important difference between nations and other kinds of community, including many ethnic communities, concerns scale.

With a few exceptions (notably mini-states in the Caribbean and the Pacific), nation-states are social systems operating on a vast scale. Tribal societies and other local communities could to a great extent rely on kinship networks and face-to-face interaction for their maintenance as systems and for the loyalty of their members. Even in the great dynastic states, most of the subjects were locally integrated; they were first and foremost members of families and villages. Socialisation and social control were largely handled locally. Armies tended to be professional, unlike in nationalist societies, where it is considered the moral duty of all to fight for their country.

Nations are communities where the citizens are expected to be integrated in respect to culture and self-identity in an abstract, anonymous manner. One of Anderson's most telling illustrations of this abstract character of the moral community of the nation is the tomb of the Unknown Soldier. Usually these tombs are deliberately left empty; they signify the universal, abstract character of the nation. 'Yet void as these tombs are of identifiable mortal remains or immortal souls, they are nonetheless saturated with ghostly *national* imaginings' (Anderson, 1991 [1983]: 9).

What are the conditions for such an abstract ideology? I have described the economic and political concomitants of nationalism, and here we shall add a technological prerequisite for it, namely communications technology facilitating the standardisation of knowledge or representations (see chapter 5). Anderson strongly emphasises print-capitalism as an important condition for nationalism. Through the spread of the printed word in cheap editions, potentially unlimited numbers of persons have access to identical information without direct contact with the originator.

More recently, newspapers, television and radio have played – and still play – a crucial part in standardising representations and language. These media also play an important part in the reproduction and strengthening of nationalist sentiments. During the Falklands/Malvinas War in 1982, for example, the British media depicted the war quite consistently as a 'simple opposition between good and evil' (J. Taylor, 1992: 30), whereas the Argentinian media depicted it as a struggle against colonialism (Caistor, 1992). Later commentary on the media's role in connection with the Gulf War (Walsh, 1995) and the war in Afghanistan (Chomsky, 2001) arrive at similar conclusions.

Studies of the role of the Internet in influencing identities, language and public discourse are also highly relevant in research on ethnicity and nationalism. By now it is clear that, contrary to some early expectations, the Internet has not contributed to a global cultural homogenisation. Although roughly half of the contents on the web are in English, this nevertheless means that there is an enormous number of web sites in other languages. Just as most Norwegians continue to watch Norwegian TV channels today, as they did before they got cable television with an almost unlimited choice, the Internet is used at least as much to confirm and strengthen existing identities as to transcend them. Long-distance nationalism involving diasporic groups, secessionists and others has become widespread on the Internet, forging bonds between people who would otherwise have been isolated from each other. Websites devoted to the Kurdish nation, the Tamil nation and so on proliferate and are important both at the level of identity and as political tools. Recently, the Chilean government has even designated a 'fourteenth region' in the country, called the region of *el exterior* or *el reencuentro* (the reunion), consisting of Chileans abroad. The main tool for creating an imagined community of diasporic Chileans (who live in 110 different countries) is the Internet (Eriksen, 2007a).

A different kind of communication technology might also be considered here, namely modern means of transportation. In the mid-nineteenth century, it could take a week to cross Trinidad; today, the journey takes less than an hour in a fast car. Modern transportation technology greatly facilitates the integration of people into larger social systems, increasing the flow of people and goods indefinitely. It creates conditions for the integration of people into nation-states, and in this way it may have important indirect effects at the level of consciousness in making people *feel* that they are members of the nation.

A metaphor appropriate to the political and cultural developments leading to nationalism is the map. Although maps existed before nationalism, the map can be a very concise and potent symbol of the nation. Country maps, present in classrooms all over the world, depict the nation simultaneously as a bounded, observable thing and as an abstraction of something which has a physical reality. Most world maps place Europe at the centre of the world. This is not a politically innocent act, as Australians and Argentinians are well aware.

Most students of nationalism emphasise its modern and abstract aspects. Anthropological perspectives are particularly valuable here, since anthropologists may throw into relief the unique and peculiar character of nationalism and nation-states through comparisons with small-scale societies. In this perspective, the nation and nationalist ideology appear at least partly as symbolic tools for the ruling classes in societies that would otherwise have been threatened by potential dissolution. Some writers have argued that nationalism and national communities can have profound roots in earlier ethnic communities or *ethnies* (Armstrong, 1982; A.D. Smith, 1986), but it would be misleading to claim that there is an unbroken continuity from the pre-modern communities or 'cultures' to the national ones. As the Norwegian example shows, folk costumes and other national symbols take on a different meaning in the modern context from that which they originally had. They become *emblems of distinctiveness* in relation to other nations.

## NATIONALISM AS METAPHORIC KINSHIP

Nationalism in itself belongs neither on the left nor on the right of the political spectrum. Through an emphasis on equality between citizens, it may be seen as an ideology of the left. By emphasising vertical solidarity and the exclusion of foreigners (and sometimes minorities), it may belong on the right. Anderson suggests that nationalism (as well as other ethnic ideologies) should be classified together with kinship and religion rather than with fascism and liberalism (1991 [1983]: 15). It is an ideology which proclaims that the *Gemeinschaft* threatened by mass society can survive through a concern with roots and cultural continuity. In Josip Llobera's words: 'In modernity, the nationalist sentiment is first of all a reaction against the cosmopolitan pretensions of the Enlightenment' (1995: 221). Llobera, in a book with the telling title *The God of Modernity* (1995), argues strongly in favour of a view of nationalism as a kind of secular religion.

   In an important study of violence and nationalism in Sri Lanka and Australia, Bruce Kapferer (1988, 1989) describes nationalism as an *ontology*; that is a doctrine about the essence of reality. Through his examples from the two very different societies, Kapferer shows how nationalism can instil passions and profound emotions in its followers. It frequently draws on religion and myth for its symbolism, which is often violent in character. (One need only think of military parades, which are common in the celebration of Independence Days in many countries.) Like other ethnic ideologies, nationalism lays claim to symbols which have great importance for people, and argues that these symbols represent the nation-state. Death is often important in nationalist symbolism: individuals who have died in war are depicted as martyrs who died in defence of their nation. If the nation is a community that one is willing to die for, reasons Kapferer, then it must be capable of touching very intense emotions. Like Anderson, Kapferer thus stresses the religious aspect of nationalism and its ability to depict the nation as a sacred community.

In his study of nationalism in Québec, Richard Handler suggests that Québecois nationalists imagine the nation as a 'collective individual'. Citing three different informant statements which support this assumption, he concludes:

> These images of the nation as a living individual – a tree, a friend, a creature with a soul – convey first of all a sense of wholeness and boundedness. They establish the integral, irreducible nature of the collectivity as an existent entity. (Handler, 1988: 40)

In general, nationalism, like other ethnic ideologies, appropriates symbols and meanings from cultural contexts which are important in people's everyday experience. During the period leading up to the Islamic Revolution in Iran in 1979, the US was depicted as an adulterous infidel who raped and mistreated Iran, which was depicted as a woman – as a mother-country (Thaiss, 1978). This kind of symbolism can be extremely powerful in mass politics.

This example also confirms the view of nationalism (and other ethnic ideologies) as a form of metaphoric kinship. Kinship terms are frequently used in nationalist discourse (motherland, father of the nation, brothers and sisters, and so on), and the abstract community postulated by nationalists may be likened to the kin group. Although principles of kinship vary, the members of every society have some notion of family obligations. Kinship and kin organisation are basic features of social organisation in most societies. Nationalism appeared, and continues to appear, in periods when the social importance of kinship is weakened. One may perhaps go so far as to say that urbanisation and individualism create a social and cultural vacuum in human lives in so far as kinship loses much of its importance. Nationalism promises to satisfy some of the same needs that kinship was formerly responsible for. It offers security and a feeling of continuity, as well as offering career opportunities (through the educational system and the labour market). As a metaphorical *pater familias*, nationalism states that the members of the nation are a large family: through the national courts it punishes its disobedient children. It is an abstract version of something concrete which every individual has strong emotions about, and nationalism tries to transfer this emotional power to the state level. In this way, nationalism appears as a metaphoric kinship ideology tailored to fit large-scale modern society – it is the ideology of the nation-state. Against this background, we see that studies of kinship, and the changing character of kinship in the contemporary era (Carsten, 2004; Wade, 2007), are profoundly relevant for research on ethnic and national identities. Since these abstract ideologies draw much of their symbolic appeal from kinship, changes in the ways people think about kinship must inevitably influence ways in which they think about national and ethnic identities. In a more literal way, Emmanuel Todd (1985) has also argued, on empirical grounds, that there is a connection between family organisation and ideology on the one hand, and political culture on the other hand, so that, for example, authoritarian, patriarchal families engender national ideologies with similar characteristics.

## THE NATION-STATE

Like other ideologies, nationalism must simultaneously justify a particular (real or potential) power structure and satisfy acknowledged needs on the part of a population. Seen from this perspective, a successful nationalism implies the linking of an ethnic ideology with a state apparatus. There are important differences between the functioning of such a state and other social systems studied by anthropologists.

The nation-state, unlike many other political systems, draws on an ideology proclaiming that political boundaries should be coterminous with cultural boundaries (although where these cultural boundaries should be drawn is a fascinating question to be discussed in the following chapters). Further, the nation-state has a monopoly on the legitimate use of violence and taxation. This double monopoly is its most important source of power. The nation-state has a bureaucratic administration and a written legislation which encompasses all citizens, and it has – at least as an ideal – a uniform educational system and a shared labour market for all its citizens. The great majority of nation-states have a national language used in all official communications; some deny linguistic minorities the right to use their vernacular for the sake of state control and social cohesion.

Political leaders in other kinds of society may also monopolise violence and taxation. What is peculiar to the nation-state is the considerable concentration of power it represents. The difference is apparent between a modern war and a feud among the Yanomamö or Nuer. In the same way as the abstract community of nationalism includes an inconceivable number of people (in Britain more than 60 million) compared with polities based on kinship (the upper limit for a Yanomamö local community is approximately 500 individuals), the modern state can be said to be modelled on social organisations based on kinship.

Having discussed general aspects of nationalist identity, ideology and organisation, we shall now consider some examples which suggest ways in which nationalism can be studied anthropologically.

## NATIONALISM AGAINST THE STATE

The cultural egalitarianism preached by nationalism in most of its manifestations can inspire counter-reactions in situations where a segment of the population does not consider itself to be part of the nation. This is extremely common, as most nation-states contain larger or smaller minorities. In chapters 7 and 8, different minority situations will be considered; here, we shall briefly consider one where a part of the minority reacts through inventing its own nation.

The egalitarian charter of French nationalism and the French Revolution emphasised that every citizen should have equal rights, equal juridical rights and, in principle, equal opportunities (women, however, were only partly included in this imagined community). Eventually all French people were to identify themselves as Frenchmen and feel loyal towards the new republic. Linguistic standardisation through the spread of the official French language has been an important aspect of this project since the eighteenth century, but linguistic minorities still exist, notably in the south and south-east and in Brittany, where the majority of the population traditionally spoke Breton, a Celtic language unrelated to French.

Breton ethnic identity is intimately connected with language; there are few other conspicuous markers available for boundary maintenance. This identity has been threatened for centuries by the dominant French language. Particularly during the first half of the twentieth century, the number of Breton-speakers declined rapidly. However, as Maryon McDonald (1989) and others have shown, there have been signs of ethnic revitalisation in later years. A plethora of organisations championing the Breton cause have emerged since the Second World War. Lois Kuter (1989) reports that young Bretons have a positive view of learning Breton, explicitly linking it with their ethnic identity. Some radio and TV programmes are now made in Breton, and many learn Breton as a foreign language at evening classes and summer schools. Links with organisations representing the cultural heritage of other groups on the 'Celtic fringe' of Europe have been forged, and annual festivals of music and dance are devoted to this more comprehensive shared identity. The language, as well as many aspects of imputed Breton custom, have largely had to be revived, since the 'acculturation' process had gone very far.

Why do the survival and revival of the Breton language seem so important to many Bretons? It would be simplistic to say, as an explanation, that their language forms an important part of their cultural identity. After all, language shift has been widespread in Brittany (and elsewhere) for centuries. The militancy concerning language can therefore be seen as an anti-French political strategy. Since the French state chose the French language as the foremost symbol of its nationalism, the most efficient and visible kind of resistance against that nationalism may be a rejection of that language. For many years it was illegal to speak Breton in public. Many Bretons are still bilingual and switch situationally between the languages. By using Breton in public contexts, Bretons signal that they do not acquiescence in French domination. A notion of cultural roots alone would not have been enough: roots were never sufficient to revive a vanishing identity.

An interesting feature of the Breton resistance against French domination is an aspect of what Eric Hobsbawm (1977) has called 'the Shetlands effect', whereby a small periphery allies itself with a major centre against its local dominator. In the case of some Breton leaders, this effect was articulated in taking a pro-German line during the Second World War (McDonald, 1989: 123).

The population of Brittany is divided over the issues of language, identity and political rights. The revitalisation movement is still largely an elite or middle-class phenomenon, as in many other similar movements, although there are indications that this is changing (see chapter 5 for Indo-Trinidadians). Cost–benefit calculations may be involved here. Had Brittany been the wealthiest part of France, Bretons might, like some Catalans in Spain, have demanded full independence. But, on the other hand, there are strong ethno-political movements in economically disadvantaged regions as well, such as Andalusia in southern Spain.

## NATIONALISM AND THE OTHER

Like other ethnic identities, national identities are constituted in relation to *others*; the very idea of the nation presupposes that there are other nations, or at least other peoples, who are not members of the nation. Nationalist dichotomisation may take many forms; it could well be argued that the main structural condition for chauvinist nationalism in our day and age is competition between nation-states on the world market. Although there have been many wars between nation-states, such wars have been comparatively rare since 1945. Instead, we may perhaps regard international sports as the most important form of metaphoric war between nation-states – containing, perhaps, most of the identity-building features of warfare and few of the violent, destructive ones (see Archetti, 1999; Giulianotti and Robertson, 2009; MacClancy, 1996). Nonetheless, boundary maintenance and ethnic contrasting certainly takes more violent forms in many parts of the world (see for example Schmidt and Schröder, 2001; Tronvoll, 2009), and this also holds good for a number of ethnic nationalisms, for example in Sri Lanka.

In his analysis of Sinhalese national symbolism, Kapferer (1988) links state power, nationalist ideology and the Sinhalese–Tamil conflict with the role of Sinhalese myth in cosmology and in everyday life. Important myths, recorded in the ancient Sinhalese chronicle of the *Mahavamsa*, are the Vijaya and Dutugemunu legends. The Vijaya myth, the main Sinhalese myth of origin, tells of a prince who arrives from India and slaughters a great number of demons in order to conquer Sri Lanka. The Dutugemunu myth, set at a later historical period, tells of a Sinhalese leader under whose military guidance the people rids itself of a foreign overlord. Later, he conquers the Tamils.

In Sinhalese political discourse, these myths are frequently 'treated as historical fact or as having foundation in fact' (Kapferer, 1988: 35). Sinhalese dominance in the Sri Lankan state, including dominance over the Tamil minority, is justified by referring to the *Mahavamsa*, which is interpreted so as to state that the Sinhalese and the Tamils have the same origins, but are now two nations, with the Sinhalese as the dominant one. The myths thus form an important element in the justification of Sinhalese nationalism. Tamils produce contradictory interpretations of the myths, which are thus actively used in reconstruction of the past aimed at justifying present political projects.

Kapferer is particularly concerned with violence and the inter-penetration of lived experience, myth and state power. When he analyses the ethnic riots of the early 1980s, he finds that 'the demonic passions of the rioting were fuelled in a Sinhalese Buddhist nationalism that involved cosmological arguments similar to those in exorcism, particularly in the rites of sorcery' (Kapferer, 1988: 29). The human–demon dualism and other – frequently violent – aspects of myth were transferred to a nationalist ideology justifying Sinhalese hegemony and violence against Tamils.

According to many nationalist myths, the nation is born, or arises, from a painful rite of passage where it has to fight its adversaries; the Other or the enemy within. Re-enactment of that violence, as in Sri Lanka, can be justified by referring to such myths, which form part of a 'cosmic logic' or ontology through which the Sinhalese experience the world (Kapferer, 1988: 79). This cosmic logic, where evil plays an important part, is congruent with the long-running ethnic hostilities and serves as a rationalisation for the use of force.

Kapferer's argument is complex and cannot be reproduced in full here. It may not be correct that violence is a more or less universal feature of nationalist imagery, but his analysis is consistent with the perspective on ethnicity and nationalism developed in this book. He shows the importance of the Other in the formation of ethnic identity and illuminates the mediating role of symbols in ethnic ideologies. They must simultaneously justify a power structure *and* give profound meaning to people's experience in order to motivate them to make personal sacrifices for the nation. Finally, Kapferer shows how the potential power of ethnic identifications is increased many times over when an ethnic identity is linked with a modern state – when ethnicity becomes nationalism. My descriptions of nationalism as a metaphoric kinship ideology and (from peaceful Québec) the depiction of the nation as a human organism, are perhaps too weak in this context. In relation to Sinhalese nationalism, appropriate metaphors may rather be war, birth and death. However, both the peaceful Québecois nationalism and the violent Sinhalese one share certain features: both refer to the past and to assumptions of shared culture in imagining their abstract communities. In other regards, of course, they may not be comparable, since the Québecois are separatist and the Sinhalese are not. In Kapferer's words:

The organizing and integrating potential of ideology, the propensity of certain ideological formations to unify, to embrace persons of varying and perhaps opposed political and social interests, and to engage them in concerted, directed action, may owe much to the logic of an ontology that the ideology inscribes ... Ideology can engage a person in a fundamental and what may be experienced as a 'primordial' way. And so the passions are fired and people may burn. (1988: 83)

Kapferer's analysis of Sri Lankan nationalism focuses on the enactment of boundary mechanisms at different interrelated levels: symbolic, practical and political. He argues that nationalisms must be studied in a truly comparative spirit, and shows that Sinhalese nationalism is qualitatively different from European nationalisms because the societies differ. Notably, he argues that it is hierarchical in nature and not inherently egalitarian. Nevertheless, Kapferer's study is consistent with the theoretical framework on ethnic organisation and identity developed in earlier chapters, as well as the theory of nationalism which stresses the link between ethnicity and the state.

## THE PROBLEM OF IDENTITY BOUNDARIES

Problems of identity and problems of boundary maintenance have usually been studied in relation to minorities or otherwise 'threatened', 'subaltern' or 'weak' groups, or in situations of rapid social change. It seems to have been an implicit assumption that identity processes and the maintenance of identity are unproblematic in dominant groups. 'Majority identities', Diana Forsythe writes, 'appear as they are seen from without, seeming ... to be strong and secure, if not outright aggressive. Certainly this is how Germanness is perceived in many parts of Europe' (1989: 137).

Forsythe's research on German identity indicates that this central and powerful identity – considered by many as *the* dominant national identity in Europe[3] – is characterised by anomalies, fuzzy boundaries and ambiguous criteria for belongingness. First of all, it is unclear *where* Germany is. Although both the inhabitants of the Federal Republic and the GDR are clearly German (Forsythe's article was written shortly before *die Wende*, the reunification), they fail to unite the nation in a nation-state. Not all West Germans

3. This is perhaps particularly true after reunification in 1990, when Germany suddenly became much bigger in terms of population, and geographically even more central, than the other large European countries.

would include the GDR as *Inland*. Even after reunification, the distinction between *Wessies* and *Ossies* is a salient one, which refers to economic as well as to imputed cultural differences. Further, many Germans would include the areas lost to Poland and the former USSR during the Second World War as German.

Second, it is difficult to justify the existence of the German nation by referring to history. With the Nazi period (1933–45) in mind, Forsythe writes: 'The German past is not one that lends itself comfortably to nostalgia, nor is it well-suited to serve as a charter for nationalists' dreams for the future' (1989: 138).

Third, more or less as a consequence, it is difficult to state what it means to be German in cultural terms. Pride in national identity has positively been discouraged since the Second World War, as many 'typical' aspects of German culture were associated with Nazism (see Dumont, 1992, for a controversial cultural–historical analysis of German national identity).

Fourth, and this is the issue which is of particular concern here, the question of *who is German* turns out to be a complicated one. In principle, 'the universe is divided into the theoretically exhaustive and mutually exclusive categories of *Deutsche* (Germans) and *Ausländer* (foreigners)' (Forsythe, 1989: 143). In practice, there are nevertheless difficult problems associated with the delineation of boundaries. The criterion for Germanness, as applied by ordinary Germans, can be either language or 'a mixture compounded of appearance, family background, country of residence, and country of origin' (Forsythe, 1989: 143). A certain number of foreigners are included in both definitions of Germanness, and the latter especially is quite inaccurate. Austrians and the majority of Swiss are German-speakers, but do not live in a German state. On the other hand, millions of people of German descent, who may or may not actually speak German, live in Central and Eastern Europe.[4] These, as well as other emigrants, fall into different categories (see Figure 6.1). The category *Ausländer* (foreign) presents similar problems, and it transpires that the Dutch and Scandinavians are considered much 'less foreign' than Turks and Jews.

These anomalies, while they pose specific problems to German identity, are general and widespread. Such problems highlight the lack of congruence between ideal models or ideologies and that

---

4. The foreign policy spokesman for the German Social Democratic Party stated, at a public lecture in 1992, that 'there are six million Germans living in the former Soviet Union'.

*Nationalism*

*Figure 6.1*   Degrees of German-ness according to emic categories

Source: Forsythe, 1989: 146.

social reality to which they ostensibly refer. Nationalist and other ethnic ideologies hold that social and cultural boundaries should be unambiguous, clear-cut and 'digital' or binary. They should also be congruent with spatial, political boundaries. This, as we have seen, is an ideal which is very difficult to uphold in practice. Some violent nationalisms may try to eradicate the anomalies; such was the case of Nazism, where millions of members of so-called lower races occupying parts of German territory were killed or forced to emigrate; and more recently, Europeans and Africans alike have witnessed 'ethnic cleansing' in ex-Yugoslavia and Rwanda. In most cases, however, complex realities are coped with more gracefully. We should here keep in mind that there is never a perfect fit between an ideology and the social reality it is about, since an ideology is a kind of theory – like a map – which necessarily simplifies the concrete.

German identity, although ideally solid, digital and well demarcated, functions in an *analog* way on the ground: differences of degree are made relevant in the classification of others even when the classificatory system in theory requires clear dichotomisation. It is possible to be 'somewhat German' or 'not really foreign'. German identity seems to have frontiers, but no boundaries (see A.P. Cohen, 1994). Perhaps official nationalist ideologies tend to be more concerned with clear-cut, unambiguous boundaries than other ethnic ideologies. An explanation for this could be that nations are territorial and political units with an inherent need to divide others into insiders and outsiders on the basis of citizenship. Cultural similarity among citizens becomes a political programme vested in the state. In this way, official national identities may, generally speaking, be more comprehensive and may place greater demands on the individual than ethnic identities in a polyethnic society, which are rarely sanctioned through state institutions. However, as the German example shows, popular perceptions of Germanness are more fine-grained and less unambiguous than the formal nationalism of the state would imply. The difference between dominant and popular discourses is thus evident not merely in the contrast between state nationalism and non-state ethnicity, but also in the contrast between state/formal and popular/informal nationalism (Banks, 1996: 155; Baumann, 1996; Eriksen, 1993a).

As the above examples indicate, although it may be correct to talk of *a* general theory of nationalism, namely that presented in the first pages of this chapter, nationalisms on the ground are quite different from each other. So far, all of the nationalisms considered have been ethnic in character. Sinhalese nationalism acknowledges the presence of Sri Lankan Tamils as a distinctive ethnic group, but places them in a subservient relationship to the Sinhalese. We shall therefore round off this chapter by considering the possibility of a kind of nationalism which is *not* based on ethnicity.

## NATIONALISM WITHOUT ETHNICITY?

So-called plural or polyethnic societies have often been described as deeply divided societies marked by perennial conflict and resource competition between discrete ethnic groups (Horowitz, 1985; M.G. Smith, 1965). Although this view may in some cases be accurate, many have argued against it for focusing too strongly on conflict and group boundaries, at the cost of underestimat-ing cooperation, identity formation along non-ethnic lines and cultural integration transcending ethnic boundaries. Mauritius is often regarded as a typical plural society (Benedict, 1965); here, I shall approach it from a different perspective, focusing on shared meaning rather than group competition.

There are two complementary trends in Mauritian nationalism, and both of them are ostensibly non-ethnic in character (Eriksen, 1988, 1998). First, the Mauritian nation may be depicted as identical with the 'mosaic of cultures' reified in the identity politics of the island. Typical expressions of this view of the nation are the cultural shows organised annually in connection with Independence Day (Republic Day since 1992). At these shows, every main ethnic category is invited to present a 'typical' song or dance from its cultural repertoire. The Sino-Mauritians are always present with a dragon of some kind, Hindus sing Indian film songs or play sitar music, and the Creoles are always represented with a *séga* (a song form associated with the Creoles). In this way, the nation is imagined as a mosaic. This trend, which we may label 'multiculturalism', is also evident in the national mass media, where every group is represented through specific radio and TV programmes, and in the educational system, where pupils may learn their 'ancestral languages' as a foreign language.

The other main trend in Mauritian nationalism depicts the nation as a supra-ethnic or non-ethnic community, which encompasses or transcends ethnicity rather than endorsing it. The flag, the national anthem and the national language express such a nationalism. The national language of Mauritius is English, which is no ethnic group's ancestral language or indeed currently spoken language outside of formal contexts – and which therefore seems an appropriate choice as a supra-ethnic compromise (Eriksen, 1992a). Colonial symbols, which cannot be associated with a particular ethnic group, are also dominant. Formal equality and equal opportunities are emphasised.

The Mauritian situation is more complex than this outline suggests. There is some ethnic tension, and there are conflicts between national and ethnic identifications. Many post-colonial states are faced with similar problems to those of Mauritius. They are obviously constructions of recent origins. When Immanuel Wallerstein asks, rhetorically, 'Does India exist?' (1991a), he must therefore answer no – or at least, that it did not exist as an imagined community prior to colonisation. Many post-colonial states, particularly in Africa, had no pre-colonial state that could be revived, and the great majority of these states are polyethnic, although it is true, as Banks (1996: 157) argues, that in many cases, they are dominated by one ethnic group. Nevertheless, two points have to be made here: first, the perhaps only African state to have collapsed institutionally in the post-colonial era, namely Somalia, is also one of the few mono-ethnic ones. In other words, shared ethnic identity is not sufficient to build nationhood. Second, in most polyethnic states, some degree of compromise between constituent groups is needed, and some degree of supra-ethnic symbolism is required – if only to avoid riots and unrest. To depict the nation as identical with a 'mosaic of ethnic groups' could, at the same time, threaten to undermine the project of nation-building since it focuses on differences instead of similarities.

In a discussion of this section as it appeared in the first edition of this book, Banks expresses serious doubt as to the notion of non-ethnic nations which 'bypass any local ethnicities' (1996: 158). Instead, he argues that 'all nationalisms, once state control is achieved, actively seek both to enhance and reify the specifically ethnic identities of deviant others within the nation state, and at the same time to efface the idea of ethnic particularism within the national identity' (1996: 158). His view is, in other words, that nations tend to be dominated by ethnic groups which deny their ethnic identity (instead presenting themselves simply as citizens or humans) and either relegate others to minority status or assimilate them. This is an important argument, and symbolic domination frequently works this way. For example, male domination often expresses itself through the tacit assumption that 'humans' are 'men' (witnessed in statements, common in classic anthropology, like 'the X'es allow their women to work outside the home'). The stereotype of the 'American' is typically a white man, and so on.

I am nevertheless not convinced of the general applicability of this argument. In Trinidad & Tobago, the dominant group since Independence has been the Afro-Trinidadians, and it could well be argued that Indo-Trinidadians have been exoticised as a minority – however, in the mid 1990s, an Indo-Trinidadian became Prime Minister of the country, and Indo-Trinidadians are appropriating and adapting symbols of Afro-ness, such as the steelband and even the calypso. The cultural boundaries are becoming increasingly blurred, and the terms of discursive hegemony are becoming unclear (see Stewart, 2007, for a thorough exploration of a particular kind of cultural mixing, namely creolisation). In the USA, the traditional hegemony of the WASPs is, if anything, being challenged from a number of directions: the anxieties and debates concerning multicultural education (see chapter 8) are a case in point; the majority of US Nobel laureates tend to be Jewish; the current President is indeed black, as was the previous Secretary of State; and one of the foremost defenders of the American societal model, Francis Fukuyama, is of Japanese descent. The situation in the UK also tends to be much more variegated in terms of physical appearance and cultural image among its elites than in the past. I am not saying that the ethnic element in nationhood is about to go away due to globalisation and the eradication of 'radical cultural difference', only that there is no *necessary* link between national identity and ethnic identity. The metaphoric kinship ideology on which national identification rests can be imputed to shared (biological) ancestry, but it can also attach itself to shared historical experiences or territory (Eriksen, 2004b).

Let us leave this debate for now, and instead see how some of the insights developed earlier may shed light on the Mauritian situation. From the study of ethnic processes on the interpersonal level – from the early Copperbelt studies onwards – we know that identities are negotiable and situational. From the Barthian emphasis on boundary processes and later studies of identity boundaries, we also know that the selection of boundary markers is arbitrary in the sense that only some features of culture are singled out and defined as crucial in boundary processes. Just as the potential number of nations is much larger than the actual number, the number of ethnic groups in the world is potentially infinite. From recent studies of nationalism, finally, we have learnt that the relationship between cultural practices and reified culture is not a simple one, and that ideologists always select and reinterpret aspects of culture and history which fit into the legitimation of a particular power constellation.

On the basis of these theoretical insights, it is possible to draw the conclusion that Mauritian nationalism may represent an attempt to create a nation in the conventional sense; that Mauritian society is currently at an early stage of the ethnogenesis of a nation. The invention of a shared history for all the ethnic groups of the island is under way, and it has been suggested that a plausible 'myth of origin' for the nation could be the last ethnic riot, in 1967–8, the 'riot to end all riots'. The homogenisation of cultural practices has gone very far, due to rapid industrialisation and capitalist integration, and by now the vast majority of Mauritians speaks the same language at home (*Kreol*, a French-lexicon creole). As an increasing part of the individual's life is determined by his or her performance in the anonymous labour market, the supra-ethnic variety of national identity may eventually replace obsolete ethnic identities.

On the other hand, a principal lesson from ethnicity studies is that doomed ethnic categories tend to re-emerge, often with unprecedented force. An often mentioned example from Europe is that of the Celts, who have been 'perennially vanishing' for a thousand years. In the USA, occasionally mentioned as a non-ethnic nation, hyphenated identities and ethnic identity politics are perhaps more important than ever at the beginning of the twenty-first century. Referring to 'primordial' values, such identifications remain capable of mobilising people – years after the social contexts where these values were enacted had vanished. And in Mauritius itself, 30 years after 'the last ethnic riot', ethnic violence briefly erupted again in February 1999, following the unexplained death, in police custody, of a popular Creole singer (Eriksen, 2004c). Mauritius may nonetheless remain a prosperous, stable and democratic society based on a plurality of ethnic identities which are compatible with national identity – and this is also a possible outcome of the ongoing process of transformation.

Nations are not necessarily more static than ethnic groups. Moreover, as suggested above, polyethnic nations may be effectively redefined historically, in order to accommodate rights claims from groups who have felt excluded from the core of the nation. In an intriguing comparison between the USA, Canada and Australia, John Hutchinson (1994) shows how the symbolism and official identities of these three 'New World' countries have been re-fashioned during the last decades of the twentieth century. He analyses a major commemorative event in each country: the centenary of the federal Canadian state (1967), the Bicentenary of the Declaration of Independence in the USA (1976) and the

Bicentenary of the settlement in Australia by Europeans (1988). In all three cases, the authorities had envisioned a consolidation of a homogeneous white national identity; and in all three cases, the national celebrations led to widespread contestation of the terms in which nationhood was framed. In Canada, the centenary marked the beginning of Québecois secessionism; in the USA, various minority activists demonstrated noisily; and in Australia, Aborigines in particular were strongly against the celebrations, declaring 'a national year of mourning' (Hutchinson, 1994: 170). Interestingly, all three countries have since embarked on official redefinitions of nationhood, now presenting themselves to the outside world as 'multicultural societies' rather than white ones. If one accepts that national identity does not have to be founded in common ethnic origins, the disruptions and conflicts surrounding the rituals may actually have strengthened national cohesion by making a wider participation possible.

## NATIONALISM AND ETHNICITY RECONSIDERED

Nationalism and ethnicity are kindred concepts, and the majority of nationalisms are ethnic in character. The distinction between nationalism and ethnicity as analytical concepts is a simple one, if we stick to the formal level of definitions. A nationalist ideology is an ethnic ideology which demands a state on behalf of the ethnic group. However, in practice the distinction can be highly problematic.

First, nationalism may sometimes express a polyethnic or supra-ethnic ideology which stresses shared civil rights rather than shared cultural roots, *jus soli* rather than *jus sanguinis*. That would be the case in many African countries as well as in France or Mauritius, where no ethnic group openly tries to turn nation-building into an ethnic project on its own behalf. A distinction between ethnic nationalisms and polyethnic or supra-ethnic nationalisms could be relevant here, overlapping with the classic, and oft-criticised, distinction between 'ethnic' (East European) and 'civic' (West European) nationalism.

Second, certain categories of people may find themselves in a grey zone between full membership in the nation and ethnic minority identity. If some of their members want full political independence, others limit their demands to linguistic and other rights within an existing state. It depends on the interlocutor whether the category is a nation or an ethnic group. Moreover, national and ethnic membership can change situationally. A Mexican in the United States belongs to an ethnic minority, but belongs to a nation when he or she returns to Mexico. Such designations are not politically innocent. Whereas the proponents of an independent Punjabi state (Khalistan) describe themselves as a nation, the Indian government sees them as ethnic rebels. Our terrorists are their freedom fighters.

Third, in the mass media and in casual conversation the terms are not used consistently. When, regarding the former Soviet Union, one spoke of the '104 nations' comprising the union, this term referred to ethnic groups. Only a handful of them, it turned out in the years following the demise of the USSR, were nations to the extent that their leaders wanted full independence.

In societies where nationalism above all is presented as an impartial and universalistic ideology based on bureaucratic principles of justice, ethnicity and ethnic organisation may appear as threats against national cohesion, justice and the state. This tension may appear as a conflict between *particularist* and *universalist* moralities. In these polyethnic societies, nationalism is frequently presented as a supra-ethnic ideology guaranteeing formal justice and equal rights for everybody.

A different kind of conflict between ethnicity and nationalism, which is perhaps more true to the conventional meaning of the term 'nationalism', can be described as a conflict between a dominating and a dominated ethnic group within the framework of a modern nation-state. In such contexts, the nationalist ideology of the hegemonic group will be perceived as a particularist ideology rather than a universalist one, where the mechanisms of exclusion and ethnic discrimination are more obvious than the mechanisms of inclusion and formal justice. This kind of duality, or ambiguity, is fundamental to nationalist ideology (Eriksen, 1991b).

This duality of nationalism has been described as 'the Janus face of nationalism' (Nairn, 1977: part 3). A conflict between ethnicity and nationalism is evident, for example, in the case of the relationship between the Bretons and the French state. This kind of situation is characteristic of the contemporary world, where states tend to be dominated politically by one of the constituent ethnic groups (see Connor, 1978) or, more accurately, by its elites. In the next two chapters I shall distinguish between two types of minority situation, that of aboriginal or indigenous populations and that of urban minorities, and differences and similarities between their respective situations will be elaborated on. Several of the themes dealt with in this chapter, including contested national identities, culture and rights, citizenship and cultural change, will then be picked up and developed further in the two kinds of context.

## FURTHER READING

Anderson, Benedict (1991) *Imagined Communities: Reflections on the Origins and Spread of Nationalism*, 2nd edn. London: Verso. Powerful, influential and beautifully written book on the emotional force that nationalism is.

Malesevič, Sinisa and Mark Haugaard, eds (2007) *Ernest Gellner and Contemporary Social Thought*. Cambridge: Cambridge University Press. An interdisciplinary, wide-ranging volume engaging in critical discussion of Gellner's seminal contributions to the theory of nationalism.

Özkirmli, Umut (2000) *Theories of Nationalism*. London: Macmillan. A tightly argued, comprehensive and usefully critical account of current theoretical approaches.

# 7
# Minorities and the State

[F]or their part, the Indians have little or nothing to put in the place of governmental administration: there are no 'typically Indian' methods of administering a hospital nor is there a 'typically Indian' way of bookkeeping or using typewriters.

Eugeen E. Roosens (1989: 72)

[T]he road from national genius to a totalized cosmology of the sacred nation, and further to ethnic purity and cleansing, is relatively direct.

Arjun Appadurai (2006: 4)

Modernisation and the establishment of a system of nation-states have created a new situation for the people nowadays known as 'ethnic minorities' or 'indigenous peoples'. Most of them have become citizens in states, whether they like it or not. The spread of capitalism has also played an important part in creating conditions for new forms of ethnicity – both through local economic and cultural change and through migration. The perspective on ethnicity and nationalism in this chapter can be described as a perspective from below, in that we focus on ethnic groups which are not hegemonic in a state. They remain distinctive despite efforts undertaken by the agencies of the nation-state to integrate them politically, culturally and economically – or, in other cases, they may try to become integrated as equal citizens, but are kept separate through a politics of segregation.

In a reassessment of *Ethnic Groups and Boundaries*, Fredrik Barth admitted that his colleagues and his '1969 analyses gave limited attention to the effects of state organization' (1994: 19). The specialisation in ethnicity studies called minority studies is, however, not guilty of this omission, since the very term 'minority' is meaningful only in the context of a state.

## MINORITIES AND MAJORITIES

An ethnic minority can be defined as a group which is numerically inferior to the rest of the population in a society, which is politically non-dominant and which is being reproduced as an ethnic category or group. Like other concepts used in the analysis of ethnicity, the twin concepts minority and majority are *relative* and *relational*. A minority exists only in relation to a majority and vice versa, and their relationship is contingent on the relevant system boundaries. In the contemporary world, these system boundaries are nearly always state boundaries. The majority–minority relationship therefore changes if state boundaries are redrawn. Whereas the Sikhs form a tiny minority in India (1.9 per cent of the total population), they form a majority (slightly over 60 per cent) in Punjab. If the militant Sikh quest for independence (supported by some, but far from all Sikhs) is eventually successful, there will still be a 35 per cent Hindu minority in the independent country of Khalistan. In other words, as soon as minorities become majorities due to redefinitions of system boundaries, new minorities tend to appear.

We should also keep in mind that groups which constitute majorities in one area or country may be minorities elsewhere. The Magyars or Hungarians, for example, form a strong majority in Hungary, but large groups of people who consider themselves and are considered by others as Hungarians live in neighbouring countries (Slovakia, Romania, Serbia and Austria) where they are minorities. Russians, a majority population in the former Soviet Union, have become minorities in many of the post-Soviet nation-states. Immigrant groups can be in a comparable situation; members of these groups belong to a majority (or a nation) in their country of origin, but to a minority (or an 'ethnic group') in the host country. A majority group can also become a minority through the inclusion of its territory in a larger system.

There are possibilities for situational switching, as well as historical change, between minority and majority status for a particular group or category. Here we should note that the group boundaries themselves may well remain more or less unchanged through such a process.

## MINORITIES AND THE STATE

In the contemporary world, virtually everybody is forced to take on an identity as a citizen – in the poignant words of David Maybury-Lewis (1984), we are living in Leviathan. Since some forms of cultural and ethnic variation must be 'matter out of place' to nationalists with their ideals of cultural (if not necessarily ethnic) homogeneity, such diversity is frequently defined by dominant groups as a problem, as something one has to 'cope with'. Downright genocide and enforced displacement are the most brutal methods employed by states in their dealings with minorities. Several instances of genocide in the Americas and Australia followed European colonialism; another familiar case was the systematic extermination of German and Central European Jews and Gypsies by the Third Reich before and during the Second World War; more recent examples include the attempts at 'ethnic cleansing' in parts of former Yugoslavia and the Hutu massacre on Tutsis in Rwanda in 1994.

Enforced displacement of whole ethnic groups has been carried out by North American colonisers as well as by the Soviet Union under Stalin and by the pre-Columbian Inca kingdom in the Andes, where the Aymara were forcefully displaced. These methods have on the whole become less widespread since the Second World War. Today, states generally use one or several of three main strategies in their dealings with minorities.

First, the state may insist on the assimilation of 'entropy-resistant groups' (Gellner's term). It may insist that, say, minorities such as Bretons and Provençals become French; that they shed their parochial languages and boundary markers and gradually come to identify themselves as French people. Although such policies of assimilation are often believed to help their target groups to achieve equal rights and to improve their social standing, they often inflict suffering and loss of dignity on the minorities, who are thus taught that their own tradition is of no value. In the previous chapter, we saw an example of an ethnic revitalisation movement, the Breton movement, which seemed to compete for no other scarce resource than cultural self-determination. Successful policies of assimilation ultimately lead to the disappearance of the minority. In recent British history, this has been the fate of the Cornish, whose descendants are indistinguishable from the English – that is to say, they *are* English.

Second, the state may opt for domination, which frequently implies segregation on ethnic grounds. This entails the minority being physically removed from the majority, and this is frequently justified by referring to the presumed cultural inferiority of the former. Ideologies of segregation often hold that it is harmful to 'mix cultures' or races, and are concerned with boundary maintenance. The context is always one of power asymmetry, although, as we shall see below, it can also be analysed in terms of negotiation. South African apartheid was a very clear case of ethnic segregation, and many North American cities are also segregated along ethnic lines. In the latter case, segregation is not necessarily the result of state policies but is caused by a combination of class differences following ethnic lines, ethnic dichotomisation and minority stigma.

The third main option for the state consists in transcending ethnic nationalist ideology and adopting an ideology of multicultural-ism, where citizenship and full civil rights are compatible with several ethnic or religious identities, a decentralised federal model providing a high degree of local autonomy, or a Republican model (as in France, not as in the American political party) where cultural identity is simply defined as irrelevant to citizenship.

Minorities may respond to state domination in three principal ways; they have the three options first described as 'exit, voice or loyalty' by Alfred Hirschmann (1970). The first option is to assimilate. This has been a very common process, whether actually chosen or not. In some cases, it is nevertheless impossible for an ethnic minority to choose assimilation. Black people in the United States have not been assimilated, largely because skin colour ('race') is an important marker of collective identity in the US. Skin colour thereby eventually becomes an ethnic characteristic, whether or not blacks themselves emphasise it. In minority–majority relations, therefore, we see the limitations of an analytical perspective on ethnicity which one-sidedly stresses the voluntary, strategic aspect. Many people are indeed *victims* of ethnic classifications which they do not themselves support.

The minorities which are denied assimilation frequently have a subordinate place in the division of labour. They could be considered the victims of ethnic segregation. Other groups, however, actively resist assimilation and react through ethnic incorporation. The second option for minorities thus consists in acquiescing in their subordination, or in other ways trying to coexist peacefully with the nation-state. They may sometimes negotiate for limited autonomy in, say, religious, linguistic or local political matters. In other cases, such groups may reproduce their boundaries and identities informally. Some, such as North American Jews, Sino-Mauritians or Freetown Creoles (in Sierra Leone; see A. Cohen, 1981), can be considered elites, and as Amy Chua (2004) has shown in a worldwide survey of ethnic elites, immigrant minorities tend to form economic elites in Third World countries, quite unlike the situation in Western Europe.

The third principal option for minorities, exit or secession, is by default incompatible with state policies. Groups which favour secession and full independence are always ethnic communities in Handelman's sense, and I have earlier described them as proto nations.

These strategies are ideal types. In practice, both state tactics and minority responses will usually combine strategies of assimilation and segregation (or ethnic incorporation), and minorities may be divided over issues of independence. A term commonly used to describe compromises between assimilation and segregation/ incorporation, is 'integration'. This implies the minority's simultaneous participation in the shared institutions of society *and* its reproduction of group identity and ethnic boundaries. As we shall see below, many majority–minority relationships may be analysed by focusing on the tension between *equality* and *difference* along these lines.

## THE CREATION OF MINORITIES IN THE MODERN WORLD

When did the Yanomamö become a minority? In Napoleon Chagnon's widely read studies (e.g. Chagnon, 1983), they do not appear as a minority. On the contrary, they appear to be a dominant group divided into clans and lineages, not into ethnic groups. Today the Yanomamö are seen, and their leaders define themselves, as an ethnic minority or an indigenous people. Drawing on international law and on a global network of indigenous peoples, they negotiate with the Venezuelan and the Brazilian governments for territorial rights. Through the dual process of integration into the state and into the capitalist mode of production and system of consumption (see chapter 5) the Yanomamö *became* a minority. Their minority situation is caused by their partial integration, whether it is willed or not, into a larger system and dominance thereby.

When this kind of integration is more or less accomplished, it usually leads to complementary reactions of assimilation and ethnic incorporation. In the case of many minorities, it is possible to trace distinct phases in their strategies. We should note here that the agenda of 'cultural rights' is a recent one in world politics, and that it is only after the Second World War that membership in an ethnic minority can, in some societies, be a political advantage. Neither the UN Charter nor the Universal Declaration of Human Rights contained paragraphs about minority rights (Young, 2004), and it was only in 2007 that the UN General Assembly adopted the United Nations Declaration on the Rights of Indigenous Peoples, after more than twenty years of discussion.

An important 'ethnicisation' of the world is currently taking place and, as argued in chapters 4 and 5, this process is linked with modernisation – it is what we could also describe as the politicisation of culture, or its commercialisation (cf. Comaroff and Comaroff, 2009, on what they call 'Ethnicity, Inc.'). The Ainu minority of Hokkaido (Japan) was for a long time defined by the dominant Japanese not as an ethnic minority, but as imperfect Japanese (Sjöberg, 1993). Recent ethnic revitalisation among the Ainu, whose leaders stress that 'we have our own culture', has established a new kind of relationship with the Japanese. Instead of being measured by the standards of Japanese society, they now present themselves as *a people*, distinct from and equal to the Japanese; as different rather than inferior. Presented with the choice between being an underclass or an ethnic minority, many groups opt for the latter.

Although this example refers to an indigenous population, the general points made so far are valid for other minorities as well. What they all have in common is a potentially conflictual relationship with the state and/or a dominant group. In the following, I shall distinguish between two main kinds of minority situations: indigenous peoples and urban immigrant minorities.

## INDIGENEITY

The term 'indigenous people' is used in anthropology to describe a non-dominant group in a delineated territory, with a more or less acknowledged claim to aboriginality (see Campbell, 2004; Paine, 1992, 2000, on the intricacies of this contested term). Aboriginal peoples are not necessarily 'first-comers'. Although the Germans and the Russians may be the oldest extant ethnic groups in parts of their respective territories, they are not considered indigenous peoples. Indigenous groups are defined as non-state people, and they are always linked with a non-industrial mode of production (Saugestad, 2001). This does not mean that members of indigenous peoples never take part in governments or work in factories, but rather that they represent a way of life which renders them particularly vulnerable in relation to modernisation and the state. Indigenous peoples have historically been subjected to massive slaughter, forceful assimilation and neglect (Australian Aborigines were not even counted in national censuses until the 1960s). Since the latter half of the twentieth century, particularly since the 1970s, many such groups have become politically organised in ways that enable them to promote their interests vis-à-vis the dominant, encompassing majority. The formation of the World Council for Indigenous Peoples (WCIP) has been important in this regard. Seen from the perspective of anthropological theory of ethnicity, the dynamics of such ethnopolitical movements have proved a very fertile ground for the study of identity processes in a situation of change (see, for example, Brass, 1985).

As noted by Nick Thomas (1992), moreover, it is a common misconception that indigenous peoples were isolated before colonialism and statehood, even if the present situation represents something new, as witnessed in

> indigenous arts and crafts in an urban souvenir shop sold to European tourists; indigenous migrant labourers moving between Mexico and California; indigenous philosophies of universal humanism; indigenous peoples in the mainstream media; indigenous performers in Paris; indigenous organizations ... (Forte, 2009)

Indigenous peoples nonetheless stand in a potentially conflictual relationship to the nation-state as an institution. Their main political project is often presented as an attempt to survive as a culture-bearing group, but they rarely envision the formation of their own nation-state. They are non-state peoples.

## TERRITORIAL CONFLICT

The most common kind of conflict between indigenous peoples and the state concerns territorial rights. A typical case of this kind is the continuing dispute between the Cree Indians and the Canadian state over a major hydroelectric project in James Bay. In the 1970s the Canadian authorities decided to build a large dam in the middle of a territory acknowledged to be a traditional hunting ground of the Indians, who protested against what they saw as an illegitimate use of force. The conflict highlighted the difficult political situation of stateless peoples when confronted with a state which formally encompasses their territory. Anthropologists who studied the James Bay dispute nevertheless emphasised the considerable skill displayed by Indian leaders as brokers and negotiators (Feit, 1985). Overall it has been seen as an important event in the formation of Canadian Indian identities (Roosens, 1989): through such confrontations with the state, the Indian groups were effectively organised and succeeded in pooling their political resources, as well as learning how to reify culture and to use it strategically in political negotiations.

A parallel case in northern Scandinavia has been studied by Robert Paine (1985; see also Thuen, 1995). This case, which was eventually lost by the indigenous people, concerned the building of a hydroelectric dam by the Norwegian government, which it was said would upset the ecology of traditional grazing areas of the transhumant mountain Sami. Paine argues that the Sami depended on mobilising support from the outside – essentially from greater Norwegian society – for their resistance to be of any consequence. The Sami, and other groups in similar situations, are crucially dependent on interethnic *brokers* who can represent their interests in greater society, who can complementarise (Eidheim's term; see chapter 2) with the authorities and with world opinion. This kind of political brokerage may increase both the standing of the minority in greater society and the self-respect of its members. In the case of the Sami, the resistance against the Alta dam, although ultimately unsuccessful, was instrumental in forging a sense of Sami unity. It laid the organisational foundation for an interesting political experiment, namely the formation in 1989 of a Sami parliament, with admittedly limited legislative powers, within the Norwegian state. Links were forged within the Sami category, strengthening its network and association aspects (see chapter 3), with Norwegian political organisations and non-governmental organisations (NGOs), and with indigenous groups in other parts of the world.

Two general points must be made here. First, there is no necessary contradiction between modernisation and retention of ethnic identity – on the contrary, it can be argued that in many cases certain aspects of modernisation are required for identity maintenance to be successful. It is not cultural change in itself that determines the chances for survival for ethnic minorities. Rather, it is the relative ability of specific minorities to master the changes and utilise new technologies and political possibilities for their own ends (Eidheim, 1992; Henriksen, 1992).

This conclusion coincides well with the perspective on ethnicity developed earlier in this book, which originally grew out of studies of interethnic relations on the Copperbelt, immigrants in the United States, boundary processes in the Sudan and in Swat, and politics in African cities. The fact that it is applicable to such a diversity of contexts ought to indicate that the anthropological perspective on ethnicity has much to recommend it.

The second point is that a minority–majority relationship may involve other agents as well as the two groups. In many conflicts of this kind, third parties may play an important part. Given their inferior military and political power, indigenous people rely to a great extent on international support. The transnational networks of indigenous peoples have been – and are, to increasing degrees

– very important in this regard. So is the role of cultural brokers or entrepreneurs: those individuals and agencies which mediate between the indigenous group, the state and international society. Such actors may themselves be formally educated members of the indigenous group, but they may also be foreign anthropologists, missionaries, or NGOs such as Amnesty, Survival International or the International Work Group for Indigenous Affairs (IWGIA) (Paine, 1971). In many cases, there may be doubts as to whose interests these brokers actually represent: in Roosens' (1989) and van den Berghe's (1975) view, they may simply be career politicians in search of power. Their role in processes of cultural change can also be an interesting topic for further investigation.

## STAGES IN ETHNOGENESIS

The process of ethnogenesis which the Greenlandic Inuits have passed through during the last four or five decades brings up a few further points.

For many years before and after the Second World War, the Greenlandic Inuit identity seemed seriously threatened. Greenland was a Danish colony, and a growing number of Inuit, traditionally hunters, were 'acculturated' to a modern way of life. Danish became an increasingly dominant language, notably as a medium of instruction in the schools. The Danes were favourable to the widespread use of Greenlandic, but the Inuit themselves 'wished to make Greenland Danish-speaking in the long run' (Berthelsen, 1990: 335).

As a part of the new trend in international ethnopolitics which gained momentum in the early 1970s, when it became politically legitimate to raise demands on behalf of ethnic minorities, a new group of spokespeople began to question the disappearance of Inuit culture. Since then, and particularly since the introduction of home rule in 1978, Greenlandic has begun to replace Danish in schools, media and officialdom. Other aspects of what is seen as traditional Inuit culture are also being revitalised, such as handicrafts and clothing.

It was only after a long period of cultural change that Inuits began to reflect systematically on their culture and thereby to turn it into a 'thing' which could be reified in books and political statements. Also, people began to assert their identity only when it could no longer be taken for granted.

The form of cultural reflexivity engendered by literacy may be a decisive variable in the ethnic revitalisation of indigenous peoples. Since 'culture as a thing' is important in ethnopolitical symbolism, and since it can most effectively be turned into a thing through writing, we can assume that minorities confronted with capitalism and the state stand a better chance of surviving as culture-bearing groups than illiterate groups. Groups which have 'discovered that they have a culture', who have invented and reified their culture, can draw on myths of origin and a wide array of potential boundary-markers that are unavailable to illiterate minorities, which may easily be turned into underclasses. As the Huron example in chapter 4 showed, a glorious and tragic past can actually be acquired if need be.

These reflections lead up to a seeming paradox of ethnopolitics, which may help to clarify the complex relationship between ethnicity and culture that has been discussed in earlier chapters. For the emphasis on literacy and negotiations with the state in ethnic survival seems to imply that in order to save 'a culture', one must first lose it! This assumption is strengthened by the fact that the leaders of a dominated group must master the cultural codes of the dominant group in order to present their case efficiently.

Modernisation may be said to reduce the scope of cultural variation in the world. However, the emerging cultural self-consciousness or reflexivity brought about through these very processes has also inspired the formation of ethnic identities stressing cultural uniqueness. Simplistically, we may put it like this: while one's grandparents may have lived as traditional Inuit (or Sami, or Scots ...) without giving it any thought,[1] and one's parents took great pains to escape from their stigmatised and shameful minority position and to become assimilated and modern, today's generation does everything in its power to revive the customs and traditions that their grandparents followed without knowing it, and which their parents tried so hard to forget (cf. Beck *et al.*, 1994, on reflexivity and modernity). Similar identity processes may result from various forms of sustained culture contact, but they become especially acute and politically important during the rapid social changes brought about by modernisation.

1. The word 'Inuit' means 'human being'. It is not, in other words, an ethnic label, nor does it suggest that its carriers see themselves as members of 'a culture'. The term 'Eskimo' was thrust upon Inuit by southern neighbours, Algonquin Indians, and had a pejorative meaning referring to imputed aspects of their culture (it seems to have meant 'the eaters of raw meat').

## FACTORS IN INDIGENOUS ETHNOGENESIS

Potential conflicts between indigenous groups and the nation-state are activated when the majority wishes to control resources – ecological, economic or human – in the territory of the indigenous population. This may partly explain why questions concerning the 'Fourth World' have grown steadily more prominent, as the nation-state and capitalism exert a direct influence on an increasing number of people in the world. The ethnopolitical movements described earlier are attempts to cope with this development. They are not necessarily directed against modernisation, but against what they see as attempts to violate their territorial rights and their rights to define their own way of life.

In Botswana, tension between indigenes and the majority has been unfolding with increasing intensity since the early 1980s (Barnard, 2007; Gulbrandsen, 1992; Wilmsen, 1989). The Bushmen (or *basarwa*, as they are called in Tswana, or San, as many anthropologists still call them) do not constitute an 'ethnic group' or even an ethnic category in the sense that we use the terms. They are socially and politically fragmented. They are a culturally heterogeneous category of hunters and gatherers, comprising a number of distinct peoples living in Botswana, but also in Namibia and South Africa).[2] The categorisation of the Bushmen (or San) as an ethnic group is imposed from the outside.

Bushmen have lost large parts of their original territory. By the early 1990s, perhaps only 5 per cent of the Bushmen were actually hunter-gatherers. Many are itinerant wageworkers, who nevertheless continue to live in a nomadic way. As compensation, the authorities of Botswana founded a development scheme in the 1980s which was intended to 'help' Bushmen to become sedentary peasants. Villages are founded for them. Schools, post offices and dispensaries are being built, and a few are offered work in local industries. The programme can be regarded as an attempt to assimilate the Bushmen (Saugestad, 2001).

Attempts to force indigenous groups to become sedentary and literate are typical of the nation-state, and nomadic peoples are almost everywhere in a difficult situation. There are two chief reasons for this. First, all territories *belong* to someone, either

2. The Inuit and the Sami may also, following standard criteria of anthropology, be described as culturally heterogeneous, in spite of their shared ethnic identities. The mode of subsistence, dress code and language varies significantly within the ethnic category – even if we do not take the facts of modernisation into account.

individuals, companies or the state in a modern country. Second, the administration and surveillance of itinerant minorities present great problems. Property rights, the judicial system, the taxation system and the notion of equal rights and duties for everybody are aspects of the modern state which are incompatible with the traditional way of life of many indigenous peoples.

Drawing on research on indigenous peoples elsewhere, we may suggest two principal possible scenarios for the Bushmen. One is their eventual assimilation, possibly as a 'low caste', into Botswana society. The other consists of ethnic revitalisation and active ethnopolitics vis-à-vis the authorities. This alternative requires that they establish a political organisation enabling them to present their demands in an efficient way. This in turn requires that they develop an indigenous elite of interethnic brokers. These two scenarios are not mutually exclusive: each of them may apply for different persons or in different situations.

Indigenous peoples may seem to be trapped between cultural genocide and the reservation. They may try to choose isolation in order to retain their tradition – and this seems impossible. They may also try to pursue their political interests through channels defined by the state – and for this to be possible they must first go through a process of cultural adaptation. My distinction between culture and ethnic identity, and the parallel distinction between tradition and traditionalism, indicate that ethnic incorporation – seemingly paradoxically – can be successful during a process of profound cultural change.

There is a problem of authenticity involved in ethnogenesis, but the job of the anthropologist consists of *studying* it rather than *asking* about it. When Roosens declared to fellow academics in Québec that he wished to study the Hurons, many advised him not to, since they were no longer 'real Indians'. His colleagues thus seemed to distinguish between 'real' and 'artificial' culture. Such a distinction cannot be anthropologically valid, since it is itself culturally produced. Criteria for authentic ethnic identity are generated intraethnically as well as interethnically, and the dynamics of these criteria are themselves part of that social reality we study. If a Sami who plays lead guitar in a rock group can present himself credibly vis-à-vis other Sami and vis-à-vis greater society *as a Sami*, then it is a social fact that one can be an authentic Sami *and* play lead guitar. At the same time, there is considerable tension within the Sami category as to who is entitled to the ethnic label. So-called 'new Sami' (Hovland, 1996) are coastal people of Sami descent who revitalise their Sami-ness through outward display of Sami symbols (especially traditional clothing) and language learning. They are not necessarily accepted as bona fide Sami by the 'more authentic' Sami-speakers of the mountain hinterland, who – for their part – have had no qualms about adapting to a modern way of life (including props such as modern houses, snowmobiles and electric music).

The tendency among anthropologists to favour 'old, authentic culture' over 'new, contaminated culture', which informed much nineteenth- and twentieth-century anthropology, has largely – if sometimes reluctantly – been abandoned (although it may still exist among ethnopolitical leaders, as we have seen). In a networked, globalised world, the isolated tribe no longer exists anyway. Anthropologists working among indigenous peoples today tend not to see their moral obligation as contributing to the preservation of an ancient way of life, but rather in helping the people to make a transition to modernity on their own terms. Terence Turner, an anthropologist who has worked among the Amazonian Kayapó for decades, has thus – in addition to his research on Kayapó society and cultural change – not only encouraged them to learn Portuguese (the official language in Brazil), but has also instructed them in the use of videocameras to enable them to present themselves to the outside world on their own terms (T. Turner, 1992).

## IMMIGRANT MINORITIES

Migrants are in several important respects different from indigenous peoples. They often lack citizenship in the host country, and they were often members of majorities in their country of origin. In many cases, immigrants are only temporarily settled in the host country. Unlike indigenous people, labour migrants tend to be totally integrated in the capitalist system of production and consumption, since they usually arrive as prospective wageworkers. By this token, refugees are a slightly different category, and it may often be useful to distinguish them from labour migrants.

This section focuses to a great extent on the situation of non-European migrants to European cities. Obviously this should not be taken to mean that labour migration and urban minorities are chiefly European phenomena, but many major anthropological studies of urban minorities of this kind have been carried out in Europe. Towards the end of this section, we shall consider the minority situation in the United States. At the outset, we should note that this kind of minority research is strongly ideologically charged – and this holds true on both sides of the Atlantic – because the studies usually deal with conflicts in the author's own society, and can thus often be interpreted as (even if they were not intended as) political statements.

As described in chapter 5, changes in the labour markets have been instrumental in the creation of permanent immigrant minorities in Europe and North America (and elsewhere in the world). Like the minority situations of 'Fourth World' populations, their relationships with dominant groups have to a great extent been studied – particularly by sociologists – as relationships marked by unequal power and economic, political and cultural domination. Studies inspired by Marxist thought have argued that ethnic discrimination in industrial societies is contingent on the class relations in those societies. Immigrant groups, which in the North Atlantic societies tend to occupy a low-ranking position in the division of labour, have thus been seen as a reserve labour force which was imported when there was a demand for labour, and which is neglected and sometimes expelled during recessions. Conflicts between immigrants and domestic working classes, sometimes taking the shape of racism and rioting, have sometimes been regarded within this framework as being 'functional' for the system as a whole, since they divert attention from the fundamental contradiction between labour and capital.

Immigrant minority studies focusing on the level of interpersonal relationships and group dynamics have often considered the power asymmetry between minority and majority as an important context. We may initially distinguish five aspects of these minority situations which have received much attention:

(i)   Discrimination and disqualification from the dominant population (Alghasi *et al.*, 2009; Cox, 1976; Fenton, 1999; Patterson, 1977; Rex, 1973). Disqualification means that the migrant's skills are unrecognised in the host country. If, for example, she speaks four African languages, that is usually not an asset in the British labour market.

(ii)  Minority strategies for the maintenance of group identity (Epstein, 1978; Glazer and Moynihan, 1963; Novak, 1971; Tajfel, 1978).

(iii) Group competition and ethnic conflict (Banton, 1983; A. Cohen, 1974a; Despres, 1975b; Schmidt and Schröder, 2001).

(iv)  Cultural change and dynamics in migrant groups, including overall changes in host society (Baumann, 1996; De Vos and Romanucci-Ross, 1975; May *et al.*, 2004).

(v)  Transnationalism (Basch *et al.*, 1994; Vertovec, 2001; Werbner, 2002; and see chapter 8).

We should keep in mind that immigrant groups may well occupy elite positions in societies – Chinese in Indonesia and the Philippines; Lebanese in Liberia; Indians in Madagascar, etc. (Chua, 2004).

I now go on to exemplify how anthropological perspectives on ethnicity may shed light on the kind of minority situation characteristic of labour migrants and their descendants in Europe.

## BOUNDARIES AND HYBRIDITY

In a classic comparison between two polyethnic areas in London, Sandra Wallman (1986) found interesting differences in majority–minority relationships. Bow in the East End (in Tower Hamlets) was marked by strong polarisation and dichotomisation between the traditional residents and immigrants, whereas ethnic relations in Battersea (south London) were much more relaxed and socially less important. Both areas could be described as working-class, and there are approximately as many immigrants from the same places (India, Pakistan, Africa, the West Indies) in both areas. How can we account for the differences?

The social networks in the two areas were differently constituted, and ethnic boundary mechanisms functioned differently. In Bow, the social networks tended to be dense and closed; people interacted with the same partners in many different contexts. In Battersea, on the contrary, people belonged to many different groups with only partly overlapping membership. In Bow, people lived and worked in the same area; people who lived in Battersea worked in other parts of London. In Bow, people characteristically worked at one of a few major factories, whereas those who lived in Battersea had a greater choice and were employed in a greater variety of smaller and larger enterprises. Bow was an area with an old, stable English population, whereas the population of Battersea was more transient. In Bow, housing was largely municipal and did not allow for the same choice as in Battersea, which offered a variety of different kinds of housing. In Bow, only old English (or Irish) families were considered full members of the local community; in Battersea, one 'belonged' the moment one moved in. Wallman describes the difference between the areas as that between a closed homogeneous system (Bow) and an open heterogeneous system (Battersea). The result was that the ethnic boundaries in Bow were much more solid than in Battersea, where ethnicity proved less important (see Figure 7.1). There were several 'gates', or independent points of entry, into the various social subsystems of Battersea, whereas in Bow one would have to pass all the 'hurdles' at once in order to be accepted:

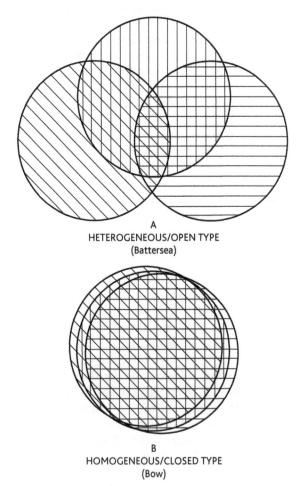

A
HETEROGENEOUS/OPEN TYPE
(Battersea)

B
HOMOGENEOUS/CLOSED TYPE
(Bow)

*Figure 7.1*   Local systems in Battersea and Bow showing boundary overlap, density and reach of local connections

Source: Wallman, 1986: 241.

When all your resources are in one overlapping local system, the possibilities for adaptation are much more limited, and your social relationships tend to be multiplex – i.e. the person you work with is also your neighbour etc. – local relations are not linked with domains or systems outside in the same way, and ethnic groups are more likely to remain distinct. (Wallman, 1986: 243)

The model suggested by Wallman, while describing relationships in a polyethnic city, may fruitfully be applied to other contexts of ethnicity. Her main point is that the salience of ethnicity varies and that this variation can be investigated by looking at *who does what with whom and for which purposes*. If ethnic networks are relevant in some domains, such as the job market, the likelihood for the development of ethnic associations increases. Surely, one may argue that the underlying causes for a particular configuration are structural. One may, for instance, show how the very presence of migrants, and the very competition for housing and jobs, is caused by the capitalist system. Such analyses may be valuable in their own right, but they are incapable of investigating the importance of ethnicity *in people's lives*.

## CULTURE AND ECONOMICS AMONG MIGRANTS

In a classic, influential study of Pakistanis in London, John Rex and Robert Moore (1967) argued that Pakistanis were 'turned into a lower class' because of systematic discrimination in the labour and housing markets. A few years later, Badr Dahya (1974) argued against this analysis, showing how the 'low' Pakistani standard of living was in fact consistent with their own economic priorities. The Pakistanis themselves, according to Dahya, regarded the British emphasis on 'good housing' as wasteful and as an irrational investment of assets. This difference in evaluation indicates a systematic difference of values between the two groups. Those social workers, politicians and researchers who defined the Pakistani areas as 'slums' and blamed the British authorities or the class system for the poor housing condition of the immigrants could thus be criticised for an ethnocentric view and for not taking the migrants' own evaluations of their situation sufficiently into account.

In this context, it might be interesting to look briefly at economic activities among immigrants in Western Europe. Very often, their economic survival depends on using ethnic networks and, perhaps, cultural skills. Tamils in Western Europe, for example, draw on caste and village networks to find jobs, and, like many migrants, they have a transnational economy where remittances to Sri Lanka are a main concern (Fuglerud 1999). This implies that even in societies where ethnicity is not a formal criterion for economic differentiation, the population may be occupationally differentiated along ethnic lines.

National immigration laws, as well as international agreements such as the Schengen Treaty, which aims at facilitating the movement of people within the European Union while limiting the influx of people from outside, encourage new strategies of entrepreneurship for migrant groups. The informal economy, where illegal immigrants form the backbone of the labour force, is probably very considerable in many rich countries (see Harris, 2002, for some estimates).

A study of Senegalese Wolof in Emilia Romagna (northern Italy) by Riccio (1999) demonstrates several important features of transnational entrepreneurship. Wolof are traditionally associated with trade in West Africa, and they have successfully adapted their skills to function in European markets (see Stoller, 2002, for a study of Wolof in New York). Riccio argues that, as in the case of the Hausa of Ibadan, Wolof in Italy are morally and socially bound by their allegiance to Muslim brotherhoods in Senegal (the Mouride), but he points out that without a strong organisation of Wolof wholesalers based in Italy offering not only goods but also sales advice, the individual Wolof pedlar would have had no chance.

The Wolof trade system studied by Riccio goes both ways. Traders live in Italy part of the year and in Senegal part of the year, and the goods offered for sale in the Senegalese markets range from hi-fi equipment and other electronic goods to the trader's own second-hand clothes. Although Riccio is at pains to describe the variations in the circumstances of migration, an unambiguous pattern emerges from his material, which shows that Wolof migrants to Italy are positioned in Italian society in a unique way, due to particular features of their culture and local organisation in Senegal. Somewhat like Gujarati traders in London (Tambs-Lyche, 1980), they draw on pre-existing social and cultural resources in developing their economic niche under new circumstances.

Transnational micro-economies have become very widespread during the last decades – so common that a study of a town in the Dominican Republic is not complete until one has explored the lives of townspeople living temporarily or permanently in New York City (cf. Krohn-Hansen, 2003); and migration must increasingly be envisioned as a transnational venture rather than as a one-way process resulting in segregation, assimilation or integration in the receiving society. The economics of transnationalism can be observed in Congolese *sapeurs* (Friedman, 1990) flaunting their wealth in Brazzaville following a frugal period of hard work in Paris, in the informal banking system whereby Somali refugees send remittances to relatives, in the flow of goods into and out of immigrant-owned shops in any European city, and most certainly in thousands of local communities, from Kerala to Jamaica, which benefit from the work of locals working overseas. Seen from a global structural perspective, this kind of transnational economics can easily be seen as a vertical ethnic division of labour whereby the exploitative systems of colonialism are continued; seen from the perspective of the local community, it may equally well be seen as a much-needed source of wealth; and seen from the perspective of the individual, it entails a new set of risks and opportunities.

In general, the role of cultural specialisations in ethnic relations has not been sufficiently studied. Whereas there is a mass of studies available which deal with power inequalities, the social reproduction of group boundaries, group competition and political identities, the 'cultural stuff' that the boundaries contain – to use Barth's formulation – has not been granted proportionate attention, except in discussions about multiculturalism (see chapter 8). We may therefore state, slightly simplistically, that anthropological and sociological ethnicity studies have dealt with political processes and identity processes, but not really with cultural processes. Cultural differences are analytically elusive – they cannot be measured. An important point for anthropologists writing on ethnicity has also been precisely that there is no one-to-one relationship between cultural variation and ethnicity – indeed, as I have repeatedly argued, ethnic differentiation may partly be an effect of cultural homogenisation. Besides, there are certain political and moral dangers associated with an analytical emphasis on cultural differences between groups. Such an emphasis may both contribute to an untenable reification of culture and contribute to reproducing native ideology and native stereotypes. Partly for these reasons, anthropologists writing on ethnic relations have tended not to stress cultural differences, focusing instead on social processes (cf. Bentley, 1987; Eriksen, 1991b; Haaland, 1992; de Heusch, 2000).

On the other hand, it is well known that the evaluations and priorities of different ethnic groups may differ. In many cases, notions of 'the good life' differ systematically between ethnic groups. Such differences, which are often recognised by the actors themselves, may form an important basis for the production of stereotypes and boundary maintenance. The Gypsy–*Gorgio* (Gypsy term for non-Gypsy) dichotomisation in contemporary European societies, for example, rests on perceptions of mutual cultural differences and value differences, the effects of which may be observed in actual social processes (Okely, 1983; Stewart, 1991). People who define themselves as Gypsies or Roma clearly have different aspirations and pursue different goals from those of the majority population. When they stereotype the *Gorgios* as unclean and dishonourable people, they generalise from their interpretations of observed *Gorgio* behaviour. Thus, ethnic relations cannot always be fully understood by way of analyses of competition or domination, but may also be regarded as 'encounters between cultures'. The goals people try to achieve are contextually or culturally defined, and in complex multi-ethnic societies members of different groups may pursue different goals.

In a study of West Indian immigrants in Bristol, Ken Pryce (1979) develops this idea further by showing how different groups of West Indians pursue very different life-projects. Two basic value-orientations are prevalent among his informants. One orientation can be labelled 'expressive–disreputable' and is cultivated by 'hustlers', Rastafarians and other groups who reject the mainstream 'respectable' British lifestyle and have a more flexible and fluid adaptation to the educational system and to the labour and housing markets. The other main orientation, which is labelled 'stable law-abiding', is prevalent among regular wageworkers and members of the small West Indian middle class. It is difficult to say to what extent these respective moralities are chosen or imposed by structural conditions. What matters here, however, is the fact that they seem highly congruent with the dual moral systems of 'respect-ability' and 'reputation' found in the Caribbean itself (P. Wilson, 1978). As in the case of the Wolof, cultural resources have been moved from one context and adapted to a new one. The outcome is a polyethnic British social system which also displays systematic cultural variations.

In modern societies where uniformity and cultural 'likeness' are either encouraged or implicitly taken for granted by the state, it is important to investigate such cultural aspects of ethnicity. In relation to official policies, this question concerns the difficult relationship between equality and difference. On the one hand, every individual is entitled to the same rights; on the other hand, ethnic minorities may be entitled to retain their identity. This potential problem, which I have already discussed in relation to indigenous peoples and the state, is also pertinent with regard to the place of immigrant minorities in greater society. Apart from shedding light on cultural dynamics and identity processes, anthropological research into these issues may provide essential insights for policy-makers.

## IDENTITIES AND CULTURE

For years, scholars assumed that second- and third-generation immigrants in European cities experience identity problems because they 'live in two cultures' (Liebkind, 1989). In talking about immigrants here, we generally mean non-European immigrants, although, for example, Finns in Sweden and South Europeans in other countries are locally categorised as immigrants 'with a distinctive culture and their own values'. Generally, only those immigrants who are locally perceived as significantly culturally distinctive are regarded as immigrants. Forsythe (1989) thus reports that some Germans protested when she classified herself as a 'foreigner', presumably because she was white and spoke German well. Similarly, a Swedish–Danish marriage is not perceived as a mixed marriage in the same way as a Croatian–Danish marriage is.

More recent research on identity processes and perceptions of self among second- or third-generation immigrants (e.g. Alghasi *et al.*, 2009; Baumann, 1996; Werbner and Modood, 1997) generally tends to confirm that (i) a clear 'acculturation' in terms of values and general orientation does take place; (ii) the people in question may switch situationally between a largely (say) 'Swedish' and a 'Turkish' identity; (iii) there is often tension between these individuals and their parents; and (iv) the boundaries preventing full assimilation may be both internally and externally constructed (in the latter case, discrimination may prevent full assimilation). There is no evidence for the assumption that it is inherently problematic to 'live in two cultures', but such ambiguous situations can certainly be difficult to handle in an environment where one is expected to have a bounded, delineated social identity. Second- or third-generation immigrants thus become anomalies, not primarily by virtue of their culture but rather because they fail to fit into the dominant categories of social classification in society.

The children (or children's children) of immigrants, while rarely fully assimilated, generally identify themselves more strongly with the values of the majority than their parents did. In some cases this kind of change may inspire revitalisation movements, but it may also lead to a diminution in the social importance of ethnicity. In societies where ethnicity is relatively important, the former option seems the more likely. Such ethnic organisations can of course be seen as expressions of identity and/or as political strategies (which is a common perspective), but they may equally well be regarded as defensive responses against discrimination and the refusal of the majority to allow them to assimilate. In these situations, as in other interethnic situations, both parties involved will attempt to define the terms for interaction, and may invoke aspects of cultural equality and difference situationally when it serves their interests.

As noted above (see also chapter 5), studies of contact between immigrants and host populations have indicated that cultural differentiae are not entirely irrelevant to ethnicity, although anthropologists have gone a long way in relativising their importance by stressing that it is only when *cultural differences make a social difference* that they contribute to the creation of ethnicity. However, it is clear that whereas language, for example, can be analysed as an ethnic boundary marker, it is also an important aspect of cultural competence in its own right and not an arbitrary ethnic symbol. For second- or third-generation immigrants in Britain, their mastery of English cultural codes necessarily gives them other options in their identity management than were available to their grandparents. The point is not, therefore, that culture and 'real cultural differences' are unimportant, but that it is the uses to which they are put – by both groups in a contact situation – that give them social relevance. The cultural content of identities changes, as does the *social relevance of cultural content*. The cultural resources that a particular immigrant group brings with it are transformed through contact and 'acculturation', but they are also put to new uses in the new context and thereby their social significance is changed. The grandchild of a Turkish immigrant in Cologne may well be Turkish, but being Turkish in Germany means something different from being Turkish in Turkey, or for that matter in Denmark.

## ETHNICITY IN THE US: RACE, CLASS AND LANGUAGE

The US is in important ways different from European countries. It has no semi-mythical history as a nation; since Indian history has been all but obliterated from collective memory. Accompanied by the destruction of traditional Indian societies, the country has been populated through successive migrations from four continents – Europe, Africa, Asia and South America – up to the present. The 1990 census revealed that of the 230 million people counted, nearly 30 million reported that they spoke another language than English at home. More than half (17 million) were speakers of Spanish. This, if nothing else, indicates that the US is not an ethnic nation in the same sense as France or Germany is. In addition, millions of Anglophone Americans have non-American 'ethnic identities', such as German, Swedish or Jewish. This form of ethnicity is sometimes spoken of as secondary ethnicity (Nash, 1988), since the people in question would probably primarily regard themselves as Americans.

The American 'ethnic revival' of the 1960s and 1970s received much scholarly attention. Many scholars argued that the 'American melting-pot', which was expected to fuse diverse populations into one (see chapter 2), never took place and that American society remained ethnically heterogeneous (Fishman *et al.*, 1966; Glazer and Moynihan, 1963; Novak, 1971). Focusing on 'European' ethnicities, these studies emphasised the dual role of ethnicity in securing political power and in strengthening personal identity.

A look at some of the different ethnic categories and groups in the United States reveals important variations, and shows that it would be oversimplifying to ask bluntly whether or not the 'melting-pot' occurred. One has to be more specific about one's contentions.

American Indians (or Native Americans) and blacks (or African-Americans) seem to be 'unmeltable' ethnic categories. They are phenotypically different from the majority and, in the case of many Indian groups, they still insist on their right not to take full part in the labour market and the American political system. Many of them have developed ethnopolitical organisations.

As regards the blacks, their colour can function effectively as an ethnic boundary since cultural stereotypes are associated with dark skin. Being what is called a visible minority, their degree of individual choice is moreover limited. A major questionnaire survey indicated that 98 per cent of white Americans agreed that blacks are in general worse off than whites (Sniderman and Hagen, 1985). William Wilson (1978) has nevertheless argued that the social significance of 'race' is declining; in other words, that class has become more important than ethnicity in accounting for vertical differentiation in American society. Wilson showed that there had been great upward mobility among blacks, and that the number of poor whites seemed to be on the increase. Wilson's critics have stressed that the rising significance of class origins in determining job opportunities and life-chances in general does not necessarily imply the decreasing significance of ethnicity or 'race' (see Banks, 1996: chapter 3; Collins, 2001; Willie, 1991). They have emphasised the need to analyse the interrelationship between the factors. However, as Comaroff and Comaroff (1992: 67) remark, Wilson's point was that 'the life chances of blacks are determined by other structural factors [than colour]; namely, class differences', even if actors would still *experience* the importance of colour strongly.

With respect to most of the European immigrant groups, the picture is different. There has been widespread intermarriage between them, and many millions of Americans could, if they wanted to, trace their origins back to several different European countries. In addition, the possibilities for the preservation of their European heritage were limited for these groups. In order to survive economically, they were forced to adapt to the American labour market and to learn English. Most immigrants lost their vernacular entirely within two generations.

These changes did not in themselves prevent the groups from recodifying their 'culture' and developing ethnic networks and associations. However, as Steinberg (1981) and others have argued, this happened only to a limited degree. The fact that, say, Americans of Scandinavian origin celebrate Scandinavian national days and publish weekly community newspapers does not imply that they are 'Scandinavian' or that ethnicity plays a crucial part in their daily life. Similarly, a New York rabbi interrogated by Epstein (1978) states that American Jews were Jews in the synagogue but 'plain Americans' the rest of the time. Often, minority identity is activated from the outside through acts of exclusion; as Hannah Arendt put it: 'If I am attacked as a Jew, I can only defend myself *as a Jew*' (cited in Bauböck 2001: 115). One may nevertheless also argue, as Nash (1988) does, that the informal ethnic associations of American Jews go a long way towards explaining their disproportionate success in the social hierarchy. It could be argued, moreover, that the divided loyalties of some Americans of non-American origin pose a potential problem of social cohesion. During the Second World War, Americans of Japanese origin were interned because they were suspected of divided loyalties. In other cases, it can be relatively unproblematic to have two or several identities. Among North Americans, there is generally no problem involved in identifying oneself in an implicitly hyphenated way as Ukrainan or Portuguese; the overarching Canadian or US identity is then taken for granted.

In a sense, the melting-pot *did* occur in that diverse immigrant groups acquired the same basic values and the same language, and intermarried to a high degree. At another level, it may *not* have occurred in so far as people still draw resources – symbolic, material or political – from ethnic identifications. Here, the importance of distinguishing between ethnic identity and culture, and between different expressions of ethnicity, is evident. For a member of a Hispanic local community in Spanish Harlem, 'ethnic identity' signifies something quite different from what it means to a Minnesota farmer of Swedish origin.

Native notions of 'race' are crucial for an understanding of American ethnicity. Whereas 'the ethnic revival' was seen as an ideological current based on voluntary identification with (real or imputed) origins, ethnic segregation based on appearance is not voluntary on the part of those who are segregated. Blacks, in particular, and later immigrants from Latin America, have largely been segregated against their own will. In their case, there is also a clear correlation between ethnicity and class membership: they occupy the lower rungs of the class system.

## MINORITIES AND MODERNITY

Immigrant minorities and indigenous people are compelled to relate to majorities, to states, and to capitalist systems of production and consumption. The recodification or reification of culture and self-conscious assertion of identity displayed by some of them cannot be entirely divorced from this historical fact, and their ways of displaying their identities are confined to modern societies. Like nationalism, modern ethnic associations and networks seek to emulate a politically useful and emotionally satisfactory *Gemeinschaft* in an historical situation where such communities have to be *created* because they do not already exist. Similarly, certain political aspects of these minority–majority situations are specific to modern societies based on literacy, wagework, capitalism and the state.

The majority of ethnicity studies deal with modern societies or modernisation processes. The number of Sami in Norway in 1940 was not significantly lower than the number in 2000, but they were far less visible and lacked shared organisation and shared collective identity (see Thuen, 1995, on the history of Sami ethnopolitics). In other words there was less Sami–Norwegian ethnicity, although it would be absurd to claim that there was 'less Sami culture'. The fact that indigenous peoples have more airtime, more organisations and more political influence does not mean that they acquire more members, but that their cultural integration into modernity and their visibility are greater. Thus they also take part in more interethnic relationships than previously.

A similar statement could be made with respect to urban migrants. The very fact that their migration is possible signifies that modernisation processes have taken place. Their displacement creates conditions for the articulation of ethnicity.

Despite the great political and cultural variations, there are interesting similarities between the ethnopolitical processes described in this and the previous chapter and the examples discussed in earlier chapters. Ethnic dichotomisation and boundary processes are implied in the very concept of ethnicity, and can be identified in all of the contexts presented. We should further note the general importance of fusing *political organisation* with the creation of a *collective identity* based on symbolic meaning in ethnic processes. These can be seen as two constitutive elements in ethnic organisation. If the Bushmen are eventually not successful in creating a politically relevant ethnic identity, they will try to pursue their goals in other ways than through ethnopolitics – possibly through individual social mobility, or through trade unionism. A relatively new, rapidly evolving way of achieving recognition and economic gain is that which Comaroff and Comaroff (2009) call 'Ethnicity, Inc.', alluding to the deliberate commercialisation of identity. Drawing largely on examples from Southern Africa, the Comaroffs show how political projects aiming for autonomy or control of land, have been transformed into commercial projects aimed chiefly at tourists, whereby tailor-made versions of 'traditional culture' are sold in the shape of dance performances, CDs of traditional music, trinkets and objects. As shown by the contributors to Erich Kasten's volume on cultural property rights (Kasten, 2004), moreover, minority spokespersons and organisations worldwide now use legal means in order to achieve control over their own cultural products, which are now seen not only as bearers of identity or symbols of political struggles, but as products in a global marketplace.

As suggested in chapter 5, there are a number of alternative ways in which ethnicity can be studied. Notably, a focus on economic processes could provide important background information accounting – at least in some cases – for the conditions in which ethnic identities form. In this chapter, I have chosen to emphasise the inner logic of ethnic group and identity formation, seen as a process involving features of greater society, but frequently giving priority to the relationships between acting individuals. This does not necessarily make the analysis a voluntaristic one where, in the words of Worsley (1984: 246), life seems like a cafeteria. Of course, an individual Bushman cannot choose whether or not he or she should be a Bushman – that much is given. He or she cannot choose away the state either, or change the dominant mode of production in society, or his or her cultural background for that matter. Such parameters are important because they indicate the social and cultural framework within which people must act, but they do not enable us to predict *how* people will act (see Bourdieu, 1977; Giddens, 1979). In focusing on options, I have chiefly wished to call attention to the ambiguity of social situations, to the historical and situational relativity of ethnicity, and to the fact that people make history, although they do not do so under conditions of their own choice. Nor is it always clear to them whose history they are making.

In suggesting that people try to improve their situation, there is no implicit assumption about people acting from 'economic' motives; and even if they do, as in the case of commercialisation, much more is at stake than mere economic gain. For the values people seek are culturally defined, and they do not always seem rational from an economist's perspective. When a Trinidadian Hindu goes to perform *puja* at the local temple, or when a Jamaican in London attends a reggae concert, they may act that way because they find it inherently meaningful, not for political reasons. Only when someone is able to exploit the symbolism surrounding the *puja* or the concert for political ends, can it be exploited in ethnic organisation.

## FURTHER READING

Comaroff, John L. and Jean Comaroff (2009) *Ethnicity, Inc.* Chicago: University of Chicago Press. A brilliant study and analysis of a number of cases whereby 'tribes' in Southern Africa are emerging as 'corporations' with corporate business interests.

Grillo, Ralph (1998) *Pluralism and the Politics of Difference: State, Culture, and Ethnicity in Comparative Perspective.* Oxford: Oxford University Press. Superb and wide-ranging historical exploration of cultural and ethnic pluralism, beginning with the Ottomans and ending with post-Thatcherite Britain.

Wimmer, Andreas (2002) *Nationalist Exclusion and Ethnic Conflict: Shadows of Modernity.* Cambridge: Cambridge University Press. Written by a sociologist, the book argues on empirical grounds that the modern state is shaped by nationalist and ethnic politics in a more fundamental way than is often believed by social theorists.

# 8
# Identity Politics, Culture and Rights

If the *modern* 'problem of identity' is how to construct an identity and keep it solid and stable, the *postmodern* 'problem of identity' is primarily how to avoid fixation and keep the options open.

Zygmunt Bauman (1996:18)

Some of the most vehement Sikh nationalists are Australians, Croatian nationalists, Canadians; Algerian nationalists, French; and Chinese, Americans.

Benedict Anderson (2001: 42)

Whereas the last chapter looked at two typical kinds of majority–minority relations – the indigenous world and that of the modern migrant – this chapter tries to take on the full complexity of contemporary polyethnic societies, from the point of view of social cohesion and minority rights. Put briefly, this chapter explores some of the central issues concerning cultural and ethnic pluralism, multiculturalism and the relationship to liberal individualism. The bulk of the chapter presents anthropological and philosophical contributions to the ongoing debates over group rights and multiculturalism versus individual rights and liberalism, interrogating notions of community, culture, diaspora and national belonging. Towards the end, I shall suggest some typical characteristics of identity politics in the contemporary era, and will argue that these features are nearly ubiquitous in the modern 'politics of recognition', whether we are dealing with the identity politics from below (from marginalised groups or minorities) or from above (from a dominant state).

## DILEMMAS OF ETHNIC DIVERSITY

Research on issues to do with cultural complexity in Western societies is not new to anthropology, but the extent of engagement with these kinds of question has intensified considerably since the late 1980s. The field of study is highly politicised, and, more often than not, the anthropologist carries out research in his or her own society. This situation requires a peculiar form of reflexivity concerning one's own subject position as a researcher and as a participant in society, since intellectual and professional engagement may very well be tied to, and difficult to disentangle from, political and moral convictions on the part of the anthropologist. There is, in short, a normative dimension to research on multicultural issues which is often absent from research in foreign countries.

A very large academic literature exists on the new ethnic diversity caused by immigration to the countries of the North Atlantic region; some of it directly policy-oriented, some of it more analytical. A substantial part of this literature addresses the dynamic relationship between minorities and a majority, often analysing official policies as part of the research agenda, and aiming to shed light on discourse and policy relating to ethnic diversity.

A fruitful starting-point may be the inherent dilemmas of the culturally complex society (looking for tensions and conflicts always generates interesting data), trying to strike a balance between unity and diversity.

Faced with a *de facto* situation of ethnic and cultural pluralism, the state may be accused of injustice both if it promotes equality *and* if it supports the retention of difference. If the state stresses equal rights and duties, minority members may feel that their cultural distinctiveness is not being respected; that their boundaries and identities are threatened. Minority reactions against French language policies, described in chapter 6, may exemplify this. Similarly, British Roma (Gypsies) may feel that the state is meddling in their affairs when it insists that they should become sedentary wageworkers (Mayall, 2003; Okely, 1983).

If, on the other hand, the dominant group emphasises cultural differences and turns difference into a positive thing, minority members may end up feeling that they are being actively discriminated against. This was the case in South Africa before the end of apartheid, where black Africans were denied the same career opportunities as the whites, who even tried to deny them command of English through encouraging the use of African languages. A similar form of hierarchical differentiation also seems to have taken place in Australia, where, in Kapferer's words, Aboriginals 'have become so close to the centre of nationalist thought that they have suffered from it' (1988: 142). They are defined from the outside as 'noble savages' whether they like it or not. In other words, they have not reached true self-determination in the sense of negotiating their identity on their own terms.

The decisive variable here is *power*. Usually the majority has the power to define when minorities should become like themselves and when they should be defined as different – when to assimilate and when to segregate. Very often, potential elites are denied the right to be different whereas low classes are denied the right to be equal. In a critique of American ethnicity studies, Stephen Steinberg asserts:

> Immigrants [from Europe] were disparaged for their cultural peculiarities, and the implied message was: 'You will become like us whether you want to or not.' When it came to racial minorities, however, the unspoken dictum was, 'No matter how much like us you are, you will remain apart.' (1981: 42)[1]

This kind of contradiction can be described as *the paradox of multiculturalism*. In some societies, such as Canada, Mauritius and Australia, ethnic diversity is positively encouraged (up to a point where some talk of 'apartheid with a human face'). As a consequence, citizens are not only given the right to 'have a culture', but in many cases they are positively forced to adorn themselves with an ethnic label, whether they want to or not. Sometimes groups are given differential treatment on the basis of presumed cultural distinctiveness – and thus some of their members may complain that they are deprived of equal treatment. In other words, both equal and differential treatment of minorities can be politically contentious.

## MULTICULTURALISM AND ITS CRITICS

Ethnic minorities are no more homogeneous than other categories of people, and there may naturally be important differences in views and values within minorities, just as there are degrees of ethnic solidarity both between and within ethnic groups. In Mauritius, it thus transpired during the 1980s that the Muslim 'community' was seriously divided over an issue of differential treatment. Up to 1987, the Muslims had been allowed to settle domestic court matters according to Muslim law even when it was at odds with Mauritian law. When the Muslim Personal Law was removed, it became evident that many Muslims, most of them women, had

1. See Gellner (1978: 149): 'The United States is notorious for the way in which its educational system has acted as an agency for transforming ethnic groups into a culturally homogeneous mass, until it failed in our time to do the same for the coloured groups.'

for years been opposed to that law. Public debates similar to these have become common in many European countries. In France, a major issue in the late 1980s concerned the right of Muslim girls at school to wear a headscarf signifying religious adherence (Modood, 1992). (French schools have been non-confessional since the French Revolution.) Debates over the use of *hijabs* have since then emerged, and re-emerged, in various European countries, and anthropologists have studied both the cultural significance of the *hijab* for its wearer and its interpretations in a wider, societal context (e.g. Bowen, 2007). Other public events which have contributed to heightened tension between minorities and majorities are the Rushdie affair, following the public burning of Salman Rushdie's novel *The Satanic Verses* in Bradford in 1988 and the subsequent *fatwa*; and, more recently, the publication of twelve cartoons depicting the Prophet Muhammad in the Danish newspaper *Jyllands-Posten* in 2005 (see Eide *et al.*, 2009). In several countries, controversies around the issue of female circumcision have emerged, and the issue of arranged (often suspected to be enforced) marriage has been a recurrent feature in European media in recent years, as are issues of domestic violence. Anthropologists, who are often experts on these kinds of cultural differences, have been engaged in such controversies in many ways, from pure scholarly research to policy advice and contributions to mainstream public debate.

Conflicts of this kind can be studied as negotiations over the situational legitimacy of ethnic boundaries. Such conflicts can be seen, optimistically, as *negotiations over meaning* involving different, culturally conditioned interpretations of social reality; or, more pessimistically, as encounters between incommensurable language games in the Wittgensteinian sense (Eriksen, 1991a). Thus we see, again, that culture is far from irrelevant in ethnicity studies. As Roosens puts it: '[A]lthough ethnicity must be distinguished from "observable or objective" culture ... it appears, paradoxically, as a privileged domain for the study of cultural dynamics' (1989: 161).

Criticism of multiculturalism has grown in Western Europe since the late 1980s, and anthropologists need to relate to it, since the models of culture developed by anthropology underlie multi-culturalism, and the tools developed to study ethnic relations may be helpful in making sense of the current situation. Now, of course 'multiculturalism' is not a simple term with a well-defined meaning. The *Oxford English Dictionary*, tracing its earliest appearance to an article about Switzerland published in 1957, defines it as '[t]he characteristics of a multicultural society; (also) the policy or process whereby the distinctive identities of the cultural groups within such a society are maintained or supported'. However lucid this definition may be, it leaves the central question unanswered. As a matter of fact, very different 'multiculturalisms' are being promoted, and this is a main reason why it is so difficult to discuss with outspoken opponents of 'multiculturalism' who tend to associate 'it' with either an exaggerated tolerance of foreign customs and beliefs or an uncritical support of any kind of immigration into the country, where immigrants are accorded many rights and few duties. In a review of the term, Stuart Hall (2000) mentions no less than six multiculturalisms: Conservative, liberal, pluralist, commercial, corporate and critical or 'revolutionary' multiculturalism. Each has its approach to the central problem in culturally complex societies, namely how to reconcile diversity with social solidarity. At the extreme ends of the spectrum are assimilationism (everybody who lives in the same country should have essentially the same culture) and difference multiculturalism (a kind not mentioned by Hall; see Turner, 1993; see also Vertovec and Wessendorf, 2009), which demands that society should not be based on one set of values, but should accommodate, recognise the equality of and indeed celebrate a great variety of cultural values. In practice, most theories of multicultural societies and most state policies in the Western world try to strike a balance between these extremes. On the one hand, too great diversity makes solidarity and democratic participation difficult to achieve. On the other hand, total cultural homogeneity is an impossible (and, to most, undesirable) goal to achieve even in ethnically homogeneous societies; there will always be religious sects and sexual minorities, to mention only two of the most obvious examples, demanding their right to be 'equal but different'.

## BEYOND THE STANDARD PARADIGM OF NATION-BUILDING

As the brief review above suggests, anthropologists specialising in the politics of identity may well contribute important conceptual clarifications here. However, philosophers and social theorists have for years discussed similar issues. One of the central controversies in contemporary political and social philosophy, which feeds directly on and into the debates over ethnic dynamics and national integration, concerns the relationship between *communitarianism* and *liberalism*. Communitarians hold that belonging to a community is a primary feature of personhood, while liberals argue the primacy of the individual. The communitarians argue that the liberal view of the individual is inadequate because people can only realise their humanity in a cohesive social and cultural community. They also hold that value, morality and the good life can only be attained within such a tight community, and thus argue that ethnic minorities should be encouraged to strengthen their cultural integration. Liberals counter this argument by pointing out that tightly integrated communities may enter into conflict with individual human rights since they give the community leadership too much power over the individual. Moreover, they say, it is necessary to have shared rules and principles in multi-ethnic societies as well, in order to avoid systematic differential treatment and power abuse by the strongest groups. If, for example, communitarianist policies encourage minorities to stick to their vernaculars, one outcome may be their inability to communicate in the dominant language, which is a considerable political handicap. Liberals insist that people living in the same society share a number of common perceptions and values (and that this must be so), while communitarians regard the groups as deeply and irreducibly different.

Few philosophers or social theorists support any of these positions in a pure form. Most search for the coveted 'middle ground' combining a respect for cultural difference with a recognition of universal rights (Cowan *et al.*, 2001; Goodale, 2009).

The recent debate in political philosophy inevitably recalls similar, long-standing debates in anthropology. The relationship between universalism and particularism has been a preoccupation and a challenge to the anthropological comparative project since the beginnings of serious anthropological thought. The communitarians' view of locally delineated communities is reminiscent of an anthropological view of culture and society as closed, more or less self-sustaining entities, which was virtually unchallenged within the mainstream of the discipline until the 1980s, when a critical mass of anthropologists began to study complex, large-scale phenomena such as transnationalism and nationhood.

The controversy naturally has a relevance extending well beyond the confines of academic philosophy – indeed well beyond academia as such. Burning political issues about racism and discrimination, religious rights, arranged marriages, refugee policies, human rights and school curricula are directly addressed by these discussions.

Most contemporary contributors to the debate argue, in one way or another, the need to transcend the opposition between a reifying multiculturalism and an unsociological individualism. Both have their political perils in a rights-based, democratic society; both, more importantly, give a misleading view of culture and society. The former position over-emphasises the social integrity and cultural cohesion of ethnic groups, and disregards the variability of individual cultural identities; while the latter position neglects the possible relevance of cultural variation for politics. It is, one might say, in the zones between liberalism and collectivism that most of the debate is focused. We now consider a few notable theoretical contributions, before moving to anthropological studies.

In an influential essay, the philosopher Charles Taylor (1992) argues in favour of what he sees as a liberalism that takes account of the intrinsic value of cultural difference. It should be noted that although Taylor is often cast as a communitarian, he describes his own 'creed' as 'a hospitable variant' of liberalism (1992: 62). His view is that 'the supposedly fair and difference-blind society is not only inhuman (because suppressing identities) but also, in a subtle and unconscious way, itself highly discriminatory' (1992: 43). Using Québécois nationalism as his main example, Taylor argues in favour of cultural pluralism, but also insists on a core of shared values.

A related, but more detailed argument is developed in Will Kymlicka's work (see, notably, Kymlicka 1995). Kymlicka regards people's 'bond to their own culture' (1995: 90) as an attachment whose causes 'lie deep in the human condition, tied up with the way humans as cultural creatures need to make sense of their world' (1995: 90). However, he rejects a static or essentialist view of culture as fixed and immutable, and sees change as sometimes inevitable. Reviewing the different claims made by minorities, mostly in North America, Kymlicka distinguishes between two kinds of minorities, just as I did in the previous chapter: on the one hand, 'nations' (meaning territorial, indigenous minorities) may justifiably claim cultural and territorial autonomy – in a word, the right to difference. On the other hand, he argues, immigrant minorities find themselves in a very different kind of situation, and what is at stake to them, he says, is integration and adaptation to the majority culture – in other words, the right to equality.

Like Kymlicka and Taylor, Bhikhu Parekh (2000) tries to reconcile liberal individualism with a recognition of cultural difference. His position is complex and based on both academic research and direct involvement in policy. In the late 1990s, Parekh directed a commission on multiculturalism in the UK, and its report (Runnymede Trust, 2000) presents a complex view of multi-ethnic society, where Britain is presented simultaneously as 'a community of citizens' and as 'a community of communities'. The 140 policy recommendations presented in the report cover a very wide range of societal areas, but the position can be summed up as the right of the individual to belong to a culturally defined (ethnic, religious or otherwise) community and his or her right to opt out (see Vertovec, 2001, for a discussion). In his major theoretical contribution from 2000, Parekh notes that while many theorists sympathetic to cultural pluralism present strong arguments for the value of belonging to a community, the intrinsic value of intergroup interaction is rarely treated – indeed, such contact is usually dealt with as a problem or challenge. Parekh thus develops what he calls a dialogic approach where the plurality of perspectives, and their cross-fertilisation, accorded by a democratic multi-ethnic society, is itself a main feature of democratic rule.

A main problem for all theorists mentioned arises when a liberal society is confronted with anti-liberal views (say, religious authoritarianism) which reveal that liberalism itself is but one of several possible perspectives. They all offer pragmatic solutions; society has to 'draw the line' somewhere against dehumanising practices, by, say, allowing traditional arranged marriages while legislating against enforced marriages. Interestingly, they all focus on education as a central battlefield (see also Grillo, 1998). Since, as Gellner, Anderson and others argued, standardised educational systems were a prerequisite for the emergence of a homogenised national identity, it stands to reason that a self-confessed culturally diverse society needs to adapt its educational system to accommodate the often contradictory demands for equality and difference. There are interesting variations regarding the solution to this problem: Some countries insist on a homogeneous educational system; some have introduced home-language instruction in the government schools, some have state-supported minority schools, and some encourage a shared educational system which stimulates tolerance and knowledge of other groups in society. The analytical point to be made here is that the Gellner–Anderson view of nationalism is difficult to reconcile with the existing, and growing, ethnic diversity in the contemporary world, where 'unmeltable ethnics' are not only here to stay, but they maintain their 'unmeltability' through transnational networks and global media.

## EMBEDDED DISCOURSES ABOUT CULTURE AND PLURALISM

Although many kinds of academics (and others) have contributed to the debates over multiculturalism and rights, anthropologists tend to feel that they speak with a special authority. They have, after all, been trained to study and make sense of cultural variation. They are also, perhaps more than any other group of academics, caught between liberal individualism and 'the love of culture'. One of the clearest statements on multiculturalism is arguably an article by anthropologist Terence Turner (1993), where he distinguishes between two kinds of multiculturalism: *critical* and *difference* multiculturalism. The latter represents, to him, a relativist position which celebrates difference, essentialises culture and renders dialogue, compromise and even translation difficult. The former, which he espouses, is a multiculturalism which aims at extending democratic rights by engaging in critical dialogue across boundaries *and* within groups, in a manner similar to Parekh's dialogic position (see also May, 1999). Turner, it will be recalled, has worked among the Kayapó in Brazil for many years, studying the dynamic relationship between their traditional culture and the impact of modernity.

The intricacies of group allegiances, multidirectional cultural impulses, role conflicts, change and divided loyalties have been explored in great ethnographic detail by anthropologists in many European cities, including Amsterdam (den Uyl and Brouwer, 2009), Berlin (Çaglar, 1995), Stockholm (Ålund, 1997) and London (Vertovec, 2007) – however, we should not think that these questions are confined to Western Europe and North America. As I have indicated intermittently in earlier chapters, the group–individual relationship and the complex issues of culture and rights are highly relevant in Mauritius and Trinidad; moreover, a major study of human rights issues in an ethnically complex society is Richard Wilson's analysis of truth and reconciliation in South Africa (2001); and in his textbook on multiculturalism, C.W. Watson (2000) draws extensively on his field experience in Malaysia. The questions of multiculturalism are thus global ones, which are nevertheless framed and expressed in uniquely local ways.

One of the most widely discussed anthropological monographs of multi-ethnic societies is Gerd Baumann's monograph from Southall, a suburb near Heathrow in south-west London (Baumann, 1996). The main categories that make up Southall's population of 60,000 are English, Irish, Indian/Pakistani and West Indian. However, allegiances are multiple and loyalties are frequently divided, based as they are on place of origin, religion (the main religions are Church of England, Roman Catholicism, Sikhism, Hinduism and Islam) and other criteria such as age, gender, place of residence and profession. Instead of concentrating on a single ethnic group, Baumann sees Southall as a single social field, and he analyses the complex, situational self-ascriptions and forms of community integration that arise from a variety of events and contexts. Unlike many studies of ethnicity, Baumann's book can be read as a running dialogue between the anthropologist's conceptualisations of culture, community and ethnicity on the one hand, and those of the ethnographic subjects on the other hand. For example, the book begins with an extensive discussion of the native meanings of the word 'community' and its relationship to 'culture', which reveals both a close kinship to standard anthropological conceptualisations and major variations within Southall. Notwithstanding the fascinating ethnographic details on everything from drinking habits to marriage practices, the main theoretical contribution of Baumann's book is his identification of two kinds of discourses about ethnicity: the *dominant* discourse and the *demotic* (popular) discourse. The dominant discourse, reproduced chiefly through the media and in the public sector, tends to equate ethnicity (often vaguely defined) with community and culture; one ethnic group comprises a community with a shared culture. Since dominant notions of 'communities' can be based on either language, religion or origin, any individual can belong to several communities, for example a Gujarati one uniting Hindus and Muslims, a Muslim one uniting people of any linguistic or regional origin, and a subcontinental one uniting Indians and Pakistanis. Be this as it may, Baumann's ethnography shows that the demotic discourse is more flexible and complex, that it recognises the situational and multifaceted character of individual identification, and contests some of the terms in which the dominant discourse is framed: alternative identifications such as blackness (which may or may not include Asians), feminism, socialism, interfaith networks and multiculturalist ideologies of tolerance contribute to softening the ethnic boundaries, creating 'frontier zones' instead.

In spite of the lack of fit between the dominant discourse and popular representations, which is moreover confirmed in the lack of a simple fit between class and ethnicity, many Southallians continue to reproduce the dominant discourse in certain situations. This could be seen as a simple effect of elite influence, but it is probably more accurate to say that since resources flow through ethnic or religious channels as defined by the authorities, people have no choice but to present their claims in ethnic or religious terms: 'The dominant discourse represents the hegemonic language within which Southallians must explain themselves and legitimate their claims' (Baumann, 1996: 192). This is not to say that Southallians are not systematically culturally different because of differing migration histories, linguistic backgrounds, 'customs' and so on, but what Baumann shows is that the classificatory system characteristic of the modern, liberal state encourages the social construction of ostensibly stable, reified, ethnic or religious *communities* (he himself italicises this word throughout the book, as if it were a problematic and untranslatable native concept). It is by virtue of their ethnic identity that minorities are discriminated against, but it is also chiefly through that identity that they can claim rights.

## STRUGGLES OVER CULTURAL IDENTITY AND SOCIAL INTEGRATION

The difference between segregation, assimilation and integration was discussed in chapter 7. Detailed ethnographies of majority/minority relations tend to show that these concepts do not form a satisfactory grid for classifying minority situations. Nor do they refer to any kind of inevitable historical process, where the ultimate outcome is bound to be the eradication of difference and full assimilation. In modern societies, sometimes spoken of as 'post-traditional societies' (Giddens, 1991), even adherence to tradition has to be chosen – albeit under pressure. Tradition, in this kind of society, no longer recommends itself; it has to be defended. Thus the institution of arranged marriages, for example, is under severe pressure from state bureaucracies and public opinion among immigrant minorities in Western Europe. Simultaneously, it can be observed that majority self-perceptions change as well. Re-definitions of Australian, Canadian and US national identities have been mentioned; in the 1990s, significant change in British identity also seemed under way, through the slogan 'Cool Britannia' and what one of Cicilie Fagerlid's Asian British informants talks of as 'a celebration of plurality of British culture' (2002: 88). Nevertheless, as I have argued elsewhere with respect to Mauritius (Eriksen, 1998), there is no one-way movement. In Mauritius, a society undergoing very rapid social and cultural change, tendencies towards de-ethnicisation and cosmopolitanism run parallel with tendencies towards increased ethnic entrenchment. In 2002, Denmark, a proverbially liberal and tolerant country, introduced very strict immigration laws and cut severely back on funding for multicultural and minority activities. In neighbouring Sweden, Ålund and Schierup (1991) showed years ago, an ostensibly benign and inclusive multicultural policy has not been capable of preventing the development of social inequalities and tensions between (reified) groups – a situation which has not been rectified in the intervening years. Counter-reactions to state policies of inclusion are also widespread, as witnessed in the resurgence of militant neo-Nazism in Sweden during the 1990s.

As Baumann and others show, the politics of identity has become a feature of the social fabric in a great number of societies, and a major political project for states worldwide – from Fiji and Malaysia to Bolivia and Canada – consists in reconciling equity and reflexively expressed cultural difference. It goes without saying that stable class differences are often more conspicuous features in these societies than the strivings towards equal rights. Since Fiji and Malaysia were mentioned: in both countries, there have been severe political tensions surrounding interethnic relations. In both countries, descendants of immigrants have been economically more successful than the indigenous populations (Chinese in Malaysia, Indians in Fiji). In both countries, moreover, this has resulted in overtly discriminatory laws favouring 'natives' over 'immigrants' – the inverted commas are deliberate, as it is difficult to define someone as an immigrant to the country in which he or she was born. In an attempt to address inequalities created during colonialism, governments in Malaysia and Fiji have thus introduced legislation and practices which discriminate in favour of the oppressed – in a manner roughly similar to the reservation system in India, which reserves generous quotas ('reservations') for low castes in the public service and the educational system. This is not the place to discuss whether or not such policies may eventually lead to greater overall equity in society; the point is that the policies and discourses surrounding them presuppose that society is divided into mutually exclusive, ascriptive groups based on descent and culture. This, ultimately, is the dilemma of multiculturalism, and it is interesting to note that the term is increasingly being replaced with the looser, less reifying 'diversity' in public discourse (cf. Vertovec and Wessendorf, 2009). In a typical endorsement of cultural diversity, the late Robin Cook said, in 2001, that 'Chicken Tikka Massala is now a true British national dish' (quoted from Christiansen and Hedetoft, 2004: 8). At the same time, concerns about gender roles, political loyalties, democratic values and religious rigidity have turned 'the question of integration' into a political issue of the first order. There are not only political issues, but also conceptual and analytical ones, to be unpacked here.

## DIASPORA AND HYBRIDITY

Indians in Fiji and Chinese in Malaysia are often seen as parts of larger diasporic populations – 20 million in the subcontinental case, 55 million as regards the Chinese. The use of the term *diaspora*, originally used to designate Jews in Europe, suggests that their primary identity connects them to their ancestral country, even if they may have lived their entire lives elsewhere. Mainly for this reason, the term – like most of the terms used in contemporary studies of identification – is contested. However, it may sometimes be analytically appropriate. The 'diaspora' term can shed light on certain groups, certain individuals or simply certain individuals in particular situations. Indians in Trinidad remain Indians in a diasporic sense – even if they no longer speak Bhojpuri, have abandoned caste, have never been to India and have invested their entire lives in the Caribbean island-state. This was evident in Klass' (1991) study of the Sai Baba movement in Trinidad (see Khan, 1997, for Trinidadian Muslims). In the introduction to a volume about the South Asian diaspora, Peter van der Veer (1995) notes how the construction of collective diasporic identities takes place in the interface between what Baumann calls dominant and demotic discourses. The term 'Asian' as a designating term for certain categories of immigrants, for example, clearly began as an dominant classificatory term in the colonial service, with no experiential relevance, but it has gradually gained significance for many immigrants of Asian descent – with, incidentally, different meanings in Britain (where it chiefly means South Asian) and in the USA (where it chiefly refers to East Asians). The phenomenal rise of an African diasporic identity since the civil rights movement should also be mentioned, as it shows the continued (and in some cases new) importance of territorial attachments centuries after the migration process.

The tension between diasporas and nations is obvious. As noted by Peter van der Veer, nationalism and migration might be seen as opposing processes – there are 'contradictions between the notion of discrete territoriality in the discourse of nationalism and the transgressive fact of migration' (1997: 2). Simultaneously, migration often leads to a reinvigoration and rephrasing of national identity, frequently with important political consequences in one or both localities. As Anderson points out (1991 [1983]), European nationalism was often developed overseas by 'creole pioneers', and many of the colonial national liberation movements were carved out by colonial subjects in European exile. The *négritude* movement of the interwar years, an interesting exercise in self-exoticisation, amounted to a romantic glorification of African culture, developed by intellectuals in Paris, many of who were *Antillais* who had never been to Africa.

A diasporic identity implies an emphasis on conservation and re-creation of the ancestral culture. Change and adaptation inevitably takes place in a new environment (how, for example, should one practise the rules of Ramadan under the Midnight Sun of northern Scandinavia?), but the project is one of continuity and frequently of cultural purism. A seemingly opposed analytical perspective is offered by the term *hybridity*, which was introduced into academia by the Birmingham School of cultural studies, and in particular Stuart Hall (see Gilroy *et al.*, 2000, for an appreciation; cf. also Bhabha, 1990; Gilroy, 1987; Werbner and Modood, 1997). An analogy from biology, the term entails cultural mixing and the emergence of 'impure', ambiguous identities which reject essentialism and rigid boundaries. In an essay on *The Satanic Verses* written in the early days of the *fatwa*, Rushdie thus offers this perspective on multi-ethnicity:

[The book] rejoices in mongrelization and fears the absolutism of the Pure. *Mélange*, hotchpotch, a bit of this and a bit of that is *how newness enters the world*. It is the great possibility that mass migration gives the world, and I have tried to embrace it. (1991: 394)

It may thus seem that diaspora and hybridity are two opposing terms; the one emphasising continuity, stable collective identities, territoriality and boundaries, the other highlighting change and flux, individual strategies, deterritorialisation and openness. In practice, the world is less tidy than this contrast may indicate, however, and any accurate ethnography grappling with multi-ethnicity has to concede that both openness and closure, both 'rootedness' and change, both continuity and adaptation are aspects of the world it describes. The emphasis varies between different studies, both because of empirical variations and theoretical differences; but it is not an either–or issue.

## TRANSNATIONALISM AND LONG-DISTANCE NATIONALISM

Typically, studies of migrant minorities focus on a particular ethnic or national migrant group, exploring both intragroup dynamics and the relationship to the majority or mainstream society, sometimes with a focus on power discrepancies and ethnic discrimination. Sometimes, as in the seminal work of Basch *et al.* (1994; see also Olwig, 2007; Vertovec, 2009), informants are pursued transnationally in order to trace their webs of reciprocity and identify the fullness of their meaning-generating life-worlds, but research is often confined to one location.

Research on transnational groups engages with the theory of ethnicity in a number of ways, often rephrasing and refining earlier debates concerning the relationship of ethnicity to culture, history and degrees of group cohesion. As in the older studies from Chicago and the Copperbelt, it has become apparent that group identities are often strengthened, not weakened, in a situation of increased interaction with others, although cultural exchanges with neighbouring groups (especially majorities) modify the worlds of everyday experience. At the same time, integration into majority society, leading to growing areas of shared experiences with the majority, create zones of tensions within these minority groups, especially at the margins. A similar argument could be made with respect to indigenous minorities which are increasingly being integrated into the state and capitalist market.

Some of the most promising new avenues of research into transnationalism concern the relationship between the new country and the old one. Research on transnational webs of reciprocity indicates that ties of moral commitment may now endure for generations, largely owing to the advent of instantaneous communication and cheap flights. Long-distance nationalism (Anderson, 1992; Fuglerud, 1999) is another, still somewhat under-studied form of transnationalism, whereby people live in one country and are politically involved in another. This phenomenon adds a new dimension to the theoretical understanding of social identification, and brings anthropology in contact with transnational law studies, political science and the interdisciplinary debate on citizenship.

Seen in the context of anthropological research on ethnicity, there is one aspect of this work which represents a break with the past, and that is its relation to normativity. When anthropologists take on issues relating to multiculturalism they often make open political or moral judgements. Many anthropologists thus come out as politically engaged, most of them defending multiculturalism in one of its many senses (see Hall, 2000), others criticising it from a perspective of human rights or women's rights (Okin, 1997). Paul Silverstein (2005) describes how diversity was, both in Europe and the USA, conflated into a 'single black–white dyad' (Silverstein, 2005: 365). He then describes how new kinds of distinctions, which are not based on assumed biological differences, have come to the fore. These distinctions, sometimes described as 'neo-racism' (Balibar, 1991), could be based on popular notions about cultural or religious differences, but are nonetheless often described in terms of racialisation (Silverstein, 2005; Stolcke, 1995; Werbner, 2005). Silverstein writes about racialisation and the 'reduction and hardening of fluid racial categories along a single black–white spectrum' (2005: 367). While this view is widespread among liberal and left-leaning intellectuals in the North Atlantic region, it needs empirical substantiation to be interesting for anthropologists. A closer look at mechanisms of inclusion and exclusion in culturally diverse European cities would doubtless reveal more nuance than this. For example, anxiety about the reluctance of Muslims to accept equal rights for women and to tolerate homosexuality should not be conflated with pejorative views of non-whites; they are based on different principles of social classification, different ideological persuasions, have different effects on social organisation and often concern different persons.

Many of those who carry out research on migration and the challenges of multi-ethnic societies have concluded that contemporary migration is often an ongoing process, which is likely to go on for generations; in other words, that any nationalist process of integration will never be fully accomplished once and for all. During the Second World War, many Norwegians active in the Resistance were refugees in neutral Sweden; nearly all returned after the war. However, many German Jews were refugees in the United States in the same period; few returned to Germany in 1945. Bosnians and Kosovars who were refugees in different European countries in the 1990s tended to return after the Balkan wars; but it is less likely that the hundreds of thousands of Somali refugees in Europe and North America will return to Somalia, partly because the prospects for political stability in Somalia are bleak. Many refugees develop an intermediate kind of identity – half refugee, half labour migrant. They learn the local language, their children may start school, they get jobs. Yet they may talk of returning.

Many minority members – immigrants, permanent diaspora and refugees – participate in two national political systems. This situation presents governments with new kinds of challenges, related to, but slightly different from the problems of culture and rights discussed above. In a study of Tamils in Norway, Fuglerud (1999) claims that it would be possible to replicate his main findings in any Western country with Tamil refugees from Sri Lanka. He analyses group dynamics within the Tamil category (or *community*), showing how leaders gather support for the independence movement fighting the Sri Lankan government, and revealing the existence of 'moderate' and 'militant' factions. He also shows how refugees are recruited along caste and kinship networks, and 'sent to Europe' with the express aim of promoting the cause. While the efforts to win over the majority are modest, financial and other forms of support for the secessionists in Sri Lanka are crucial. Now, Tamils are generally considered a well-integrated immigrant minority in Norway. A large number of them have jobs, and they are rarely involved in illegal activities. What Fuglerud shows is that integration into the majority society is scarcely an issue for most Tamils themselves: Their primary interest lies in furthering the cause of independence in Sri Lanka, and their adaptation takes place with that in mind. State efforts aiming to 'make them more Norwegian' are thus bound to fail.

This kind of transnational political activity has been called *long-distance nationalism* (Anderson, 1992). It must be distinguished from attempts to win sympathy for a political cause in the host country, which are activities confined to the host society. There are nevertheless many examples of contemporary long-distance nationalism. The Indian *hindutva* movement has received valuable support – not least in terms of money – from Indian immigrants in the West. Americans of Irish descent provide important support for the IRA, and the USA's policy towards Israel would almost certainly have been very different without the efforts of American Jews. Long-distance nationalism, or politics via remote control, can be effective and illustrate how transnational connections weaken the authority of the nation-state.

A different kind of transnationalism is described in Karen Fog Olwig's important work on Caribbean islanders. She has carried out long-term fieldwork both in the Caribbean (chiefly Nevis) and in locations they migrate to, such as London and Toronto (Olwig, 1993, 1997). Like others who have written on the Caribbean, Olwig notes that migration is not a single act with a clear departure and an equally clear arrival. Put briefly, many people travel back and forth. This can also be observed in the Turkish and subcontinental minorities in Western Europe, where many own and maintain two houses, one in each country. However, Olwig has gone on to explore the creation of place, memory and cultural identity among long-term migrants and even their children, who may scarcely ever have been to the Caribbean. They nevertheless have very clear notions of their place of origin, often associating it with particular people and tangible places such as a family plot or a grandmother's house. In spite of being physically, socially and professionally embedded in a metropolitan city, they continue to consider themselves Nevisian and to maintain networks with others from the Caribbean. With the spread of the Internet from the early 1990s, transnational connections of this kind have become much easier to maintain, and will need considerable attention from anthropologists in years to come (Eriksen, 2007a; Miller and Slater, 2000).

The symbolic reconstruction of a distant homeland is not an inevitable outcome of migration. Research among British youths of West Indian and subcontinental origins (e.g. Westwood, 1995) shows that their sense of territorial identity is not necessarily linked with their ancestral country, nor with Britain (where their sense of belonging is ambivalent anyway), nor with religion, but with locality. Sallie Westwood's research in Leicester describes the amalgamation of West Indians and South Asians around a youth organisation featuring activities such as football; the emergence of a collective identity which is neither diasporic nor transnational nor ethnic, but defined through locality and the fact of exclusion from English majority society.

So far, this chapter has shown how some of the dilemmas of multiculturalism are expressed in social philosophy, in anthropological theory and in social practice. A multicultural society, however defined, is a less tidy place than Gellner's socially engineered nation-states or Anderson's imagined communities, not to mention the cohesive ethnic corporations of the classic literature. The amount of variation in, say, Southall seems potentially nearly infinite (Steven Vertovec [2007] calls it 'super-diversity'), and the dual issues of finding a common ground within a country and effectively sealing it off from transnationalism and long-distance politics seem irresolvable. Identity politics in one form or another, I have shown in the last chapters, is a common solution, whether at the level of the ethnic category or at the level of the state. We shall now consider a recent attempt at identity politics on a very large scale, and I will subsequently go on to suggest a number of general features of contemporary identity politics.

## THE MODERNITY OF *HINDUTVA*

India is a tough case for any scholar trying to develop a general theory of ethnicity or nationalism. India is hardly a state based on cultural similarity or even equality in the Western sense; it is a country with deeply embedded hierarchies and a very considerable degree of internal cultural variation. Its population of nearly a billion is divided by language, religion, caste and culture, and it has often been argued that India is culturally more complex than continents such as sub-Saharan Africa or Europe. Although 80 per cent of the population are Hindus in one meaning of the word or another, India also has the third largest Muslim population in the world and more Christians than all the Scandinavian countries put together. Since independence (and partition) in 1947, India has been defined in Gandhian/Nehruvian terms as a secular, federal country using English and Hindi as national languages, but with another dozen or so official regional languages.

Since the early 1980s – but particularly forcefully during the 1990s – a formerly marginal political movement has steadily increased its influence in India, culminating in its victories in the successive general elections of 1998 and 1999. This is the movement often referred to as *hindutva*, meaning roughly 'Hindu-ness', which rallies behind slogans to the effect that India should be redefined as a Hindu country. The *hindutva* movement, led by an organisation called the Rashtriya Swayamsevak Sangh (RSS) began modestly in the interwar years, and its more recent parliamentary wing, the Bharatiya Janata Party, 'The Indian People's Party' (BJP) is now in power not only federally, in New Delhi, but in several of the states as well.

The rhetoric of *hindutva* is strongly reminiscent of European ethnic nationalism. It invokes ancient myths of bitter defeats and noble sacrifices, re-framing them to fit a contemporary political scene. It quotes liberally from nineteenth-century poets and sacred texts, and it redefines history to make the past conform to a redefined present. It advocates a return to the roots, condemns Westernisation and its adverse moral effects on the young, praises the family as the key institution of society and seeks to promote the vision of India as a *hindu rashtra* – a Hindu nation. While the late Rajiv Gandhi allowed himself to be photographed wearing a Lacoste shirt and khaki shorts, BJP leaders always wear traditional Indian clothes. The main enemy image is nevertheless not the West but Islam, which is depicted as a martial and cruel religion alien to the subcontinent, and Indian Muslims (the descendants of converts, like Bosnian Muslims) are represented partly as traitors to Hinduism, partly as foreign invaders. The demolition of a mosque in the northern town of Ayodhya in December 1992, the ensuing riots in several Indian cities and the call for the rebuilding of a Hindu temple devoted to Ram, allegedly destroyed by a Mughal ruler four centuries ago, marked a climax of sorts in this respect (see Hansen, 1999; van der Veer, 1994, for details).

The phenomenal rise of this traditionalist movement is a result of several connected processes of sociocultural change or modernisation. First, the very notion of *hindutva*, Hindu-ness, is a modern one. Hinduism is not a 'religion of the Book'. It is an uncentralised religion with scores of holy scriptures, thousands of *avatars* (incarnations of divinities), and very many ways of worshipping them. The idea of the Hindu identity as an imagined community based on cultural similarity is alien to Hinduism as such, which is a religion based on complementarity, difference and hierarchy. Regarding political Hinduism, some Indian commentators actually speak of a *Semitisation* of Hinduism, whereby it takes on structural characteristics from the great religions of West Asia.

Second, the *hindutva* movement is explicitly modelled on European nationalism – some early *hindutva* ideologists were even warm admirers of Hitler – which has been, for 150 years, an attempt to reconcile change and continuity by talking of roots and traditions in a situation of industrialisation and urbanisation. This is obvious in *hindutva* practice, whereby issues regarding national anthems, dress and foreign foods are given prominence, while profound social changes continue to affect everyday life as before. There is a clear connection between the rise of the BJP and the liberalisation of the Indian economy, the rise of a substantial new middle class with a strong consumerist orientation, and the rapid spread of new mass media including the Rupert Murdoch-controlled Star TV Network. While liberalisation of this kind stimulates consumerism (perceived as Westernisation), it also indirectly boosts traditionalism since the new patterns of consumption and the new media scene may indicate that cherished traditions are under threat.

Third, the 'contagious' influence from political Islam is obvious; *hindutva* is the assertion of Hindu identity *as opposed to* Muslim identity both in Pakistan and in India itself. Doubly ironically, *hindutva* has double origins in European Romanticism and West Asian political Islam. When its first ideologist, Dr Veer Savarkar, wrote in the 1920s that 'Hindutva is not the same thing as Hinduism', he was therefore right, but not for the reasons he believed. Savarkar saw *hindutva* as a wide-ranging social movement emanating from Hindu faith and practices, while a more historically correct account sees it as the result of cultural diffusion from Europe and West Asia.

Fourth, and perhaps most importantly, the *hindutva* movement can be seen as a reaction against a growing egalitarianism in Indian society. Already in the 1950s, policies attempting to improve the conditions of the 'Untouchables' (the lowest castes), were introduced, and during the 1990s, very radical measures have been proposed to this effect – and in some cases carried out. About half of India's population are now defined as being either *Dalits* ('Untouchables'), tribals, low-caste people or 'OBCs' (Other Backward Classes), and in theory, all of 49.5 per cent of jobs in the public sector should be reserved for these groups, following the recommendations of the government-appointed Mandal Commission. Since the early 1990s, this principle has been enforced in many areas. Naturally, many members of the 'twice-born', upper castes feel their inherited privileges eroding away, and *hindutva* is largely a movement representing the interests of the disenchanted upper castes. It is largely a reaction against the movement towards greater equality in Indian society. Although *hindutva* seems to promote equality among Hindus, an implication of its traditionalist Hinduism is the reinvigoration of the caste system, which may only benefit the 'twice-born' castes. For this reason, Frøystad (2000) argues, it is an unstable popular ideology which is frequently overruled by caste ideology, since the latter is more deeply embedded in everyday practices than *hindutva*. Only so long as an effective enemy image of Muslims can be kept activated, can *hindutva* retain its appeal.

## SOME GENERIC FEATURES OF IDENTITY POLITICS

Let us now see to what extent it is possible to generalise from the *hindutva* case, comparing it implicitly to other instances of identity politics with which we are familiar (see Eriksen, 2001b, for a fuller analysis). I shall propose three social and five cognitive features which seem to be nearly universal.

First, there is *competition over scarce resources*. As Horowitz (1985) and many others writing about group conflict in contemporary societies have shown, such conflicts invariably involve perceptions of scarcity and struggles to retain or attain hegemony or equality. Successful mobilisation on the basis of collective identities presupposes a widespread belief that resources are unequally distributed along group lines. 'Resources' should be interpreted in the widest sense possible, and could in principle be taken to mean economic wealth or political power, recognition or symbolic power – although what is usually at stake are either economic or political resources. This feature is easy to identify here: *hindutva* is an attempt to defend the political and economic interests of 'Hindus' in secular India.

Second, *modernisation actualises differences and triggers conflict.* With the integration of formerly discrete groups into shared economic and political systems, inequalities are made visible, as comparison between the groups becomes possible. Contemporary ethnicity can be described as the process of making cultural differences comparable, and to that extent, it is a modern phenomenon. The rise of the Dalit movement, struggling for recognition and equal rights on behalf of 'Untouchable' groups, is an expression of the modern value of equality, and the counter-reaction from the Hindu right is an attempt to stop egalitarianism from spreading, as well as reflecting – almost with the accuracy of a mirror-image – symbolic competition with Muslims within and (especially) outside India.

Third, *the groups are largely self-recruiting.* Inter-religious marriages are rare in India. Although biological self-reproduction is by no means necessary for a strong collective identity to come about, it should be kept in mind that kinship remains an important organising principle for most societies in the world, and a lot of what passes for ethnicity at the local level is really kinship. Kinship has an important social dimension in addition to its symbolic side, which is highlighted in ideologies of fictive or metaphoric kinship. Symbolic boundaries are never effective unless underpinned by social organisation.

Now to the cognitive features.

First, at the level of ideology, *cultural similarity overrules social equality.* Political Hinduism depicts the in-group as homogeneous, as people 'of the same kind'. Internal differences are undercommuni-cated, and, moreover, in the wider political context, equality values are discarded for ostensible cultural reasons. (Although it could be argued that *hindutva* is a Trojan horse concealing upper-caste interests with all-Hindu rhetoric, the point is that it stresses the commonalities of all Hindus irrespective of caste or language.)

Second, *images of past suffering and injustice are invoked.* Hindu leaders have been at great pains to depict Mughal (Muslim) rule in India from the 1500s as bloody and authoritarian, just as, for example, Serbs bemoan the defeat at the hands of the Turks in

Kosovo in 1389, indigenous Fijian leaders compare their plight to that of other indigenous peoples that have suffered foreign invasions, Scottish nationalism elaborates on English oppression, and so on. Violence targeting the descendants of the invaders can therefore be framed as legitimate revenge. *Hindutva* leaders, who claim to represent 80 per cent of India's population, still complain that Hinduism is under siege and needs to defend itself by all available means.

Third, *the political symbolism and rhetoric evokes personal experiences*. This is perhaps the most important ideological feature of identity politics in general. Using myths, cultural symbols and kinship terminology in addressing their supporters, promoters of identity politics try to downplay the difference between personal experiences and group history. In this way, it became perfectly sensible for a Serb, at the height of the Kosovo conflict, to talk about the legendary battle of Kosovo in the first person ('*We* lost in 1389'), and the logic of revenge is extended to include metaphorical kin, in many cases millions of people. The intimate experiences associated with locality and family are thereby projected onto a national screen. This general feature of social integration has been noted by Handelman (1990), analysing national rituals, and earlier in Turner's (1967) studies of ritual among the Ndembu of Zambia.

Fourth, *first-comers are contrasted with invaders*. Although this ideological feature is by no means universal in identity politics, it tends to be invoked whenever possible, and in the process, historical facts are frequently stretched. There is nothing to suggest that the ancestors of Indian Muslims were more recent arrivals than the ancestors of Christians or Hindus, although Islam is a relatively recent import. What is interesting here is how the varying depth of cultural genealogies ('roots') is used to justify differential treatment. The historical location of the self along the dimensions of descent and place is thereby invested with political significance. This, we have seen, is a central feature of indigenous movements as well as Malay and Fijian ethnopolitics.

Fifth, and finally, *the social complexity in society is reduced to a set of simple contrasts*. As Adolf Hitler already wrote in *Mein Kampf*, the truly national leader concentrates the attention of his people on one enemy at a time. Since cross-cutting ties reduce the chances of violent conflict, the collective identity must be based on relatively unambiguous criteria (such as place, religion, mother-tongue, kinship). Again, internal differences are undercommunicated in the act of delineating boundaries in relation to the demonised Other. This mechanism is familiar from a wide range of interethnic situations, from social classification in Zambian mining towns (Epstein 1992) to Norwegian–Sami relations in sub-Arctic Scandinavia (Eidheim 1971), the Sinhalese–Tamil conflict (Kapferer 1988) and Québécois nationalism (Handler 1988): the Other is reduced to a minimal set of 'traits', and so is the collective Self.

As the first parts of this chapter indicated, the simplifications of identity politics are countered by the complexities of experience. No serious social scientist writing about minority issues today can afford to assume that 'all X'es are the same'. As Hall puts it, 'all of us are composed of multiple social identities' (1991: 57). When the reifications, simplifications and rigid boundary maintenance of identity politics function, it may be precisely because they simultaneously offer a meaningful ordering of the world *and* a promise of resources: they have, as I put it in an earlier chapter, elements of both meaning and politics.

The final chapter of this book will illuminate the perspectives discussed previously through looking at that which is not ethnic. For ethnicity is created, and it is not only created by the people we study, but also by ourselves. If a researcher looks for ethnicity, he or she will find it – possibly at the cost of missing out on other kinds of relationship which are also 'there'.

## FURTHER READING

Baumann, Gerd (1999) *The Multicultural Riddle: Rethinking National, Ethnic and Religious Identities*. London: Routledge. An anthropologist engages with the philosophical problems of multiculturalism and rights, from a distinctly anthropological perspective.

Watson, C.W. (2000) *Multiculturalism*. Buckingham: Open University Press. Introduces the issues with particular emphasis on education, religious tolerance and the impact of globalisation.

Wilson, Richard A. and Jon Mitchell, eds (2003) *Human Rights in Global Perspective: Anthropological Studies of Rights, Claims and Entitlements*. London: Routledge. Excellent introduction to the anthropology of human rights, indicating the problems of cultural particularism and universalism in an ethnographically grounded way.

# 9
# The Non-Ethnic

*Habit of seeing opposites.* – The general imprecise way of observing sees everywhere in nature opposites (as, for example, 'warm and cold') where there are, not opposites, but differences in degree. This bad habit has led us into wanting to comprehend and analyse the inner world, too, the spiritual–moral world, in terms of such opposites. An unspeakable amount of pain, arrogance, harshness, estrangement, frigidity has entered into human feelings because we think we see opposites instead of transitions.

Friedrich Nietzsche (*Der Wanderer und sein Schatten*, § 67, [The Wanderer and his Shadow, 1880] in Nietzsche, 1988)

It is a feature of the contemporary world that people appear to become more similar and more different at the same time, due to the forces of modernity and globalisation. More than thirty years ago, Gellner noted that 'modern society is *both* more homogeneous *and* more diversified than those which preceded it' (1978: 141). Anthropological perspectives on ethnicity as process enable us to see this contradiction as a fundamental duality between similarity and difference, between inclusion and exclusion, between homogenisation and fragmentation. Although people in a certain sense become more similar because of modernisation, they simultaneously become more distinctive, and ethnicity is one principal expression of this differentiation. Ethnicity amounts to making cultural differences comparable, and thus presupposes a shared language for talking about those differences. Matching and contrasting, the main ways of expressing distinctiveness, entail comparison. Furthermore, since ethnicity usually has an aspect of resource competition, there needs to be agreement over the desirability of particular resources for there to be ethnic competition. Finally, ethnic groups tend to use the toolkit of modern mass communication both to strengthen the internal cohesion and to present their claims (or goods, as in the case of 'Ethnicity, Inc.') to the outside world. It could in fact be said, slightly facetiously, that globalisation makes people more and more similar; but the more similar we become, the more different we try to be. However, the more different we try to be, the more similar we become, since ethnic movements everywhere draw on the same 'grammar of uniqueness', as suggested towards the end of chapter 8.

Ethnic differentiation thus draws upon social, cultural and political resources which presuppose a prior institutionalisation of the contacts between the groups and their integration into a single system in certain respects. However, as chapters 7 and 8 in particular have shown, stability and boundedness in interethnic systems of interaction can no longer be taken for granted. Recent research on transnationalism, long-distance nationalism and related phenomena has shown that ethnic relations must increasingly be studied in the compass of a large-scale, unbounded, dynamic system rather than as a stable relationship. Instead of summing up what has already been said, I shall use this final, brief chapter to ask about the overall significance of ethnicity and nationalism studies in the contemporary world; whether, perhaps, the postmodern world has become so irreducibly complex and mixed that it can no longer be studied through a focus on the relatively stable identifications and group formations presupposed by ethnicity. This would be the view of some of the theorists writing from a postmodern perspective, as well as sociologists like Brubaker (2002), and it has been problematised by Jenkins (2007, 2008) and others.

## GLOBALISATION

It would be difficult to argue against the view that the world is more interconnected today than at any earlier historical period – through satellite TV, Internet and mobile telephony, migration and tourism, trade and an intensified traffic in signs and meanings. The culinary capital of India may be London, that of China San Francisco. In order to carry out anthropological fieldwork in a village in the Dominican Republic, one has to spend at least a few months in New York City, since half of the villagers are at any time working and living in The Big Apple. The little trolls, 'Scream' t-shirts and expensive knitted sweaters sold as Norwegian souvenirs to tourists visiting Oslo, are made in Taiwan, Pakistan and Sri Lanka, respectively. The largest city in the English-speaking Caribbean is London. And if the classical patriarchal kinship system of the Taiwanese had been unable to withstand the pressure of individualism from modernisation, several shopowners in Silicon Valley might still have been in business: The patriclan is an efficient economic unit where interest-free loans and free services are available, and when shops in California (and elsewhere) have to close down because their customers have lost their jobs, this is partly a result of competition from East Asia.

Globalisation is dual and operates, one might say, through dialectical negation: it *shrinks* the world by facilitating fast contact across former boundaries, and it *expands* the world by creating an awareness of difference. It *homogenises* human lives by imposing a set of common denominators (state organisation, labour markets, consumption, etc.), but it also leads to *heterogenisation* through the new forms of diversity emerging from the intensified contact. Globalisation is *centripetal* in that it connects people worldwide; and it is *centrifugal* in that it inspires a heightened awareness of, and indeed (re-)constructions of local uniqueness. It centralises power and prompts movements, among indigenous peoples, small nations and others, fighting for local autonomy and self-determination. Finally, globalisation makes a universalist *cosmopolitanism* possible in political thought and action because it reminds us that we are all in the same boat and have to live together in spite of our mutual differences; but it also encourages *fundamentalism* and various forms of missionary universalism as well as parochial localism, because global integration leads to a sense of alienation, threatening identities and notions of political sovereignty.

Third ways or third alternatives are often created through the working out of these tensions. This is, among other things, where the term *glocalisation* comes into its own, but also terms like *alter-globalisation*, that is 'alternative' globalisation or, if one prefers, 'the globalisation of the Other', which is to say NGO-based or grassroots initiatives aiming to use the technology and networks enabled by globalisation for the benefit of the disenfranchised.

Modernisation and increasing scale in social organisation are marked by a complex process of simultaneous homogenisation and differentiation. Some differences vanish, whereas others emerge.

Truly global processes affect the conditions of people living in particular localities, creating new opportunities and new forms of vulnerability. Risks are globally shared in the era of the nuclear bomb, transnational terrorism and potential ecological disasters. On the same note, the economic conditions in particular localities frequently (some would say always) depend on events taking place elsewhere in the global system. If there is an industrial boom in Taiwan, towns in the English Midlands will be affected. If oil prices rise, that means salvation for the oil-exporting Trinidadian economy and disaster for the oil-importing, neighbouring Barbadian one.

Patterns of consumption also seem to merge in certain respects; people nearly everywhere desire similar goods, from cellphones to readymade garments. Now, a precondition for this to happen is the more or less successful implementation of certain institutional dimensions of modernity, notably that of a monetary economy – if not necessarily evenly distributed wagework and literacy. The ever-increasing transnational flow of commodities, be they material or immaterial, creates a set of common cultural denominators which appear to eradicate local distinctions. The hot-dog, the pizza and the hamburger (or, in India, the lamb-burger) are truly parts of world cuisine; identical pop songs are played in identical discotheques in Costa Rica and Thailand; the same Coca-Cola commercials are shown with minimal local variations at cinemas all over the world, Dan Brown volumes are ubiquitous wherever books are sold, and so on. Investment capital, military power and world literature are being disembedded from the constraints of space; they no longer belong to a particular locality. With the development of the jet plane, the satellite dish and more recently, the Internet, distance no longer seems a limiting factor for the flow of influence, investments and cultural meaning.

Yet, disembedding is never total, and it is always counteracted by *re-embedding* attempts, which often appear as manifestations of ethnicity. Sometimes, re-embedding does not even seem to be required – if one cares to look, the social world in which most of humanity live remains embedded in important respects, notwithstanding decades of intensive, technology-driven globalisation. The impact of globalisation – or, rather, its significance for the lives we lead – is considerable, but every one-sided account is ultimately false. Warning against the view of globalisation as somehow 'the outcome', or the 'end product' of modernity, James Mittelman (2001: 7) writes that if 'globalization is a contested and political phenomenon, then it cannot have a predetermined outcome. A political agenda of inevitability overlooks the fact that globalization was made by humans, and, if so, can be unmade or remade by humankind'. It is far-reaching and consequential, but globalising processes are always full of contradictions which are not likely to go away soon. Some people are globalising, some are just being globalised, and many are scarcely affected directly by globalisation.

## SOCIAL THEORY AND THE POSTMODERN WORLD

Much research on ethnicity implicitly presupposes that the nation-state is the 'pre-eminent power-container of the modern era', to use Giddens' (1985: 120) formulation. This is generally true of minority studies whether aboriginal or urban, studies of secessionist movements or 'proto-nations', or studies of power struggles or identity processes in 'plural societies'. Many social scientists have questioned this assumption in recent years, and argue that the world has changed in such a way that the nation-state is no longer an appropriate synonym for 'greater society'. Perhaps Eric Hobsbawm (1990) was correct when attributing the currently great academic interest in nationalism to the Hegelian notion that 'the owl of Minerva flies at dusk' – in other words, that the age of the nation-state is nearly over. And perhaps Ulf Hannerz (1992, 1996), Arjun Appadurai (1996) and other anthropologists are correct in suggesting that many contemporary men and women tend to seek their identifications and social alignments along different axes than was formerly the case – largely because capitalism and modern communications technology, from the satellite dish to the jet plane, have relativised the spatial dimension in human life. In Roland Robertson's (1994) somewhat hyperbolic phrase, the world has become a single place.

Even more radical conclusions have been reached by social theorists such as Anthony Giddens (1990, 1991), Immanuel Wallerstein (1991b; Wallerstein *et al.* 1996) and John Urry (2000), who argue the need for a profound rethinking of the categories of social science. In Wallerstein's view, the very concept of 'society' has become obsolete (see the debate in Ingold 1996) – it may have been a useful nineteenth-century metaphor but, in his view, it is a misleading one in the seamless world system of the late twentieth century. Urry, in his *Sociology beyond Societies* (2000), develops an entire new sociology based on movement rather than structure as a founding epistemological principle; and Robertson speaks of 'the present sense of the world as a single place' (1994: 184)

Starting from an opposite direction, several theorists have questioned the category of the individual. A common notion here is that individuals in the present world are less 'integrated' and somehow more transient – situationally shifting, really – than was formerly the case. I have theories of postmodernism or postmodernity in mind here (see Bauman, 1993; Lash and Friedman, 1991; B. Turner, 1990). An interesting interpretation of this 'condition' is given by Marilyn Strathern (1992), who has argued that it is *our cultural fiction* of the integrated and bounded individual, who is presumed to be a member of 'a culture' and who lives his or her life as a continuous, directed person, which is about to lose its credibility.

Much of this theorising seems to concern only a small, rich part of the world's population – bored urban secularised Western intellectuals and heavy consumers – however, the globalisation of culture and the relativisation of boundaries has a very widespread, if uneven, effect. At the time of the nuclear disaster in Chernobyl in 1986, I was doing fieldwork in Mauritius and found that rural Indo-Mauritian cane-cutters discussed its consequences in the rum shop. Similarly, knowledge about possibilities for emigration to particular countries is widespread in many rural areas in poor countries – and everybody listens to American pop music. Unlike the globalisation of earlier times (from plantation economies onwards), this form of globalisation stimulates the emergence of a reflexive consciousness about the global system. In brief, many of the local communities of the world seem to become increasingly integrated into the global system on a political, economic and cultural level, and are increasingly aware of it; and this is now being amply documented by ethnographic studies more recent than the theories cited above, such as Comaroff and Comaroff (2009), Tsing (2005) and Olwig (2007). If an earlier orthodoxy in anthropology consisted in isolating the unit of study for analytical purposes, it may seem as if it has been replaced by the belief that no anthropology is worthwhile which does not take in global interconnectedness (see also Eriksen, 2003, 2006, 2007b).

On the other hand, severe criticism has also been directed at the tendencies towards 'globabble' (Kapferer, 2001; cf. also Friedman, 1994) and the celebration of a hybrid world where 'the space of flows' (Castells, 1996) replaces 'the space of places', and where scholarly discourse can be described facetiously as a 'postblur blur' (Appadurai, 1996: 51). In previous chapters, I have discussed criticisms of the constructivist perspectives on ethnicity; it deserves mentioning that the new, post-Marxist and post-Durkheimian social theory, with its emphasis on change, flexibility and choice, can also be seen as a scholarly parallel to the neoliberal ideology which was so pervasive during the 1990s. The Swiss anthropologist Hans-Rudolf Wicker, noting that 'the epistemology of totalities is succeeded by the epistemology of process' (1997: 21), thinks so, and claims that the postmodernist, deconstructivist and post-structuralist trend 'yields to the Zeitgeist and chooses its position in the camp of (neo-) liberal ideology' (1997: 21). Many share this view.

## CHANGES IN THE WORLD OF INTERGROUP RELATIONS

Be this as it may, there is little doubt that social identities in many parts of the world, in the post-Cold War era, seem to be more open to negotiation than they were in the decades following the Second World War, at the same time as the emphasis on 'primordial', ethnic or national identities is stronger than it used to be. The changes in British Asian identities (see e.g. Brah, 1996) illustrate this. Largely perceived in class terms in the 1950s and 1960s, a culturalisation and ethnification of their collective identities occurred in the following decades, and during the 1990s, many British citizens of Asian descent invested enormous amounts of energy to liberate themselves from stereotypical depictions of their 'culture and identity', while others sought to strengthen them. All over Europe, from Ireland and Norway to the Caucasus and Andalusia, there is a recurrent, lively discourse about which collective identities to attach oneself to. New nation-states have been formed in Eastern Europe and elsewhere, and new minority problems arise. Ideologically, state communism has been replaced by tensions between forms of liberalism and forms of nationalism (see Mach, 1993, for Poland; Holy, 1996, for the Czech Republic; Verdery, 1996, for Romania; Hann, 2002, for several East European countries). Old European nation-states, which are growing by number every decade, transfer their power to a new supranational unit, the European Union. New regionalist, ethnic or downright xenophobic movements emerge on both sides of the EU boundary, and people are torn between what they see as the old and the new. Elsewhere in the world, there are also powerful ideological movements competing for people's adherence – politicised Islam in the Middle East and increasingly, after the Gulf War, elsewhere in the Muslim world, including the diasporas in Europe; indigenous and 'ethnic minority' movements in North and South America; *bhumiputra* ('sons of the soil') ideology in Malaysia and celebrations of pre-Columbian culture in the Bolivian highlands. A great many of these movements share the crucial feature of appealing to people's sense of primordial bonds and cultural authenticity. Russia is divided between Slavophiles and Westernisers in addition to being torn by various ethnic conflicts (Tishkov, 1997); American intellectuals are divided between multiculturalists and integrationists (Schlesinger, 1992); India between *hindutva*, political Islam and secessionist movements on the one hand, secularists on the other hand. No political movement based on gender or class has been able to wield a global influence even remotely comparable to that of identity politics in the last decades.

On the one hand, then, we witness powerful centripetal waves of cultural homogenisation, tighter economic integration (Held *et al.*, 1999), increasing participation in wagework and the monetary economy, increasing consumption of global cultural merchandise (from soap operas to Coca-Cola), and an increased flow of people to and from various destinations. The widespread establishment of satellite television in the 1980s created conditions for simultaneity on a global scale: events could now be witnessed anywhere no matter where they took place. The phenomenal spread of the Internet a decade later (see Castells, 2001; Eriksen, 2001a), which at the latest count (spring 2010) had more than a billion users, is a related form of global 'shrinking', functioning simultaneously as a mass medium and, increasingly through the virtual 'social network' services, at the level of interpersonal communication.

On the other hand, as we have seen, new 'localisms' or particularisms – usually of an ethnic, religious or regional nature – continue to emerge and to assert their demands vis-à-vis the centres. Perhaps the most spectacular assertion of this kind so far, also a deeply transnational act, was the terrorist assault on the USA on 11 September 2001. It was justified, by militant Muslims of Arab origin, within the framework of a classic, however violent, discourse of identity politics. Osama bin Laden referred not to the West's exploitation of poor peoples (a Marxist perspective), but to its humiliating treatment of Muslims, its encroachment on Muslim territory, and the arrogance of the USA – in other words, he defended continued anti-US terrorism as a form of resistance and as a 'politics of recognition'. As I have argued at length in earlier chapters, processes of modernisation or homogenisation are necessary conditions for such movements – moderate or militant, as the case might be – to develop and to articulate their demands effectively. As regards nationalism, the very idea of nationalism is a globalised one, which was initially developed in Europe and the European diaspora. Besides, social integration into wider systems is a condition for their identities to become relevant at all, since it is contact and not isolation that engenders social identity. This is obvious enough – the majority of the examples discussed in this book have indicated the importance of social change and contact with others for the emergence of new social identities. The question is nevertheless: what will such identities look like in the near future?

## GLOBALISATION AND LOCALISATION

Students of ethnic and national identities and ideologies are, if anything, at the centre of the theoretical and historical upheavals which I have alluded to. It has been said that the nation-state is too small to accomplish certain tasks and too big to accomplish others – too big to give people a sense of community, too small to solve the problems facing humanity – and this entails the continued relevance of the analytical concern with identification and group cohesion, but also suggests the necessity for new frameworks. The perhaps most spectacular growth industry in social sciences and cultural studies during the 1990s addressed this challenge. The term 'globalisation', first used by the sociologist Roland Robertson in the 1980s (see Robertson, 1994), became an instant success in the post-Marxist, post-structuralist and somewhat postmodernist world of the early 1990s, offering a conceptualisation of the world as a processual, fluid and complex 'network of networks' (Ulf Hannerz's term). The trend of globalisation studies was met with mixed reactions by anthropologists, who worried about the future of ethnography in a world where nothing seemed local any more. However, it soon became clear that global phenomena more often than not could be studied in their local expressions, and that cultural globalisation was always tantamount to *glocalisation*, that is creative fusions of local and non-local elements. This is not the place to go more deeply into anthropological globalisation studies, but it must be said that the most pervasive feature of cultural globalisation may be the fact that reflexive modernity may now be encountered anywhere. Two of the leading defenders of cultural relativism, Marshall Sahlins and Clifford Geertz, each wrote an essay in the mid 1990s, slightly self-ironically describing the loss of 'radical difference' and the ability of contemporary 'natives' to talk about, and politicize, their 'culture', or *kastom* in Sahlins' Melanesian case, in terms reminiscent of anthropological theory of culture (Geertz, 1994; Sahlins, 1994; see also Eriksen and Nielsen, 2001: chapter 9). Sahlins nevertheless responds to the assumption of growing cultural uniformity by coining the term 'indigenisation of modernity', which covers the same ground as 'glocalisation'. The realities studied by ethnographers are primarily built around experience, and experience is always personal and usually localised. This implies that typical anthropological studies of globalisation will be more likely to focus on, say, the importance of Country & Western music for life politics in rural Norway, or the impact of the post-Gulf War ideological discourse on Malay fishing villages, than on, say, the global power of Microsoft or McDonald's. What is new about this is chiefly an increased awareness of the importance of contextualising one's research in a wider universe than, say, the village, the region or the nation.

In this world, which may be described as post-traditional for a growing number of its inhabitants, individuals are faced with more options and fewer scripts than before. To take an example familiar to many of the readers, the second generation of immigrants in Western Europe may plausibly opt for three main kinds of strategies: *purist* identities, preserving and reproducing (as best they can) tradition; *hyphenated* identities, 'living in two worlds' juxtaposing their ancestral identity with that of the host society, or *hybrid* or *creole* identities acknowledging irreducible mixing as a fact of life. The tools used to study ethnic relations are necessary to make sense of this kind of setting, but they are not sufficient, since the boundary presupposed by ethnic studies is exactly what is challenged in these discourses of identity.

In an ambitious series of articles, Jonathan Friedman (1987, 1990, 1991) starts from the assumption that globalisation and localisation are two mutually dependent, interrelated processes. As Ulf Hannerz (1990) argued in a similar context, cosmopolitans depend on locals in order to be able to conceive themselves to be, and to be regarded as, cosmopolitan. We may also add that perhaps it is true that the world is a single place (as Giddens, 1990, puts it) – but if so, it is largely locally constructed.

Friedman then outlines five major strategies, which he calls 'life-strategies, models for satisfying the structures of desire that emerge in the different niches of the global system'. The first is *modernist*. According to this view, society can be governed effectively on moral and sensible principles; and self, society and the world can develop according to presently conventional criteria.

The four remaining strategies build on the assumption that this kind of social and political identity is untenable because it has not delivered the goods. The first of these is plainly *postmodern* and can assume two, complementary shapes: a cynical distancing from all identification, but an acute awareness of the lack of identity; and a narcissistic dependence on consumption as a means for the presentation of self. A great number of critical analyses of modern society accuse capitalism and large-scale society of encouraging this fragmented, unpolitical and nihilistic kind of social identity; indeed, a sense of uprootedness and alienation following the Industrial Revolution was a main motivating force for many of the classic sociologists, from Marx to Durkheim and Weber.

The next strategy is *traditionalist*. It can be religious and/or ethnic, and it includes many if not most of the ethnic and nationalist movements I have described in this book. According to Friedman, this kind of project is caused by an experienced need among individuals in modern societies to 'engage [themselves] in a larger project in which identity is concrete and fixed despite mobility, success and other external changes in social conditions' (Friedman, 1991: 361). Ecopolitical movements are related to these strategies (see Giddens, 1990, on 'green' traditionalism). Many ethnic movements may thus, within this analytical framework, be lumped with 'deep ecologists' and religious fundamentalists as 'traditionalists'. Although they frequently appear as anti-modern, modernity is a condition for their emergence.

The following strategy is labelled *Third World*, and is developed in order to attract wealth and power through clientship. Patron–client chains operate both domestically and internationally. Consumption is deemed important by the adherents of this strategy; the development of national infrastructure is abandoned.

The final strategy is called *Fourth World*, and is the strategy of 'exit from the system' – the formation of politically autonomous communities which aim at re-establishing a formerly repressed identity and lifestyle.

These five life-strategies are not mutually exclusive, but they do suggest (i) great qualitative variations within the global system, and (ii) that there *is* a global system which one has to relate to. In an earlier chapter, I stated that virtually every inhabitant of the contemporary world is forced to be a citizen. In line with globalisation theory, one might add that virtually everybody is forced to be a consumer in some way or other. Combinations of 'Third' and 'Fourth World' strategies seem common among indigenous peoples, who simultaneously strive for self-determination and for a higher material standard of living. Immigrant groups in Europe may combine 'traditionalist/ethnic/religious' and 'postmodern' strategies. Similarly, combinations of 'modernist' and 'postmodernist' strategies may be common in Western Europe, where people are simultaneously strongly concerned with their own lifestyle and the condition of their society.

What is remarkable about this kind of perspective is the conviction that the world has indeed changed in such a way as to allow for other kinds of social alignments than those which were formerly viable. Some of these alignments will have an ethnic tag, others will not. The Islamic movement of the Middle East and North Africa can scarcely be considered an ethnic one. It aims at including a great number of peoples who are acknowledged to be culturally diverse and having different origins. However, it shares many features with ethnic movements: it is anti-modernist and traditionalist, it aims at a reconstitution of seemingly vanishing aspects of society, culture and identity, and it can also, at the same time, be seen as a strategy of modernisation on one's own terms (Gellner, 1992).

## IDENTITIES AND LOYALTIES

On the subject of segmentary identities, I.M. Lewis writes: 'A committed internationalist condemns parochial nationalism (little Englanderism) just as unequivocally as a nationalist condemns tribalism, a tribalist clannishness, and a clansman familism' (1985: 359). Since Evans-Pritchard's (1940) depiction of the segmentary lineage among the Nuer, this way of thinking has been with us in social anthropology. As we have seen in earlier chapters, this perspective on identity and groups can be very illuminating in ethnicity studies. We shall nevertheless move one step further. For Evans-Pritchard did not merely deal with the segmentary character of identities – political identities as concentric circles, so to speak – he also indicated that conflicting loyalties may reduce tensions and prevent conflicts between lineages.

The Nuer are patrilineal. If a sufficient number of Nuer men in lineage X have affines in lineage Y – either because they are married to women from lineage Y, or because their sisters are married to men from that lineage – this is a strong incentive not to start a feud with that lineage. If only a few men are so aligned, and the feud is a fact, the minority may experience conflicting loyalties – they may feel ill at ease whether they take part in the fighting or stay at home. Multiple or conflicting loyalties, moreover, do not only operate on the basis of kinship; enduring bonds are also formed on the basis of age-group fellowship, trade and personal friendship. According to Evans-Pritchard's own analysis, and particularly in Gluckman's (1982 [1956]) use of his material, this criss-crossing web of conflicting loyalties seems to create a relatively stable social system among the potentially perennially warlike Nuer groupings.

In terms of ethnicity, multiple loyalties may be a problem for minorities, whose members may often be loyal to – and indeed members of – two ethnic groups or nations, or one ethnic group and one nation. But why ought this to be a problem? Clearly because the ideology of the nation-state remains hegemonic and the relationship between states is seen as one of potential conflict. Here, we should perhaps remember that the United *Nations* (sic) is an organisation of states which is usually not entitled to meddle in internal affairs. When Saddam Hussein entered Kuwait in August 1991, he broke the international rules; but when he tried out new chemical weapons on Iraqi Kurds, he did not. During the 1990s, these principles were stretched greatly through a series of international interventions in conflicts which might be seen as internal – Somalia, Rwanda, Yugoslavia, Afghanistan and Iraq – a process which witnesses a growing recognition of the transnational nature of conflict, and which also doubtless contributes to weakening the nation-state.

Many people in the contemporary world are structurally placed so as to have multiple loyalties in ethnic terms. Apart from labour migrants, refugees and expatriates, transnational families are an obvious, increasingly common example. However, multiple loyalties need not follow ethnic lines. Kenneth Little (1978) has shown how gender loyalty – between women – can cut across ethnic lines in African societies, mitigate potential conflict and create problems for attempts at ethnic group formation. If women perceive that they have shared interests against the men, across ethnic boundaries, then their gender identity will situationally overrule the ethnic identity. Another basis for loyalty and identity can be social class membership. Even in Mauritius, where there is general agreement that ethnic divisions are the most important ones, solidarity along class lines occasionally forms; in 1970 and in 1979 there were major strikes uniting Creoles, Hindus and Muslims against their employers, and political parties occasionally succeed in transcending ethnicity. In this case, class solidarity obviously overruled ethnic solidarity, since several of the employers belonged to the same ethnic categories as the strikers.

In the contemporary world, social identities can form along several other lines as well. Employees of transnational companies are trained to be loyal to their company rather than their country, and many thousands may be assigned to appointments in foreign countries. Networks of professional solidarity are also transnational and cut across ethnic lines. An English anthropologist would definitely have something in common with an Indian anthropologist which she does not have in common with her neighbour. There are transnational networks, nowadays frequently mediated by the Internet, connecting a lot of more or less deterritorialised interest groups with various degrees of commitment. This kind of network obviously provides opportunities for the expression of shared identity. And we could go on. The question that must be asked pertains to whether or not ethnic identities are, by default, more 'basic' than others. Some would say yes, others would say no – and that is the state of the art.

We should stress here that multiple identities are not the same as segmentary identities. Multiple identities cannot be placed in concentric circles in orderly ways; they can scarcely be represented graphically at all. They cut across each other in the same manner as Sandra Wallman's open heterogeneous networks (chapter 7): one has a shared identity with different people at different times. In this kind of social setting, the status sets of individuals are not clustered around intricate social relationships with a limited number of people; they are diverse and flexible.

## GENDER, ETHNICITY AND NATIONHOOD

In other words, non-ethnic identities and principles of social differentiation can be highly important. The relationship between class and ethnicity has already been discussed, particularly in chapters 3 and 5. *Gender* identity is arguably also of great social importance in every human society, although gender-based political organisations are comparatively rare. Just as recent research on ethnicity has indicated that ethnicity should be distinguished from culture, recent research on gender has argued that gender should not be seen as primarily biological, but rather as a cultural construction whose legitimacy is justified through references to biology (see Strathern, 1988: chapters 1–2). According to these perspectives, gender is also most fruitfully seen as a social relation and not as an essence consisting of 'properties' or 'personality traits' – again, there are striking parallels with research on ethnicity.

The relationship between gender and ethnicity varies to such an extent, and can be so complex, that it would require another book to do justice to the subject. I shall therefore only give a bare outline of some central issues.

Sexual stereotyping is in many societies related to ethnicity in the sense that some ethnic categories of men (such as blacks in the United States) may have a reputation for sexual prowess and some categories of women similarly may have reputations as prudish or wanton. Gender imagery is often used to describe ethnic groups as a whole ('the Xs are effeminate'; 'the Ys are crude brutes with no manners', and so on).

In some societies in the Caribbean, there is a strong symbolic interrelationship between class, ethnicity and gender in social classification. In Trinidad, the (emic) classificatory poles are African–Indian, male–female and working-class–middle-class. In general, women, Indians and members of the middle class are held to share certain characteristics – they are considered more 'respectable' than men, Africans and members of the working class, who are considered strong individualists with little sense of responsibility. If somebody does not turn up for an appointment, for example, this may be explained by referring to the fact that he is a man, an African and/or a member of the working class.

Regarding the structural position in society, there are interesting similarities between women in some societies and some indigenous groups to the extent that they are 'muted' categories (Ardener's, 1989c [1975] expression) with little formal power. Both oppressed women and oppressed indigenes are compelled to use the language of the dominators in order to be able to express their interests; neither has the power to define the terms of discourse. Both groups are taught that their specific social identity is immutable and (at least in the case of women) biological, and as a consequence that their subordination is 'natural'. Both groups may be told that their contribution to society is negligible and that they should therefore remain subordinated.

There is nevertheless a fundamental difference between gender systems and other systems of differentiation, including ethnicity. In every human society, there is an ideology to the effect that men and women need each other; that they are complementary. Ethnic minorities may be expelled, exterminated or ignored – women cannot be treated in the same way if the political leaders plan for societal continuity. Physical segregation along gender lines is also much more difficult to achieve than segregation along ethnic lines. In every society where it makes sense to talk of domestic and public fields of interaction, both genders will be represented in the domestic fields.

Some interesting perspectives on gender imagery in ethnic and nationalist ideology are discussed in Anthias and Yuval-Davies (1989), one of the few books which discuss the relationship between nationalism and gender (see also Mosse, 1985; Parker et al., 1992;

B. Williams, 1996; Wilford and Miller, 1998; Yuval-Davies 1997).
The contributors show that in so far as gender relations are made
symbolically relevant in nationalist ideology, they tend to reproduce
a patriarchal view of the family. If the nation is regarded as a
metaphoric kin group, then the mother's metaphorical role must be
to reproduce – to raise children and to provide domestic services. In
war imagery, this passive role of women is particularly evident. 'The
fathers have fought/and the mothers have wept' goes a famous line
in the Norwegian national anthem. If the nation-state is symbolically
depicted as a family writ large, then it makes sense to investigate
actual family relations in the society in question to find the sources
of nationalist imagery. Here we may find that nationalism tends to
reproduce and strengthen the gender relations already prevalent in
a society, albeit placing them at a more abstract level.

Finally, it should be mentioned that a field which may be
particularly fertile (if the metaphor is allowed) for an investigation
of the dynamics between group loyalties and gender, is sport.
Spectator sports are in most countries male dominated, and bring
out a rich symbolism which has so far not been properly analysed
in relation to nationalism, violence and sexuality (but see Archetti
1999; Giulianotti and Robertson, 2009; MacClancy, 1996).

It can be about as difficult for a man to join a militant feminist
group as it would be for him to change his ethnic membership in
absolute terms. The point is not, therefore, that all notions of gender
differences or cultural differences are pure inventions, but that every
distinction – no matter how 'objective' or 'natural' it may seem to
us – needs to be codified culturally in order to be recognised.

## BEYOND ETHNICITY?

Studies of ethnicity have tended to accentuate the enactment of
boundary mechanisms and the use of overt markers of distinctiveness in the reproduction of ethnic identities. However, as we have
seen, the social world can rarely be neatly divided into fixed groups
with clear boundaries, unambiguous criteria for membership and
an all-encompassing social relevance. Therefore, a one-sided focus
on ethnicity may prevent a researcher from seeing social systems
in other ways which may also be relevant.

First of all, the existence of ethnic anomalies or liminal categories
should serve as a reminder that group boundaries are not
unproblematic. These are groups or individuals who are 'betwixt
and between', who are neither X nor Y and yet a bit of both. Their

actual group membership may be open to situational negotiation, it may be ascribed by a dominant group, or the group may form a separate ethnic category.

Second, non-ethnic criteria for group membership are situationally relevant in every society, and in complex modern societies they proliferate and can be identified as multiple identities. Different forms of group loyalty and membership may be largely congruent with ethnic membership, or they may cut across it.

Is it still analytically fruitful to think about the social world in terms of ethnicity? Perhaps a wider term, such as 'social identity', would be more true to the flux and complexity of social processes, and would allow us to study group formation and alignments along a greater variety of axes than a single-minded focus on 'ethnicity' would. As Ulf Hannerz has stressed, cultural complexity combined with group differentiation is not necessarily linked with ethnicity: 'Complex societies have other kinds of interfaces between varieties of common sense, other kinds of marginality [as well as ethnicity]' (1992: 133).

A problem concerning the concept of ethnicity is that it seems to imply that there exists *an ethnic phenomenon* (van den Berghe, 1981) in the world which requires a single explanation – which has biological or other shared and objective origins. We should be cautious of reifying the concept of ethnicity in this way. Rather, we would be well advised to follow Comaroff and Comaroff (1992: 54), who state that ethnicity 'describes both a set of relations and a mode of consciousness'. As a mode of consciousness, however, 'it is one among many ... each of which is produced as particular historical structures impinge themselves on human experience and condition social action' (1992: 54).

A related question concerns the ways in which we think about ethnic boundaries. Many of the examples discussed in earlier chapters show that such boundaries are frequently ambiguous. In this regard, the theory of the plural society seems to be flawed in that it assumes, in a rather axiomatic way, that ethnic alignments are the most basic ones in polyethnic societies. It is not always obvious who is a member of a group and who is not, and it is not always obvious which kinds of groups count and which do not. We cannot assume a priori that ethnic alignments are more important than others.

Research on group formation and social identities has tended to regard groups as mutually exclusive in a *digital* way: either one is a member of X or one is not. I have nevertheless shown that people can often be *somewhat* X. The digital way of thinking about groups and identities may be influenced by nationalist ideology and practice, according to which one cannot simultaneously be and not be a citizen in a state. However, in real life people do not normally classify each other just by referring to their citizenship. Many other statuses are relevant. Therefore, it may, perhaps, be more appropriate to think of identity in general as an *analogue* phenomenon than as a *digital* one. Conceptualised in this way, degrees of sameness and difference, of inclusion and exclusion, may be identified. People may be a bit of this and a bit of that.

Empirically, social identities appear fluid, negotiable, situational, analogic (or gradualist) and segmentary. It is therefore an empirical question whether different identities are mutually exclusive, and certainly ethnic communities are social and cultural creations. As shown in previous chapters, identity is elastic and negotiable, but not infinitely flexible. Finally, it is a universal fact that not everybody can take part in a given community. All categorisations of group membership must have boundaries; they depend on *others* in order to make sense.

In my final empirical example, I shall outline a contemporary, social process where it may seem as if ethnicity is losing its relevance.

## THE END OF ETHNICITY?

Whether or not ethnic identities become politically relevant depends on the wider social context. I have shown how ethnicity can assume different forms and may arise from different historical circumstances. I have argued that ethnic 'revitalisation' may be an inherent feature of modernity, and that many modernisation theorists who held that ethnic alignments were becoming obsolete, were wrong. However, we should also remember that, when all is said and done, ethnicity does not *necessarily* arise from modernity, and it is not necessarily an end-product. As Gerd Baumann (1999) reminds us, all identity is identification, and as David McCrone puts it, 'identities should be seen as a concern with "routes" rather than "roots", as maps for the future rather than trails from the past' (1998: 34).

The Mauritian labour market was traditionally strongly ethnically segregated. Because of industrialisation (during and after the 1980s) and democratisation of the political system (from 1947 onwards), this segregation is in many areas giving way to a labour market recruiting its employees on the basis of individual merit rather than ethnic membership. A great number of the new factories and hotels are owned by foreigners with no ethnic commitments. Merit rather than connections becomes a criterion for recruitment.

Simultaneously, the democratisation of education is deepening. A growing number of Mauritians receive higher education abroad and later return to the island. Before independence, higher education was generally reserved for a handful of wealthy families. In the towns, people increasingly live in neighbourhoods appropriate to their class instead of ethnic neighbourhoods. Also, new venues for informal social life appear: snackbars, new sports clubs, parties organised by the larger employers and so on. Most of these new arenas are not primarily constituted on an ethnic basis.

From the individual Mauritian's point of view, his or her opportunities appear very different from what they would have been thirty years ago. Individual achievement is highly praised in official rhetoric. One can no longer rely on one's family. One competes as an individual on an equal footing with members of every 'community', including one's own. At school and at work, one encounters people from other ethnic categories and has important shared experiences with them.

From the societal perspective, industrial Mauritius is compelled to compete in the world market in unprecedented ways. Employees are thus being taught that their country's welfare depends on their achievement. The other groups relevant for one's own social identity therefore tend to become foreign states rather than domestic ethnic groups. Such a shift in identity focus, if it is successful, can be seen as an indication of integration at a higher systemic level, where new sets of relationship are created. A good illustration of this was the spontaneous upsurge of nationalist sentiment in Mauritius following the international sports tournament Les Jeux des Iles de l'Océan Indien in 1985. Suddenly, dichotomisations between Mauritians and foreigners were becoming more relevant than those distinguishing Mauritians from each other (Eriksen, 1988: chapter 5; cf. also Eriksen, 1998).

There has been a perceptible growth in interethnic marriages. When the family has little to offer by way of material security, 'love marriages' become more viable than they were. What will be the identity of the children of such alliances? In many cases, the children are classified as 'some kind of Creoles', since the Creoles are regarded as a 'mixed' ethnic category. For many of these children, it would be a hopeless project to trace their genealogies and thereby establish their ancestry. There are individuals like the journalist who can count no less than nine different 'peoples' among his ancestors – from Brittany to Canton!

If the trend of interethnic marriages continues, an ultimate effect may be the end of ethnicity as we know it today. There will be too many 'anomalous' individuals around to maintain clear-cut distinctions. As a consequence, loyalties may be increasingly related to local history, culture and identities rather than to 'ancestral cultures'. Maybe the majority of Mauritians will regard their 'ancestral culture' as that mixture of influences that has shaped Mauritius. And perhaps a majority of the population will regard Kreol – the only language which grew out of the interethnic encounters in Mauritius – as their ancestral language. A woman of Tamil origin explains that her ancestral language was Kreol, since her parents as well as her grandparents spoke it, 'and as far as I'm concerned, they are ancestral enough'. (How many generations must one go back in time in order to establish one's 'ancestry'? This, of course, is socially defined.)

This kind of scenario is possible but not inevitable. Calls for religious purity are common and new traditionalist movements are being formed, particularly in the countryside. The leaders of these movements rail against what they see as the decadence associated with urbanism, modernity and cultural homogenisation or 'Creolisation' (Eriksen, 2007c). The potential appeal of such movements depends on what they have to offer. If they can convince a sufficiently large number of people that they offer economic security and/or personal integrity, they may be successful. However, such a 'new wave of ethnicity' may divide the Mauritian population along unfamiliar lines, since its main base will probably be the countryside. The rural/urban or industrial/agricultural opposition may become more salient than the Creole/Hindu dichotomy.

There are two main factors militating against the fusion of ethnic categories. First, the family is still important in Mauritius, and parents are not likely to encourage mixed marriages. Second, religion is a strong factor in boundary maintenance. If the parties to an interethnic marriage practise different religions, the chances that the marriage will endure are relatively slim. The majority of stable mixed marriages involve couples who either belong to the same religion (by birth or by conversion) or for whom religion does not play an important part in their lives.

In addition, many Mauritians dislike the idea of the disappearance of distinctive 'cultures'. 'Keep the colours of the Mauritian rainbow distinct, and it will remain beautiful,' was the advice of the Catholic Archbishop of Mauritius at a meeting in 1991.

If it is easy to discern the end of ethnicity in persons, social contexts and the social structure of Mauritius, it is almost as easy to discover ethnic revitalisation. That, in fact, is what many anthropologists studying social change have done in various societies. Movements of ethnic revitalisation are much more spectacular than the quiet daily movement towards mutual accommodation in complex societies, and they are perhaps therefore more attractive as objects of study. This does not necessarily mean, however, that such movements are more representative than moves towards the end of ethnicity in particular societies. After all, seen through the perspective of *la longue durée*, the eventual disappearance of ethnic groups is no less certain than their appearance.

## THE EYE OF THE BEHOLDER

During the heyday of Marxist social science in the 1970s, numerous well-researched studies were published on classic 'plural societies' such as the US, Mauritius, Trinidad and Malaysia. Many of these studies seemed to show unequivocally that ethnic conflict and ethnic identity were surface phenomena which were ultimately determined by domestic class relations or by international imperialism. Few would argue in the same manner twenty years later, although the societies themselves may not have changed profoundly. This should serve as a reminder that the choice of an analytical perspective or 'research hypothesis' is not an innocent act. If one goes out to look for ethnicity, one will 'find' it and thereby contribute to constructing it. For this reason, a concern with the non-ethnic dimensions of polyethnic societies can be a healthy corrective and supplement to analyses of ethnicity.

The anthropological interest in ethnicity is not universal. In French anthropology, the concept of *ethnicité* has never caught on in the same way as the word ethnicity has in British and American anthropology (A.-C. Taylor, 1991; cf. de Heusch, 2000). The connotations of *ethnie* ('ethnic group') in French are sometimes uncomfortably close to obsolete notions of race or reifying notions of 'cultures'. This does not merely concern a difference in the choice of words; differences in terminology may (as we have seen in the case of ethnic labels) indicate differences in epistemology. When mainstream French anthropologists study what we would speak of as political ethnicity, they may subsume it under the study of politics in general; when concerned with ethnic identity processes and ideology, they may connect these issues with studies of identity and ideology in general (for example, Lévi-Strauss, 1977), rather than assuming that there is such a thing as an 'ethnic phenomenon' which merits elevation to the status of a comparative concept. Thus, in Pierre Bonté's and Michel Izard's massive *Dictionnaire de l'ethnologie et de l'anthropologie* (1991), there is no entry on *ethnicité*, but the subject is briefly treated under keywords such as *ethnie* and *ethnies minoritaires*. This difference should remind us that, when all is said and done, ethnicity is a social and cultural product which anthropologists contribute to creating. If we go to Mauritius, the Copperbelt or to the Peruvian highlands in search of gender, we shall no doubt find gender; the same holds good for, say, class, ideology and kinship systems. This reservation does not imply that the concept of ethnicity is not useful, only that the researcher's choice of key concepts directs the research in a way which influences the nature of the data.

A focus on ethnic processes enables us to investigate topics which are of crucial importance in social anthropology: the relationship between culture, identity and social organisation; the relationship between meaning and politics; the multivocality of symbols; processes of social classification; exclusion and marginalisation at the group level; the relationships between action and structure; structure and process; and continuity and change. Research on ethnicity has opened up exciting new fields in social anthropology, and it still has much to offer. Nonetheless, we ought to be critical enough to abandon the concept of ethnicity the moment it becomes a straitjacket rather than a tool for generating new understanding.

## FURTHER READING

Appadurai, Arjun (1996) *Modernity at Large: Cultural Dimensions of Globalization*. Minneapolis: University of Minnesota Press. A theoretically stimulating collection of articles on consumption, identity and the construction of place in an era characterised by mass migration and electronic mediation.

Urry, John (2000) *Sociology beyond Societies: Mobilities for the Twenty-first Century*. London: Routledge. One of the most accessible and lucid overviews of recent social theory, presenting important challenges to any research on groups and identities.

# Bibliography

Alghasi, Sharam, Thomas Hylland Eriksen and Halleh Ghorashi, eds (2009) *Paradoxes of Cultural Recognition: Perspectives from Northern Europe.* Aldershot: Ashgate.

Allen, Tim and John Eade (1998) 'Understanding ethnicity'. In Tim Allen and John Eade, eds, *Divided Europeans: Understanding Ethnicities in Conflict*, pp. 11–41. The Hague: Kluwer.

Ålund, Aleksandra (1997) *Multikultiungdom: Kön, etnicitet, identitet* (Multiculti youth: Gender, ethnicity, identity). Lund: Studentlitteratur.

—— and Carl-Ulrik Schierup (1991) *Paradoxes of Multiculturalism: Essays on Swedish Society.* Aldershot: Gower.

Anderson, Benedict (1991 [1983]) *Imagined Communities: Reflections on the Origins and Spread of Nationalism*, 2nd edn. London: Verso.

—— (1992) *Long-distance Nationalism: World Capitalism and the Rise of Identity Politics.* Amsterdam: Centre for Asian Studies.

—— (2001) 'Western nationalism and Eastern nationalism'. *New Left Review*, vol. 9, pp. 31–42.

Anthias, Floya and Nira Yuval-Davies, eds (1989) *Woman – Nation – State.* London: Macmillan.

Appadurai, Arjun (1996) *Modernity at Large: Cultural Dimensions of Globalization.* Minneapolis: University of Minnesota Press.

—— (2006) *Fear of Small Numbers: An Essay on the Geography of Anger.* Durham, NC: Duke University Press.

Archetti, Eduardo P. (1999) *Masculinities: Football, Polo and the Tango in Argentina.* Oxford: Berg.

Ardener, Edwin (1989a [1972]) 'Language, ethnicity and population'. In Edwin Ardener, *The Voice of Prophecy and Other Essays*, ed. Malcolm Chapman, pp. 65–71. Oxford: Blackwell.

—— (1989b [1974]) 'Social anthropology and population'. In Edwin Ardener, *The Voice of Prophecy and Other Essays*, ed. Malcolm Chapman, pp. 109–27. Oxford: Blackwell.

—— (1989c [1975]) 'Belief and the problem of women'. In Edwin Ardener, *The Voice of Prophecy and Other Essays*, ed. Malcolm Chapman, pp. 72–85. Oxford: Blackwell.

Arens, William (1978) *The Man-eating Myth: Anthropology and Anthropophagy.* Oxford: Oxford University Press.

Armstrong, John (1982) *Nations before Nationalism.* Chapel Hill: University of North Carolina Press.

Asante, Molefi Keti (1988) *Afrocentricity.* Trenton, NJ: Africa World Press.

Atran, Scott (1990) *Cognitive Foundations of Natural History: Towards an Anthropology of Science.* Cambridge: Cambridge University Press.

Bader, Veit (2001) 'Culture and identity'. *Ethnicities*, vol. 1 (2), pp. 251–73.

Bailey, F.G. (1968) 'Parapolitical systems'. In M.J. Swartz, ed., *Local-level Politics: Social and Cultural Perspectives*, pp. 281–93. Chicago: Aldine.

Balibar, Etienne (1991) 'Class racism'. In Etienne Balibar and Immanuel Wallerstein, *Race, Nation, Class: Ambiguous Identities*, pp. 204–16. London: Verso.

Bank, Leslie (2009) *Home Spaces, Street Styles: Contesting Power and Identity in a South African City*. London: Pluto.

Banks, Marcus (1996) *Ethnicity: Anthropological Constructions*. London: Routledge.

Banton, Michael (1967) *Race Relations*. London: Tavistock.

—— (1983) *Racial and Ethnic Competition*. Cambridge: Cambridge University Press.

—— (1987) *Racial Theories*. Cambridge: Cambridge University Press.

Barker, Martin (1981) *The New Racism: Conservatives and the Ideology of the Tribe*. London: Junction Books.

Barnard, Alan (2007) *Anthropology and the Bushman*. Oxford: Berg.

Barth, Fredrik (1956) 'Ecological relations of ethnic groups in Swat, north Pakistan'. *American Anthropologist*, vol. 58 (6), pp. 1079–89.

—— (1969a) 'Introduction'. In Fredrik Barth, ed., *Ethnic Groups and Boundaries: The Social Organization of Culture Difference*, pp. 9–38. Oslo: Universitetsforlaget.

—— ed. (1969b) *Ethnic Groups and Boundaries: The Social Organization of Culture Difference*. Oslo: Universitetsforlaget.

—— (1994) 'Enduring and emerging issues in the analysis of ethnicity'. In Hans Vermeulen and Cora Govers, eds, *The Anthropology of Ethnicity: Beyond 'Ethnic Groups and Boundaries'*, pp. 11–32. Amsterdam: Het Spinhuis.

Basch, Linda, Nina Glick Schiller and Cristina Szanton Blanc (1994) *Nations Unbound: Transnational Projects, Postcolonial Predicaments, and Deterritorialized Nation-States*. Langhorn, PA: Gordon & Breach.

Bateson, Gregory (1972a) 'Culture contact and schismogenesis'. In G. Bateson, *Steps to an Ecology of Mind*, pp. 61–72. Chicago: University of Chicago Press.

—— (1972b) *Steps to an Ecology of Mind*. New York: Chandler.

—— (1979) *Mind and Nature: A Necessary Unity*. Glasgow: Fontana.

Bauböck, Rainer (2001) 'Cherishing diversity and promoting political community'. *Ethnicities*, vol. 1 (1), pp. 109–15.

Bauman, Zygmunt (1993) *Postmodern Ethics*. Cambridge: Polity.

—— (1996) 'From pilgrim to tourist, or A short history of identity'. In Stuart Hall and Paul Du Gay, eds, *Questions of Cultural Identity*, pp. 18–36. London: SAGE.

Baumann, Gerd (1996) *Contesting Culture: Discourses of Identity in Multi-ethnic London*. Cambridge: Cambridge University Press.

—— (1999) *The Multicultural Riddle: Rethinking National, Ethnic and Religious Identities*. London: Routledge.

—— (2001) 'Culture and collectivity'.

Beck, Ulrich, Anthony Giddens and Scott Lash (1994) *Reflexive Modernization: Politics, Tradition and Aesthetics in the Modern Social Order*. Cambridge: Polity.

—— (2001) 'Culture and collectivity'. *Ethnicities*, vol. 1 (2), pp. 274–81.

Benedict, Burton (1965) *Mauritius: Problems of a Plural Society*. London: Pall Mall.

Benoist, Jean-Marie (1977) 'Facettes de l'identité'. In Claude Lévi-Strauss, ed., *L'Identité*, pp. 13–23. Paris: Presses Universitaires Françaises.

Bentley, G. Carter (1987) 'Ethnicity and practice'. *Comparative Studies in Society and History*, vol. 29 (1), pp. 24–55.

Berman, Marshall (1982) *All That is Solid Melts into Air: The Experience of Modernity*. London: Verso.

Berthelsen, Christian (1990) 'Greenlandic in schools'. In Dirmid R.F. Collis, ed., *Arctic Languages: An Awakening*, pp. 333–40. Paris: Unesco.

Bhabha, Homi K., ed. (1990) *Nation and Narration*. London: Routledge.

Billig, Michael (1995) *Banal Nationalism*. London: SAGE.

Birch, Anthony H. (1989) *Nationalism and National Integration*. London: Unwin Hyman.

Blom, Jan-Petter (1969) 'Ethnic and cultural differentiation'. In Fredrik Barth, ed., *Ethnic Groups and Boundaries: The Social Organization of Culture Difference*, pp. 75–85. Oslo: Universitetsforlaget.

Bonté, Pierre and Michel Izard, eds (1991) *Dictionnaire de l'ethnologie et de l'anthropologie*. Paris: Presses Universitaires Françaises.

Boswell, Rosabelle (2006) *Le Malaise Créole: Ethnic Identity in Mauritius*. New York: Berghahn.

Bourdieu, Pierre (1977) *Outline of a Theory of Practice*, trans. Richard Nice. Cambridge: Cambridge University Press.

—— (1984) *Distinction: A Social Critique of the Judgement of Taste*, trans. Richard Nice. London: Routledge.

Bowen, John (2007) *Why the French Don't Like Headscarves: Islam, the State, and Public Space*. Princeton, NJ: Princeton University Press.

Boyer, Dominic and Claudio Lomnitz (2005) 'Intellectuals and nationalism: Anthropological engagements'. *Annual Review of Anthropology*, vol. 34, pp. 105–20.

Brah, Avtar (1996) *Cartographies of Diaspora: Contesting Identities*. London: Routledge.

Brass, Paul, ed. (1985) *Ethnic Groups and the State*. London: Croom Helm.

Brereton, Bridget (1979) *Race Relations in Colonial Trinidad 1870–1900*. Cambridge: Cambridge University Press.

Bringa, Tone (1996) *Being Muslim the Bosnian Way: Identity and Community in a Central Bosnian Village*. Princeton, NJ: Princeton University Press.

Bromley, Yuri (1974) 'The term "ethnos" and its definition'. In Yuri Bromley, ed., *Soviet Ethnology and Anthropology Today*, pp. 55–72. The Hague: Mouton.

Brubaker, Rogers (2002) 'Ethnicity without groups'. *Archives Européennes de Sociologie*, vol. 43 (2), pp. 163–89.

Bulmer, Ralph (1967) 'Why is the cassowary not a bird? A problem of zoological taxonomy among the Karam of the New Guinea highlands'. *Man* (n.s.), vol. 2 (1), pp. 5–25.

Buss, David M., ed. (2005) *The Handbook of Evolutionary Psychology*. Hoboken, NJ: Wiley.

Çaglar, Ayse (1995) 'McDöner: Döner Kebap and the social positioning struggle of German Turks'. In Janeen A. Costa and Gary J. Bamossy, eds, *Marketing in a Multicultural World*, pp. 209–30. London: SAGE.

Caistor, Nick (1992) 'Whose war is it anyway? The Argentine press during the South Atlantic conflict'. In James Aulich, ed., *Framing the Falklands War: Nationhood, Culture and Identity*, pp. 50–7. Milton Keynes: Open University Press.

Campbell, Ben (2007) 'Media storylines of culturally hybrid persons and nation'. In Peter Wade, ed., *Race, Ethnicity and Nation: Perspectives from Kinship and Genetics*, pp. 169–86. Oxford: Berghahn.

Campbell, John R. (2004) Ethnic minorities and development: A prospective look at the situation of African pastoralists and hunter-gatherers. *Ethnicities*, vol. 4 (1), pp. 5–26.

Carsten, Janet (2004) *After Kinship*. Cambridge: Cambridge University Press.

Castells, Manuel (1996) *The Rise of the Network Society*. Oxford: Blackwell.

—— (2001) *The Internet Galaxy: Reflexions on the Internet, Business and Society*. Oxford: Oxford University Press.

Cavalli-Sforza, Luca, Paolo Menozzi and Alberto Piazza, eds (1994) *The History and Geography of Human Genes*. Princeton, NJ: Princeton University Press.

Chagnon, Napoleon (1983) *Yanomamö: The Fierce People*, 3rd edn. New York: Holt, Rinehart & Winston.

Chapman, Malcolm, Maryon McDonald and Elizabeth Tonkin (1989) 'Introduction – history and social anthropology'. In Elizabeth Tonkin, Maryon McDonald and Malcolm Chapman, eds, *History and Ethnicity*, pp. 1–21. London: Routledge.

Chomsky, Noam (2001) *9–11*. New York: Seven Stories Press.

Christiansen, Flemming and Ulf Hedetoft (2004) 'Introduction'. In Flemming Christiansen and Ulf Hedetoft, eds, *The Politics of Multiple Belonging: Ethnicity and Nationalism in Europe and East Asia*, pp. 1–23. Aldershot: Ashgate.

Chua, Amy (2004) *World on Fire: How Exporting Free Market Democracy Breeds Ethnic Hatred and Global Instability*. New York: Anchor.

Cohen, Abner (1969) *Custom and Politics in Urban Africa*. London: Routledge.

—— (1974a) 'Introduction: the lesson of ethnicity'. In Abner Cohen, ed., *Urban Ethnicity*, pp. ix–xxii. London: Tavistock.

—— (1974b) *Two-dimensional Man*. London: Tavistock.

—— (1981) *The Politics of Elite Culture: Explorations in the Dramaturgy of Power in a Modern African Society*. Berkeley: University of California Press.

Cohen, Anthony P. (1985) *The Symbolic Construction of Community*. London: Routledge.

—— (1994) *Self Consciousness: An Alternative Anthropology of Identity*. London: Routledge.

—— ed. (2000) *Signifying Identities: Anthropological Perspectives on Boundaries and Contested Values*. London: Routledge.

Cohen, Ronald (1978) 'Ethnicity: Problem and focus in anthropology', *Annual Review of Anthropology*, vol. 7, pp. 379–404.

Collins, Patricia Hill (2001) 'Like one of the family: Race, ethnicity, and the paradox of US national identity'. *Ethnic and Racial Studies*, vol. 24 (1), pp. 3–28.

—— (2004) 'Black nationalism and African American ethnicity'. In Stephen May, Tariq Modood and Judith Squires, eds, *Ethnicity, Nationalism, and Minority Rights*, pp. 96–119. Cambridge: Cambridge University Press.

Comaroff, John and Jean Comaroff (1992) *Ethnography and the Historical Imagination*. Boulder, CO: Westview Press.

—— (2009) *Ethnicity, Inc*. Chicago: University of Chicago Press.

Connor, Walker (1978) 'A nation is a nation, is a state, is an ethnic group, is a …' *Ethnic and Racial Studies*, vol. 1 (4), pp. 378–400.

Cowan, Jane, Marie-Bédédicte Dembour and Richard A. Wilson, eds (2001) *Culture and Rights: Anthropological Perspectives*. Cambridge: Cambridge University Press.

Cox, Oliver (1976) *Race Relations: Elements and Social Dynamics*. Detroit, MI: Wayne State University Press.

Crèvecoeur, J. Hector St John (1904 [1788]). *Letters from an American Farmer*. New York: Fox, Duffield.

Dahya, Badr (1974) 'The nature of Pakistani ethnicity in industrial cities in Britain'. In Abner Cohen, ed., *Urban Ethnicity*, pp. 77–118. London: Tavistock.

Davis, Mike (2006) *Planet of Slums*. London: Verso.

De Vos, George and Lola Romanucci-Ross, eds (1975) *Ethnic Identity: Cultural Communities and Change*. Palo Alto, CA: Mayfield.

Despres, Leo (1975a) 'Ethnicity and resource competition in Guyanese society'. In Leo Despres, ed. *Ethnicity and Resource Competition in Plural Societies*, pp. 87–118. The Hague: Mouton.

—— ed. (1975b) *Ethnicity and Resource Competition in Plural Societies*. The Hague: Mouton

Douglas, Mary (1966) *Purity and Danger*. London: Routledge.

—— (1970) *Natural Symbols*. London: Barrie & Rockliff.

Dumont, Louis (1992) *L'Idéologie allemande*. Paris: Seuil.

Durkheim, Emile and Marcel Mauss (1964 [1903]) *Primitive Classification*, trans. Rodney Needham. London: Cohen & West.

Duroselle, Jean-Baptiste (1990) *Europe – A History of its Peoples*. Harmondsworth: Penguin.

Eidheim, Harald (1969) 'When ethnic identity is a social stigma'. In Fredrik Barth, ed., *Ethnic Groups and Boundaries: The Social Organization of Culture Difference*, pp. 39–57. Oslo: Universitetsforlaget.

—— (1971) *Aspects of the Lappish Minority Situation*. Oslo: Universitetsforlaget.

—— (1992) *Stages in the Development of Sami Selfhood*. Working Paper no. 7. Dept. of Social Anthropology, University of Oslo.

Eide, Elisabeth, Risto Kunelius and Angela Phillips, eds (2009) *Transnational Media Events: The Mohammed Cartoons and the Imagined Clash of Civilizations*. Gothenburg: Nordicom.

Epstein, A.L. (1958) *Politics in an Urban African Community*. Manchester: Manchester University Press.

—— (1978) *Ethos and Identity: Three Studies in Ethnicity*. London: Tavistock.

—— (1992) *Scenes from African Urban Life: Collected Copperbelt Essays*. Edinburgh: Edinburgh University Press.

Eriksen, Thomas Hylland (1986) 'Creole culture and social change'. *Journal of Mauritian Studies*, vol. 1 (2), pp. 59–72.

—— (1988) *Communicating Cultural Difference and Identity: Ethnicity and Nationalism in Mauritius*. Occasional Papers in Social Anthropology, 16. Dept. of Social Anthropology, University of Oslo.

—— (1991a) 'The cultural contexts of ethnic differences'. *Man*, vol. 26 (1), pp. 127–44.

—— (1991b) 'Ethnicity versus nationalism'. *Journal of Peace Research*, vol. 28 (3), pp. 263–78.

—— (1992a) *Us and Them in Modern Societies: Ethnicity and Nationalism in Trinidad, Mauritius and Beyond*. Oslo: Universitetsforlaget.

—— (1992b) 'Multiple traditions and the problem of cultural integration'. *Ethnos*, vol. 57 (1–2), pp. 5–30.

—— (1993a) 'Formal and informal nationalism'. *Ethnic and Racial Studies*, vol. 16 (1), pp. 1–25.

—— (1993b) 'In which sense do cultural islands exist?' *Social Anthropology*, 1, pp. 133–46.

—— (1998) *Common Denominators: Politics, Ideology and Compromise in Mauritius*. Oxford: Berg.

—— (2000) 'Ethnicity and culture: A second look'. In Herman Roodenburg and Regina Bendix, eds, *Managing Ethnicity*, pp. 185–205. Amsterdam: Het Spinhuis.

—— (2001a) *Tyranny of the Moment: Slow and Fast Time in the Information Age*. London: Pluto.

—— (2001b) 'Ethnic identity, national identity and intergroup conflict: The significance of personal experiences'. In Richard D. Ashmore, Lee Jussim and David Wilder, eds, *Social Identity, Intergroup Conflict, and Conflict Reduction*, pp. 42–70. Oxford: Oxford University Press.

—— (2001c) 'Between universalism and relativism: A critique of the UNESCO concept of culture'. In Jane Cowan, Marie-Bénédicte Dembour and Richard A. Wilson, eds, *Culture and Rights*, pp. 127–48. Cambridge: Cambridge University Press.

—— ed. (2003) *Globalisation – Studies in Anthropology*. London: Pluto.

—— (2004a) 'Traditionalism and neoliberalism: The Norwegian folk dress in the 21st century'. In Erich Kasten, ed., *Properties of Culture – Culture as Property*, pp. 267–87. Berlin: Dietrich Reimer Verlag.

—— (2004b) 'The case for non-ethnic nations'. *Nations and Nationalism*, vol. 10 (1–2): 49–62.

—— (2004c) 'Ethnicity, class and the 1999 Mauritian riots'. In Stephen May, Tariq Modood and Judith Squires, eds, *Ethnicity, Nationalism, and Minority Rights*, pp. 78–95. Cambridge: Cambridge University Press.

—— (2006) *Engaging Anthropology: The Case for a Public Presence*. Oxford: Berg.

—— (2007a) 'Nationalism and the Internet'. *Nations and Nationalism*, vol. 13 (1), pp. 1–18.

——(2007b) *Globalization: The Key Concepts*. Oxford: Berg.

—— (2007c) 'Creolization in anthropological theory and in Mauritius'. In Charles Stewart, ed., *Creolization: History, Ethnography, Theory*, pp. 153–77. Walnut Creek, CA: Left Coast Press.

—— and Finn Sivert Nielsen (2001) *A History of Anthropology*. London: Pluto.

—— and Richard Jenkins, eds (2007) *Flag, Nation and Symbolism in Europe and America*. London: Routledge.

Evans-Pritchard, E.E. (1940) *The Nuer*. Oxford: Clarendon Press.

Fagerlid, Cicilie (2002) 'Beyond ethnic boundaries? British Asian cosmopolitans'. M.Phil. thesis, University of Oslo.

Fallers, Lloyd A. (1974) *The Social Anthropology of the Nation-State*. Chicago: Aldine.

Fardon, Richard (1987) '"African ethnogenesis": Limits to the comparability of ethnic phenomena'. In Ladislav Holy, ed., *Comparative Anthropology*, pp. 168–88. Oxford: Blackwell.

Featherstone, Mike, ed. (1990) *Global Culture: Nationalism, Globalization and Modernity*. London: SAGE.

Feit, Harvey (1985) 'Legitimation and autonomy in James Bay – Cree responses to hydro-electric development'. In Noel Dyck, ed., *Indigenous Peoples and the Nation-State*, Memorial University of Newfoundland papers, no. 14, pp. 27–60. St John's, Newfoundland: Memorial University of Newfoundland.

Fenton, Steve (1999) *Ethnicity: Racism, Class and Culture*. London: Macmillan.

Ferguson, James (1999) *Expectations of Modernity: Myth and Meanings of Urban Life on the Zambian Copperbelt*. Berkeley: University of California Press.

Fishman, Joshua A., V.C. Nahirny, J.E. Hofman and R.G. Hayden (1966) *Language Loyalty in the United States*. The Hague: Mouton.

Fitzgerald, Thomas K. (1993) *Metaphors of Identity: A Culture–Communication Dialogue*. New York: SUNY Press.

Forsythe, Diana (1989) 'German identity and the problem of history'. In Elizabeth Tonkin, Maryon McDonald and Malcolm Chapman, eds, *History and Ethnicity*, pp. 137–56. London: Routledge.

Forte, Maximilian (2009) 'Introduction: Indigeneities and cosmopolitanism'. In Maximilian Forte, ed., *Indigenous Cosmopolitans: Transnational and Transcultural Indigeneity in the Twenty-first Century*. New York: Peter Lang.

Fox, Jonathan (1999) 'Clash of civilizations or clash of religions: Which is a more important determinant of ethnic conflict?', *Ethnicities*, vol. 1 (3), pp. 295–366.

Friedman, Jonathan (1987) 'Prolegomena to the adventures of Phallus in Blunderland: An anti-anti discourse'. *Culture and History*, vol. 1, pp. 31–49.

—— (1990) 'Being in the world: Globalization and localization'. In Mike Featherstone, ed., *Global Culture*, pp. 311–28. London: SAGE.

—— (1991) 'Narcissism, roots and postmodernity: The constitution of selfhood in the global crisis'. In Scott Lash and Jonathan Friedman, eds, *Modernity and Identity*, pp. 331–66. Oxford: Blackwell.

—— (1994) *Global Culture and Local Process*. London: SAGE.

Frøystad, Kathinka (2000) 'Beneath Hindu nationalism: Caste, class and shifting faces of "Hinduness" in a North Indian city'. PhD thesis, University of Oslo.

Fuglerud, Øivind (1999) *Life on the Outside: The Tamil Diaspora and Long-distance Nationalism*. London: Pluto.

Furnivall, John S. (1948) *Colonial Policy and Practice: A Comparative Study of Burma and Netherlands India*. Cambridge: Cambridge University Press.

Gans, Herbert J. (1979) 'Symbolic ethnicity: The future of ethnic groups and cultures in America'. *Ethnic and Racial Studies*, vol. 2 (1), pp. 1–20.

Geertz, Clifford (1973 [1963]) 'The integrative revolution: Primordial sentiments and civil politics in the new states'. In Clifford Geertz, *The Interpretation of Cultures*, pp. 255–310. New York: Basic Books.

—— (1988) *Works and Lives: The Anthropologist as Author*. Cambridge: Polity.

—— (1994) 'The uses of diversity'. In Robert Borofsky, ed., *Assessing Cultural Anthropology*, pp. 454–65. New York: McGraw-Hill

Gellner, Ernest (1964) *Thought and Change*. London: Weidenfeld & Nicolson.

—— (1978) 'Scale and nation'. In Fredrik Barth, ed., *Scale and Social Organization*, pp. 133–49. Oslo: Universitetsforlaget.

—— (1983) *Nations and Nationalism*. Oxford: Blackwell.

—— (1991) 'Le Nationalisme en apesanteur'. *Terrain*, vol. 17, pp. 7–16.

—— (1992) *Postmodernism, Reason and Religion*. London: Routledge.

—— (1997) *Nationalism*. London: Weidenfeld & Nicolson.

Giddens, Anthony (1979) *Central Problems in Social Theory*. London: Macmillan.

—— (1984) *The Constitution of Society*. Cambridge: Polity.

—— (1985) *The Nation-state and Violence*. Cambridge: Polity.

—— (1990) *The Consequences of Modernity*. Cambridge: Polity.

—— (1991) *Modernity and Self-identity*. Cambridge: Polity.

Gilroy, Paul (1987) *There Ain't No Black in the Union Jack*. London: Routledge.

—— (2000) *Between Camps: Race, Identity and Nationalism at the End of the Colour Line*. London: Allen Lane.

—— Lawrence Grossberg and Angela McRobbie, eds (2000) *Without Guarantees: In Honour of Stuart Hall*. London: Verso.

Giulianotti, Richard and Roland Robertson (2009) *Globalization and Football*. London: SAGE.

Glazer, Nathan and Daniel A. Moynihan (1963) *Beyond the Melting-pot*. Cambridge, MA: Harvard University Press.

—— , eds (1975) *Ethnicity: Theory and Experience*. Cambridge, MA: Harvard University Press.

Gluckman, Max (1961) 'Anthropological problems arising from the African industrial revolution'. In Aidan Southall, ed., *Social Change in Modern Africa*, pp. 67–83. London: Oxford University Press.

—— (1982 [1956]) *Conflict and Custom in Africa*. Oxford: Blackwell.

Goffman, Erving (1959) *The Presentation of Self in Everyday Life*. New York: Doubleday.

Goodale, Mark, ed. (2009) *Human Rights: An Anthropological Reader*. Oxford: Blackwell.

Goody, Jack (1977) *The Domestication of the Savage Mind*. Cambridge: Cambridge University Press.

Grillo, Ralph (1980) 'Introduction'. In Ralph Grillo, ed., *'Nation' and 'State' in Europe*. London: Academic Press.

—— (1998) *Pluralism and the Politics of Difference: State, Culture, and Ethnicity in Comparative Perspective*. Oxford: Oxford University Press.

Grønhaug, Reidar (1974) *Micro–Macro Relations: Social Organization in Antalya, Southern Turkey*. Bergen: Bergen Studies in Social Anthropology, no. 7.

Guibernau, Montserrat (2004) 'Anthony D. Smith on nations and national identity: A critical assessment', *Nations and Nationalism*, vol. 10 (1/2), pp. 125–42.

—— and John Rex, eds (1997) *The Ethnicity Reader: Nationalism, Multiculturalism and Migration*. Cambridge: Polity.

Gulbrandsen, Ørnulf (1992) 'On the problem of egalitarianism: The Kalahari San in transition'. In Reidar Grønhaug, Gunnar Haaland and Georg Henriksen, eds, *The Ecology of Choice and Symbols: Essays in Honour of Fredrik Barth*, pp. 81–110. Bergen: Alma Mater.

Haaland, Gunnar (1969) 'Economic determinants in ethnic processes'. In Fredrik Barth, ed., *Ethnic Groups and Boundaries: The Social Organization of Culture Difference*, pp. 58–74. Oslo: Universitetsforlaget.

—— (1992) 'Cultural content and ethnic boundaries'. In Reidar Grønhaug, Gunnar Haaland and Georg Henriksen, eds, *The Ecology of Choice and Symbols: Essays in Honour of Fredrik Barth*, pp. 155–79. Bergen: Alma Mater.

Haley, Alex (1998 [1976]) *Roots*. New York: Vintage.

Hall, Stuart (1991) 'Old and new identities, old and new ethnicities'. In Anthony D. King, ed., *Culture, Globalization and the World-System*, pp. 41–68. London: Macmillan.

—— (2000) 'Conclusion: The multi-cultural question'. In Barnor Hesse, ed., *Un/settled Multiculturalisms: Diasporas, Entanglements, Transruptions*, pp. 201–41. London: Zed.

Handelman, Don (1977) 'The organization of ethnicity'. *Ethnic Groups*, vol. 1, pp. 187–200.

—— (1990) *Models and Mirrors: Towards an Anthropology of Public Events*. Cambridge: Cambridge University Press.

Handler, Richard (1988) *Nationalism and the Politics of Culture in Quebec*. Madison: University of Wisconsin Press.

—— and Daniel Segal (1992) 'How European is nationalism?', *Social Analysis*, vol. 32, pp. 1–15.

Hann, Chris, ed. (2002) *Postsocialism: Ideals, Ideologies and Practices in Eurasia*. London: Routledge.

Hannerz, Ulf (1980) *Exploring the City: Inquiries Toward and Urban Anthropology*. New York: Columbia University Press.

—— (1990) 'Cosmopolitans and locals in world culture'. In Mike Featherstone, ed., *Global Culture: Nationalism, Globalization and Modernity*, pp. 237–52. London: SAGE.

—— (1992) *Cultural Complexity: Studies in the Social Organization of Meaning*. New York: Columbia University Press.

—— (1996) *Transnational Connections*. London: Routledge.

Hansen, Thomas Blom (1999) *The Saffron Wave: Democracy and Hindu Nationalism in Modern India*. Princeton, NJ: Princeton University Press.

Harris, Nigel (2002) *Thinking the Unthinkable: The Immigrant Myth Exposed*. London: I.B. Tauris.

Harrison, Simon (1999) 'Identity as a scarce resource'. *Social Anthropology*, vol. 7 (3), pp. 239–52.

—— (2002) 'The politics of resemblance: Ethnicity, trademarks, head-hunting'. *Journal of the Royal Anthropological Institute*, 8, pp. 211–32.

Heiberg, Marianne (1989) *The Making of the Basque Nation*. Cambridge: Cambridge University Press.

Held, David, Anthony McGrew, David Goldblatt and Jonathan Perraton (1999) *Global Transformations: Politics, Economics and Culture*. Cambridge: Polity.

Henriksen, Georg (1992) 'The experience of social worth as a force in inter-ethnic relations'. In Reidar Grønhaug, Gunnar Haaland and Georg Henriksen, eds, *The Ecology of Choice and Symbols: Essays in Honour of Fredrik Barth*, pp. 407–25. Bergen: Alma Mater.

Herzfeld, Michael (1987) *Anthropology through the Looking-glass: Critical Ethnography in the Margins of Europe*. Cambridge: Cambridge University Press.

—— (1997) *Cultural Intimacy: Social Poetics in the Nation-State*. New York: Routledge.

Heusch, Luc de (2000) '*L'Ethnie:* The vicissitudes of a concept'. *Social Anthropology*, vol. 8 (2), pp. 99–116.

Hirschfeld, Lawrence (1998) *Race in the Making: Cognition, Culture, and the Child's Construction of Human Kinds*. Cambridge, MA: MIT Press.

Hirschmann, Alfred O. (1970) *Exit, Voice, Loyalty: Responses to Decline in Firms, Organizations and States*. Cambridge, MA: Harvard University Press.

Hobsbawm, Eric (1977) 'Some reflections on "The Break-up of Britain"'. *New Left Review*, vol. 105, pp. 3–23.

—— (1983) 'Introduction: Inventing traditions'. In Eric Hobsbawm and Terence Ranger, eds, *The Invention of Tradition*, pp. 1–14. Cambridge: Cambridge University Press.

—— (1990) *Nations and Nationalism since the 1780s: Programme, Myth, Reality*. Cambridge: Cambridge University Press.

Holy, Ladislav (1996) *The Little Czech and the Great Czech Nation: National Identity and the Post-Communist Social Transformation*. Cambridge: Cambridge University Press.

—— and Milan Stuchlik (1983) *Actions, Norms and Representations: Foundations of Anthropological Inquiry*. Cambridge: Cambridge University Press.

Horowitz, Donald L. (1985) *Ethnic Groups in Conflict*. Berkeley, CA: University of California Press.

Hovland, Arild (1996) *Moderne urfolk: Samisk ungdom i bevegelse* (Modern indigenes: Sami youth on the move). Oslo: Cappelen Akademisk Forlag.

Howell, Signe and Marit Melhuus (2007) 'Race, biology and culture in contemporary Norway: Identity and belonging in adoption, donor gametes and immigration'. In Peter Wade, ed., *Race, Ethnicity and Nation: Perspectives from Kinship and Genetics*, pp. 53–72. Oxford: Berghahn.

—— and Roy Willis, eds (1989) *Societies at Peace*. London: Routledge.

Hutchinson, John (1994) *Modern Nationalism*. London: Fontana.

Huntington, Samuel (1996) *The Clash of Civilizations and the Making of a New World Order*. New York: Simon & Schuster.

Ingold, Tim (1993) 'The art of translation in a continuous world'. In Gísli Pálsson, ed., *Beyond Boundaries: Understanding, Translation and Anthropological Discourse*, pp. 210–30. Oxford: Berg.

—— (1996) 'The concept of society is theoretically obsolete'. In Tim Ingold, ed., *Key Debates in Anthropology*, pp. 55–98. London: Routledge.

Jenkins, Richard (1986) 'Social anthropological models of inter-ethnic relations'. In John Rex and David Mason, eds, *Theories of Race and Race Relations*, pp. 170–86. Cambridge: Cambridge University Press.

—— (2002) 'Ethnicity and nationalism in the modern world'. In Jeremy MacClancy, ed., *Exotic No More: Anthropology on the Front Lines*, pp. 114–28. Chicago: University of Chicago Press.

—— (2007) *Social Identity*, 3rd edn. London: Routledge.

—— (2008) *Rethinking Ethnicity*, 2nd edn. London: SAGE.

Joyce, James (1984 [1922]) *Ulysses*. Harmondsworth: Penguin.

Just, Roger (1989) 'Triumph of the ethnos'. In Elizabeth Tonkin, Maryon McDonald and Malcolm Chapman, eds, *History and Ethnicity*, pp. 71–88. London: Routledge.

Kapferer, Bruce (1988) *Legends of People, Myths of State: Violence, Intolerance and Political Culture in Sri Lanka and Australia*. Washington, DC: Smithsonian Institute Press.

—— (1989) 'Nationalist ideology and a comparative anthropology'. *Ethnos*, vol. 54, pp. 161–99.

—— (2001) 'Star Wars: About anthropology, culture and globalisation'. *Suomen Antropologi*, vol. 26 (3), pp. 2–29.

Kasten, Erich, ed. (2004) *Properties of Culture – Culture as Property*. Berlin: Dietrich Reimer Verlag.

Khan, Aisha (1997) 'Homeland, motherland: Authenticity, legitimacy and ideologies of place among Muslims in Trinidad'. In Peter van der Veer, ed., *Nation and Migration*, pp. 93–131. Philadelphia: University of Pennsylvania Press.

Klass, Morton (1991) *Singing with Sai Baba: The Politics of Revitalization in Trinidad*. Boulder, CO: Westview Press.

Kroeber, Alfred and Clyde Kluckhohn (1952) *Culture: A Critical Review of Concepts and Definitions*. Cambridge, MA: Harvard University Press.

Krohn-Hansen, Christian (2003) 'Into our time: The anthropology of political life in the era of globalisation'. In Thomas Hylland Eriksen, ed., *Globalisation – Studies in Anthropology*, pp. 77–98. London: Pluto.

Kuper, Adam (2005) *The Invention of Primitive Society. Transformations of an Illusion*, 2nd edition. London: Routledge.

Kuter, Lois (1989) 'Breton vs. French: Language and the opposition of political, economic, social and cultural values'. In Nancy Dorian, ed., *Investigating*

*Obsolescence: Studies in Language Contraction and Death*, pp. 75–90. Cambridge: Cambridge University Press.

Kymlicka, Will (1995) *Multicultural Citizenship*. Oxford: Oxford University Press.

La Piere, R. (1934) 'Attitudes versus actions'. *Social Forces*, vol. 13, pp. 230–7.

Lal, Barbara Ballis (1986) 'The "Chicago School" of American sociology, symbolic interactionism, and race relations theory'. In David Mason and John Rex, eds, *Theories of Race and Ethnic Relations*, pp. 280–99. Cambridge: Cambridge University Press.

Lash, Scott and Jonathan Friedman, eds (1991) *Modernity and Identity*. Oxford: Blackwell.

Leach, Edmund R. (1954) *Political Systems of Highland Burma*. London: Athlone.

Lévi-Strauss, Claude (1962) *La Pensée sauvage*. Paris: Plon. (English edition: *The Savage Mind*, University of Chicago Press, 1966.)

—— ed. (1977) *L'Identité*. Paris: Presses Universitaires Françaises.

Lewis, Ioan M. (1985) *Social Anthropology in Perspective: The Relevance of Social Anthropology*, 2nd edn. Cambridge: Cambridge University Press.

Liebkind, Karmela, ed. (1989) *New Identities in Europe*. Aldershot: Gower.

Lien, Marianne E. and Marit Melhuus, eds (2007) *Holding Worlds Together: Ethnographies of Knowing and Belonging*. New York: Berghahn.

Little, Kenneth (1978) 'Countervailing influences in African ethnicity: A less apparent factor'. In Brian du Toit, ed., *Ethnicity in Modern Africa*, pp. 175–89 Boulder, CO: Westview Press.

Llobera, Josip (1995) *The God of Modernity: The Development of Nationalism in Western Europe*. Oxford: Berg.

Lock, Margaret (1990) 'On being ethnic: The politics of identity breaking and making in Canada, or, *Nevra* on Sunday'. *Culture, Medicine and Psychiatry*, vol. 14, pp. 237–54.

Lowenthal, David (1985) *The Past Is a Foreign Country*. Cambridge: Cambridge University Press.

MacClancy, Jeremy, ed. (1996) *Sport, Identity and Ethnicity*. Oxford: Berg.

McCrone, David (1998) *The Sociology of Nationalism: Tomorrow's Ancestors*. London: Routledge.

McDonald, Maryon (1989) *'We are not French!' Language, Culture and Identity in Brittany*. London: Routledge.

Mach, Zdzislav (1993) *Symbols, Conflict, and Identity. Essays in Political Anthropology*. New York: SUNY Press.

Maleseviç, Sinisa and Mark Haugaard, eds (2007) *Ernest Gellner and Contemporary Social Thought*. Cambridge: Cambridge University Press.

May, Stephen, ed. (1999) *Critical Multiculturalism*. London: Routledge.

—— Tariq Modood and Judith Squires, eds (2004) *Ethnicity, Nationalism, and Minority Rights*. Cambridge: Cambridge University Press.

Mayall, David (2003) *History of Gypsy Identities*. London: Routledge.

Maybury-Lewis, David (1984) 'Living in Leviathan: Ethnic groups and the state'. In David Maybury-Lewis, ed., *The Prospects for Plural Societies*, pp. 220–31. Washington, DC: American Ethnological Society.

Mayer, Philip (1961) *Townsmen or Tribesmen: Conservatism and the Process of Urbanization in a South African City*. Cape Town: Oxford University Press.

Miller, Daniel and Don Slater (2000) *The Internet: An Ethnographic Approach*. Oxford: Berg.

Minority Rights Group (1990) *World Directory of Minorities*. London: Longman.

Mitchell, J. Clyde (1956) *The Kalela Dance*, Rhodes-Livingstone papers no. 27. Manchester: Manchester University Press.
—— (1966) 'Theoretical orientations in African urban studies'. In Michael Banton, ed., *The Social Anthropology of Complex Societies*, pp. 37–68. London: Tavistock.
—— (1974) 'Perceptions of ethnicity and ethnic behaviour: An empirical exploration'. In Abner Cohen, ed., *Urban Ethnicity*, pp. 1–26. London: Tavistock.
Mittelholzer, Edgar (1979 [1950]) *A Morning at the Office*. London: Heinemann.
Mittelman, James (2001) 'Globalization: Captors and Captives'. In James Mittelman and Norani Othman, eds, *Capturing Globalization*, pp. 1–17. London: Routledge.
Modood, Tariq (1992) 'British Asian Muslims and the Rushdie affair'. In James Donald and Ali Rattansi, eds, *'Race', Culture and Difference*, pp. 260–77. London: SAGE.
Moerman, Michael (1965) 'Who are the Lue? Ethnic identification in a complex civilization'. *American Anthropologist*, vol. 67, pp. 1215–29.
Mosse, George L. (1985) *Nationalism and Sexuality*. Madison: University of Wisconsin Press.
Naipaul, V.S. (1969) *The Loss of El Dorado*. London: André Deutsch.
—— (1973) *The Overcrowded Barracoon*. Harmondsworth: Penguin.
Nairn, Tom (1977) *The Break-up of Britain*. London: New Left Books.
Nash, Manning (1988) *The Cauldron of Ethnicity in the Modern World*. Chicago: University of Chicago Press.
Neumann, Iver B. and Jennifer M. Welsh (1991) 'The Other in European self-definition: A critical addendum to the literature on international society'. *Review of International Studies*, vol. 17 (4), pp. 327–48.
Nietzsche, Friedrich (1988 [1880]) *A Nietzsche Reader*, ed. and trans. R.J. Hollingdale. Harmondsworth: Penguin.
Nimni, Ephraim (1991) *Marxism and Nationalism*. London: Pluto.
Novak, Michael (1971) *The Rise of the Unmeltable Ethnics*. New York: Macmillan.
O'Brien, Jay (1986) 'Toward a reconstitution of ethnicity: Capitalist expansion and cultural dynamics in Sudan'. *American Anthropologist*, vol. 88, pp. 898–906.
Okamura, Jonathan (1981) 'Situational ethnicity'. *Ethnic and Racial Studies*, vol. 4, pp. 452–63.
Okely, Judith (1983) *The Traveller-Gypsies*. Cambridge: Cambridge University Press.
Okin, Susan (1997) 'Is multiculturalism bad for women?' *Boston Review*, Oct./Nov.
Olwig, Karen Fog (1993) *Global Culture, Island Identity: Continuity and Change in the Afro-Caribbean Community of Nevis*. Chur, Switzerland: Harwood.
—— (1997) 'Cultural sites: Sustaining a home in a deterritorialised world'. In Kirsten Hastrup and Karen Fog Olwig, eds, *Siting Culture*, pp. 17–38. London: Routledge.
—— (2007) *Caribbean Journeys: An Ethnography of Migration and Home in Three Family Networks*. Durham, NC: Duke University Press.
Özkirimli, Umut (2000) *Theories of Nationalism: A Critical Introduction*. London: Macmillan.
Paine, Robert, ed. (1971) 'Patrons and brokers in the east Arctic'. Memorial University of Newfoundland, Social and Economic Papers, no. 2. St John's, Newfoundland: Memorial University of Newfoundland.
—— (1985) 'Ethnodrama and the "Fourth World": The Saami action group in Norway'. Memorial University of Newfoundland, social and economic papers, no. 14. St John's, Newfoundland: Memorial University of Newfoundland.

—— (1992) 'The claim to aboriginality: Saami in Norway'. In Reidar Grønhaug, Gunnar Haaland and Georg Henriksen, eds, *The Ecology of Choice and Symbols: Essays in Honour of Fredrik Barth*, pp. 388–407. Bergen: Alma Mater.

—— (2000) 'Aboriginality, authenticity and the Settler world'. In Anthony P. Cohen, ed., *Signifying Identities: Anthropological Perspectives on Boundaries and Contested Values*, pp. 77–116. London: Routledge.

Parekh, Bhikhu (2000) *Rethinking Multiculturalism: Cultural Diversity and Political Theory*. London: Macmillan.

Park, Robert E. (1950) *Race and Culture*. Glencoe, IL: Free Press.

—— (1955 [1921]) 'Sociology and the social sciences'. In Robert E. Park, *Society, Collective Behaviour, News and Opinion, Sociology and Modern Society*. Glencoe, IL: Free Press.

Parker, Andrew, Mary Russo, Doris Sommer and Patricia Yaeger, eds (1992) *Nationalism and Sexualities*. London: Routledge.

Parkin, David (1974) 'Congregational and interpersonal ideologies in political ethnicity'. In Abner Cohen, ed., *Urban Ethnicity*, pp. 119–57. London: Tavistock.

Patterson, Orlando (1977) *Ethnic Chauvinism: The Reactionary Impulse*. New York: Stein & Day.

Peel, John D.Y. (1989) 'The cultural work of Yoruba ethnogenesis'. In Elizabeth Tonkin, Maryon McDonald and Malcolm Chapman, eds, *History and Ethnicity*, pp. 198–215. London: Routledge.

—— (2000) *Religious Encounter and the Making of the Yoruba*. Bloomington: Indiana University Press.

Pryce, Ken (1979) *Endless Pressure: A Study of West Indian Life-styles in Bristol*. Bristol: Bristol Classical Press.

Renan, Ernest (1992 [1882]) *Qu'est-ce qu'une nation?* Paris: Presses Pocket.

Rex, John (1973) *Race, Colonialism and the City*. London: Routledge.

—— and David Mason, eds (1986) *Theories of Race and Ethnic Relations*. Cambridge: Cambridge University Press.

—— and Robert Moore (1967) *Race, Community and Conflict: A Study of Sparkbrook*. Oxford: Oxford University Press.

Riccio, Bruno (1999) 'Senegalese transmigrants and the construction of immigration in Emilia-Romagna, Italy'. D.Phil. thesis, University of Sussex.

Robertson, Roland (1994) *Globalization*. London: SAGE.

Romanucci-Ross, Lola and George DeVos, eds (1995) *Ethnic Identity: Creation, Conflict and Accommodation*, 3rd edn. Walnut Creek, CA: AltaMira Press.

Roosens, Eugeen E. (1989) *Creating Ethnicity*. London: SAGE.

Rosaldo, Michelle Z. (1984) 'Towards an anthropology of self and feeling'. In Richard A. Shweder and Robert LeVine, eds, *Culture Theory*, pp. 137–54. Cambridge: Cambridge University Press.

Runnymede Trust (2000) *The Future of Multi-Ethnic Britain: Report of the Commission on the Future of Multi-Ethnic Britain*, edited by Bhikhu Parekh. London: Profile Books.

Rushdie, Salman (1991) *Imaginary Homelands*. London: Granta.

Sahlins, Marshall D. (1994) 'Goodbye to tristes tropes: Ethnography in the context of modern world history'. In Robert Borofsky, ed., *Assessing Cultural Anthropology*, pp. 377–94. New York: McGraw-Hill.

Said, Edward (1978) *Orientalism*. London: Routledge.

Salvierda, Tijo (2009) 'Sugar, Sea and Power: A study of the Franco-Mauritian elite and the multidimensionality of elite maintenance'. PhD thesis, Free University of Amsterdam.

Sartre, Jean-Paul (1943) *L'Être et le néant*. Paris: Gallimard.

Saugestad, Sidsel (2001) *The Inconvenient Indigenous: Remote Area Development in Botswana, Donor Assistance, and the First People of the Kalahari*. Uppsala: Nordic African Institute.

Schlesinger, Arthur M. (1992) *The Disuniting of America*. New York: Norton.

Schmidt, Bettina E. and Ingo W. Schröder, eds (2001) *Anthropology of Violence and Conflict*. London: Routledge.

Scott, James (1998) *Seeing Like a State: How Certain Schemes to Improve the Human Condition Have Failed*. New Haven, CT: Yale University Press.

Shils, Edward (1980) *Tradition*. Glencoe, IL: Free Press.

Shore, Cris (2000) *Building Europe: The Cultural Politics of European Integration*. London: Routledge.

Silverstein, Paul A. (2005) 'Immigrant racialization and the new savage slot: Race, migration, and immigration in the new Europe'. *Annual Review of Anthropology* vol. 34, pp. 363–84.

Sjöberg, Katarina (1993) *The Return of the Ainu: Cultural Mobilization and the Practice of Ethnicity in Japan*. Chur, Switzerland: Harwood.

Smith, Anthony D. (1986) *The Ethnic Origin of Nations*. Oxford: Blackwell.

—— (1995) *Nations and Nationalism in a Global Era*. Cambridge: Polity.

Smith, Michael G. (1965) *The Plural Society of the British West Indies*. London: Sangster's.

—— (1984) *Culture, Race and Class in the Commonwealth Caribbean*. Mona, Jamaica: Institute of Social and Economic Research (ISER).

Sniderman, Paul M. and Michael Gray Hagen (1985) *Race and Inequality: A Study in American Values*. Chatham, NJ: Chatham House.

Southall, Aidan (1970) 'The illusion of tribe'. *Journal of Asian and African Studies*, vol. 5: 28–50.

—— (1976) 'Nuer and Dinka are people: Ecology, ethnicity and logical possibility'. *Man*, vol. 11 (4), pp. 463–91.

Steinberg, Stephen (1981) *The Ethnic Myth: Race, Ethnicity and Class in America*. New York: Atheneum.

Stewart, Charles, ed. (2007) *Creolization: History, Ethnography, Theory*. Walnut Creek, CA: Left Coast Press.

Stewart, Michael (1991) 'Un peuple sans patrie'. *Terrain*, vol. 17, pp. 39–52.

Stolcke, Verena (1995) 'Talking culture: New boundaries, new rhetorics of exclusion in Europe'. *Current Anthropology*, vol. 36 (1), pp. 1–24.

Stoller, Paul (2002) *Money Has no Smell: The Africanization of New York City*. Chicago: University of Chicago Press.

Strathern, Marilyn (1988) *The Gender of the Gift: Problems with Women and Problems with Society in Melanesia*. Berkeley: University of California Press.

—— (1992) *After Nature: English Kinship in the Late Twentieth Century*. Cambridge: Cambridge University Press.

Tajfel, Henri (1978) *The Social Psychology of Minorities*, report no. 38. London: Minority Rights Group.

Tambiah, Stanley J. (1989) 'The politics of ethnicity'. *American Ethnologist*, vol. 16 (2), pp. 335–49.

Tambs-Lynch, Harald (1980) *London Patidars*. London: Routledge.

Taylor, Anne-Christine (1991) 'Ethnie'. In Pierre Bonté and Michel Izard, eds, *Dictionnaire de l'ethnologie et de l'anthropologie*, pp. 242–4. Paris: Presses Universitaires Françaises.

Taylor, Charles (1992) *Multiculturalism and 'The Politics of Recognition'*, edited by Amy Gutmann. Princeton, NJ: Princeton University Press.

Taylor, John (1992) 'Touched with glory: Heroes and human interest in the news'. In James Aulich, ed., *Framing the Falklands War: Nationhood, Culture and Identity*, pp. 13–32. Milton Keynes: Open University Press.

Thaiss, Gustav (1978) 'The conceptualization of social change through metaphors'. *Journal of Asian and African Studies*, vol. 13 (1), pp. 1–13.

Thomas, Nick (1992) 'The inversion of tradition'. *American Ethnologist*, vol. 19 (2), pp. 213–32.

Thuen, Trond (1995) *Quest for Equity: Norway and the Saami Challenge*. St John's: Institute of Social and Economic Research.

Tinker, Hugh (1974) *A New Form of Slavery: The Export of Indian Labour Overseas 1880–1920*. Oxford: Oxford University Press.

Tishkov, Valery (1997) *Ethnicity, Nationalism and Conflict in and after the Soviet Union: The Mind Aflame*. London: SAGE.

Todd, Emmanuel (1985) *The Explanation of Ideology: Family Structures and Social Systems*. Oxford: Blackwell.

Todorov, Tzvetan (1989) *Nous et les autres: La réflexion française sur la diversité humaine*. Paris: Seuil.

Tonkin, Elizabeth, Maryon McDonald and Malcolm Chapman, eds (1989) *History and Ethnicity*. London: Routledge.

Tronvoll, Kjetil (2009) *War and the Politics of Identity in Ethiopia: The Making of Enemies and Allies in the Horn of Africa*. London: James Currey.

Tsing, Anna Lowenhaupt (2005) *Friction: An Ethnography of Global Connection*. Princeton, NJ: Princeton University Press.

Turner, Bryan S., ed. (1990) *Theories of Modernity and Postmodernity*. London: SAGE.

Turner, Terence (1992) 'Defiant images: The Kayapo appropriation of video'. *Anthropology Today*, vol. 8 (6), pp. 5–16.

—— (1993) 'Anthropology and multiculturalism: What is it about anthropology that multiculturalists should be mindful of it?' *Cultural Anthropology*, vol. 8 (4), pp. 411–29.

Turner, Victor (1967) *The Forest of Symbols*. Ithaca, NY: Cornell University Press.

—— (1969) *The Ritual Process: Structure and Anti-structure*. Chicago: Aldine.

Urry, John (2000) *Sociology beyond Societies: Mobilities for the Twenty-first Century*. London: Routledge.

Uyl, Marion den and Lenie Brouwer (2009) 'Mix, just mix and see what happens: Girls in a super-diverse Amsterdam neighbourhood'. In Sharam Alghasi, Thomas Hylland Eriksen and Halleh Ghorashi, eds, *Paradoxes of Cultural Recognition*, pp. 201–18. Aldershot: Ashgate.

Van den Berghe, Pierre L. (1975) 'Ethnicity and class in highland Peru'. In Leo Despres, ed., *Ethnicity and Resource Competition in Plural Societies*, pp. 71–85. The Hague: Mouton.

—— (1981) *The Ethnic Phenomenon*. New York: Elsevier Press.

—— (1983) 'Class, race and ethnicity in Africa'. *Ethnic and Racial Studies*, vol. 6 (2), pp. 221–36.

Veer, Peter van der (1994) *Religious Nationalism*. Berkeley: University of California Press.
—— ed. (1995) *Nation and Migration: The Politics of Space in the South Asian Diaspora*. Philadelphia: University of Pennsylvania Press.
Verdery, Katherine (1996) *What Was Socialism, and What Comes Next?* Princeton, NJ: Princeton University Press.
Vermeulen, Hans and Cora Govers, eds (1994) *The Anthropology of Ethnicity: Beyond 'Ethnic Groups and Boundaries'*. Amsterdam: Het Spinhuis.
Vertovec, Steven (1991) 'Religion and ethnic ideology: The Hindu youth movement in Trinidad'. *Ethnic and Racial Studies*, vol. 13 (2), pp. 225–49.
—— (1992) *Hindu Trinidad*. London: Macmillan.
—— (2001) 'Transnational challenges to the "new" multiculturalism'. Paper presented at the 2001 ASA Conference, University of Sussex, 30 March–2 April.
—— (2007) '*Super-diversity* and its implications'. *Ethnic and Racial Studies*, vol. 30, pp. 1024–54.
—— (2009) *Transnationalism*. London: Routledge.
—— and Susanne Wessendorf, eds (2009) *The Multiculturalism Backlash*. London: Routledge.
Wade, Peter (1997) *Race and Ethnicity in Latin America*. London: Pluto.
—— (2002) *Race, Nature and Culture: An Anthropological Perspective*. London: Pluto.
—— ed. (2007) *Race, Ethnicity and Nation: Perspectives from Kinship and Genetics*. Oxford: Berghahn.
Wallerstein, Immanuel (1991a) 'Does India exist?' In Immanuel Wallerstein, *Unthinking Social Science: The Limits of Nineteenth-century Paradigms*, pp. 130–4. Cambridge: Polity.
—— (1991b) *Unthinking Social Science: The Limits of Nineteenth-century Paradigms*. Cambridge: Polity.
—— *et al.* (1996) *Open the Social Sciences: Report of the Gulbenkian Commission on the Restructuring of the Social Sciences*. Palo Alto, CA: Stanford University Press.
Wallman, Sandra (1986) 'Ethnicity and the boundary process in context'. In John Rex and David Mason, eds, *Theories of Race and Ethnic Relations*, pp. 226–35. Cambridge: Cambridge University Press.
Walsh, Jeffrey, ed. (1995) *The Gulf War Did Not Happen: Politics, Culture and Warfare Post-Vietnam*. Aldershot: Arena.
Watson, C.W. (2000) *Multiculturalism*. Buckingham: Open University Press.
Weber, Eugen (1976) *Peasants into Frenchmen: The Modernization of Rural France 1870–1914*. Palo Alto, CA: Stanford University Press.
Weber, Max (1980 [1921]) *Wirtschaft und Gesellschaft*. Tübingen: Mohr (English trans.: *Economy and Society*).
Weiner, Annette (1992) *Inalienable Possessions: The Paradox of Keeping-While-Giving*. Berkeley: University of California Press.
Werbner, Pnina (1997) 'Introduction: The dialectics of cultural hybridity'. In P. Werbner and T. Modood, eds, *Debating Cultural Hybridity*, pp. 1–26. London: Zed Books.
—— (2002) *Imagined Diasporas among Manchester Muslims: The Public Performance of Pakistani Transnational Identity Politics*. Oxford: James Currey.
—— (2005) 'Islamophobia'. *Anthropology Today*, vol. 21 (1), pp. 5–9.
—— and Tariq Modood, eds (1997) *Debating Cultural Hybridity: Multicultural Policies and the Politics of Anti-Racism*. London: Zed Books.

Westwood, Sallie (1995) 'Gendering diaspora: Space, politics and South Asian masculinities in Britain'. In P. van der Veer, ed., *Nation and Migration*, pp. 197–221. Philadelphia: University of Pennsylvania Press.

Wicker, Hans-Rudolf (1997) 'Introduction: Theorizing ethnicity and nationalism'. In Hans-Rudolf Wicker, ed., *Rethinking Nationalism and Ethnicity: The Struggle for Meaning and Order in Europe*, pp. 1–43. Oxford: Berg.

Wieviorka, Michel (1991) *L'Espace du racisme*. Paris: Seuil.

—— (1997) 'Is it so difficult to be anti-racist?' In Pnina Werbner and Tariq Modood, eds, *Debating Cultural Hybridity*, pp. 139–53. London: Zed Books.

Wilford, Rick and Robert L. Miller, eds (1998) *Women, Ethnicity and Nationalism: The Politics of Transition*. London: Routledge.

Williams, Brackette (1989) 'A class act: Anthropology and the race to nation across ethnic terrain'. *Annual Review of Anthropology*, vol. 18, pp. 401–4.

—— (1991) *Stains on My Name, War in My Veins: Guyana and the Politics of Cultural Struggle*. Durham, NC: Duke University Press.

—— ed. (1996) *Women Out of Place: The Gender of Agency and the Race of Nationality*. London: Routledge.

Williams, Raymond (1976) *Keywords*. London: Flamingo.

Willie, Charles V. (1991) 'Caste, class and family life chances'. In Rutledge M. Dennis, ed., *Research in Ethnic Relations*, vol. 6, pp. 65–84. London: JAI Press.

Wilmsen, Edwin N. (1989) *Land Filled with Flies: A Political Economy of the Kalahari*. Chicago: University of Chicago Press.

Wilson, Godfrey (1941–2) *An Essay on the Economics of Detribalization in Northern Rhodesia, Parts I–II*. Livingstone: Rhodes-Livingstone Institute.

Wilson, Peter J. (1978) *Crab Antics*, 2nd edn. New Haven, CT: Yale University Press.

Wilson, Richard (2001) *The Politics of Truth and Reconciliation in South Africa*. Cambridge: Cambridge University Press.

—— and Jon Mitchell, eds (2003) *Human Rights in Global Perspective: Anthropological Studies of Rights, Claims and Entitlements*. London: Routledge.

Wilson, William J. (1978) *The Declining Significance of Race*. Chicago: University of Chicago Press.

Wimmer, Andreas (2002) *Nationalist Exclusion and Ethnic Conflict: Shadows of Modernity*. Cambridge: Cambridge University Press.

Wirth, Louis (1956 [1928]) *The Ghetto*. Chicago: University of Chicago Press.

Wolf, Eric (1964) *Anthropology*. Englewood Cliffs, NJ: Prentice Hall.

—— (1982) *Europe and the People without History*. Berkeley: University of California Press.

Worsley, Peter (1984) *The Three Worlds: Culture and World Development*. London: Weidenfeld & Nicolson.

Yelvington, Kevin (1991) 'Ethnicity as practice? A comment on Bentley'. *Comparative Studies in Society and History*, vol. 33 (1), pp. 158–68.

Young, Iris Marion (2004) 'Two concepts of self-determination'. In Stephen May, Tariq Modood and Judith Squires, eds, *Ethnicity, Nationalism, and Minority Rights*, pp. 176–95. Cambridge: Cambridge University Press.

Yuval-Davis, Nira (1997) *Gender and Nation*. London: SAGE.

# Index

*Compiled by Sue Carlton*